THIS BOOK IS DEDICATED TO

the sixth worst singer in Scotland.

A LITTLE PREAMBLE

If I were to bump into my nineteen-year-old self, I'm pretty sure I would have thought *'cocky little upstart, what makes you think you're good enough to join the police?'*

In truth, I wasn't as confident or self-assured as I let on. I was just a naïve wee laddie with no real life experience. As immature as the next randy wee nineteen-year-old who wants to earn some pennies to buy enough beer to help pluck up the courage to ask a girl out.

After thirty years as a police officer, I retired. Still immature and naïve but much less of a cocky little upstart than when I joined. How many of you can say that?

It was weird being in the police, I mean you wouldn't believe the things that happened; like the time Officer Dribble taught me the most unusual way of catching a housebreaker or the time we raced around a garden on a ride-on lawnmower.

There were weird people; like Irene, an alcoholic nude model, who kept something in her display cabinet that had every new probationer scheming to take a better look.

There were weird situations; like when two drunk detectives woke up on a train, somewhere in the middle of England, to see a pair of handcuffs sitting where their prisoner had been.

I learned lots of weird things too; like how to fool the breathalyser, how 'Bumjar' got his nickname and why some people don't come quietly.

There was an awful lot of practical jokes played on yours truly; although the worst prank in the world was a despicable creation of my own.

It was an interesting career. I blundered into countless out-of-the-ordinary situations. It was exciting. There were funny incidents and strange goings-on. Sometimes it was a house of horrors, and we turned to humour to stay sane.

So here they are, written for my amusement. Warts and all. The stories that made me laugh, cry and shake my head.

There's just one problem.

I might give you a bad impression of the police in Scotland, which isn't my intention. These recollections are about many of the characters and events, which took place over many years. More often than not, I am the butt of the joke. It is a gift to be able to laugh at yourself, it is a wonderful remedy for all forms of pretentiousness, self-importance, intellectual twaddle and humbug.

Nowadays, police officers have neither the time nor inclination for such high jinks. They work long and hard in difficult circumstances. The constraints on them make it hard to have any nonsense at all. Yet it is important for police officers to engage in the occasional mischief. There is a shelf life to dealing with the world's ills. A good giggle from time to time helps them get through it.

Laughter is a powerful healing elixir.

I would like to apologise up front to any colleagues who recognise themselves and take offence because I have embellished a story about them. If the story is true, and you still take offence, then you only have yourself to blame.

Malky McEwan

My thanks go to Donald for his sensible advice to take out the more controversial stories. Thanks also to Gerry for his suggestion to put all the stuff back in that Donald advised me to remove.

Not least, my sincere thanks to you for reading.

LATE ONE NIGHT

"Your mum?"

"Seriously?"

"Your mum!"

"You are not funny."

"You laughed the first time."

"You can't keep saying 'your mum' and expect it to be funny every time, it's not funny anymore. Anyway, it begins with B, my 'mum' doesn't begin with B," I tried again, "I spy with my little eye something beginning with B."

"Your bum?"

"Nope."

"I give in."

"Badger."

"Badger? Where do you see a badger?"

"Back there, in the woods."

It had been a long night with my partner, PC Barbeque Bill, we hadn't had a single call and it reduced us to playing 'I spy'. It was times like that I wondered why I joined the police. I was young and naïve. I craved for something to do. Hoping someone needed us. When nothing happened, boredom became the enemy. Out on patrol, seeking injustice and all we saw were black clouds and bumper stickers. I lied about the badger, I didn't see a badger - but he hadn't seen my mum either.

We wanted to do something other than play 'I spy' but we weren't prepared for what happened next.

Our radio crackled to life.

"Alpha Charlie to all officers, make your way 'Grade 1' to Boswell Place."

"Boswell Place!" said Barbeque Bill, with a sig-

nificant look; I nodded and replied, "Brian S. McNutt,"
saying what he was thinking, "What has he been up to
now?"

When you telephone the police, we grade your call by
its seriousness.

A 'Grade 1' call requires an emergency response.
A 'Grade 2' is a priority response but unlike a 'Grade 1'
call officers cannot use their blue lights or sirens. The
grading system goes all the way to a 'Grade 5', which
is like getting a Christmas card from a distant relative
in Timbuktu, whom you have never met nor are ever
likely to meet.

I turned on our blue lights did a quick U-turn and
headed off toward Boswell Place. Speeding through the
town, the lights reflected in the shop windows. We
were two miles away, traffic was light, and I reckoned
on getting there in under five minutes. It gave me time
to collect my thoughts and speculate on what we were
getting ourselves into.

Brian S. McNutt stayed in Boswell Place and was
one of our regulars. His father, Neville I. McNutt, had
thought it amusing for him to continue the McNutt
family tradition of christening their first-born son
with a stupid middle name. Thus the 'S' in Brian S.
McNutt stood for 'Stupid,' the result of which only
reminded everyone that Brian S. McNutt was worth
watching.

Neville I. McNutt was an 'Idiot.'

When sober, Brian was a reasonable human
being. With a drink, however, he was a police officer's
nightmare. It was now 10 p.m. and, considering Brian
opened his first bottle of extra strong cider around
noon, we knew by now he would not be a reasonable

human being. Alcohol made him a tad tetchy.

Getting any sense from a drunk Brian S. McNutt was somewhere in between speaking to a brick wall and explaining quantum theory to a chicken in Swahili. The only sure-fire way to get Brian calm and level-headed again meant arresting him and locking him in a cell until sober (him not the cops, although that did help too).

"DO NOT ENTER BOSWELL PLACE!"

The radio barked.

"To all officers heading to Boswell Place, do not enter Boswell Place, your rendezvous point is Hill Street. I repeat DO NOT ENTER BOSWELL PLACE!"

The Control Room Inspector had taken command of the situation, the normal radio operator demoted to record the events as they took place. A Control Room Inspector taking charge meant only one thing - whatever we were being sent to was serious.

Not knowing what we were going into was a normal ingredient in the package of being a police officer. We did it all the time. Sometimes it was the innocuous calls that turned out to be the ones that gave us the most issues.

We knew something was up, a Control Room Inspector doesn't take charge of the normal run-of-the-mill calls. Added to this, we weren't allowed to go to where the crisis was unfolding.

All of this meant that, without any conscious effort, our adrenal glands pumped its hormone into our blood. This biological process is the body's natural reaction to prepare us for the 'fight or flight' response. My blood sent the adrenaline through my veins altering my body's metabolism to prepare for what was to come. I could already feel my pulse quicken, and the air in my lungs expand. I did not know what was to come, but I was now alert to the slightest danger we might face.

My grip tightened on the steering wheel.
A few minutes later, we arrived in Hill Street and scrambled out of our car to join the duty sergeant and another crew, who had arrived moments before us. All of showing signs of agitated energy as the chemical mediators flooded through our bloodstream.

A taut Sergeant Brown explained what was going on.

"Brian S. McNutt's girlfriend has phoned to say he is drunk and has threatened her with a handgun. He is in the house now, and we don't know if it is a real handgun or not. We don't know what the situation is in the house because the phone was cut off and when the operator phoned back, it was engaged. I think he has taken it off the hook."

It is difficult to get your hands on a handgun in Scotland. It is not like America where kids need only dip their hand into their mother's purse.

In Scotland, kids are lucky if they get to put their hands on a badly calibrated, underpowered air rifle at the fairground. We have strict laws on the use and ownership of guns. Brian S. McNutt had an extensive criminal history, which disqualified him from obtaining a licence for any firearm. It is one reason there are so few deaths from firearms in Scotland. We don't let just anyone own a gun. Even if you are a fine upstanding member of the community, you still need to have a good reason to get a licence. Not that Brian didn't acquire one through illegal means.

Our adrenaline levels kicked higher.

We got our instructions.

Barbeque Bill and I were to sneak around to the back of Brian S. McNutt's house where we were to maintain discrete observations.

We got back in our police van and drove off. I took the first right, and then right again. One hundred yards from the back of Brian S. McNutt's house I did another U-turn and parked facing back towards the way I came. If I had to run back to my vehicle, I wanted to make sure it was facing in the right direction for my 'flight' response.

We stepped out of our vehicle and made our way to the rear of his house. My earpiece blasted out a warning: "SHOT FIRED! SHOT FIRED!" screamed Sergeant Brown.

Sergeant Brown had edged his way towards the front of the house to take up observations and almost had a heart attack when he saw a flash of light from the front window of Brian's house and heard the instantaneous sound of a gunshot.

Barbeque Bill and I stopped in our tracks, unsure of our next step. The radio was silent for about a minute. We remained rooted to the spot.

"Control room to Sergeant Brown, update, update, what's going on?" The Control Room Inspector asked with some urgency.

"I think I heard a gunshot from his house. It sounded like a gun going off, but I can't be certain, I've positioned myself at the side of a house diagonally opposite," said Sergeant Brown.

This information did nothing to reduce the flow of adrenaline in our bodies.

The Control Room Inspector moved things forward.

The firearms team were on their way. From my experience, that could mean anything from two to six hours.

Then, he instructed all other police personnel to move into Boswell Place, park their marked police vehicles fifty yards away from Brian S. McNutt's house and to activate their blue lights. No sirens. He wanted to let Brian know we were there. It was a strategy designed to contain him in his house. Brian could have walked out and pointed the gun at us and there would have been a scramble to exit the scene, but at least then we would know what he was doing.

So Barbeque Bill and I waited. With no new instructions, we followed our last order and sidled our way towards the back of Brian's building.

Brian S. McNutt lived with his girlfriend and two-year-old son (George M. McNutt) in the downstairs unit in a block of four council-owned flats.

There was only one entrance at the side of the building. It had a shared front and rear garden, large by today's standards. The rear garden extended across an unkempt lawn with clotheslines and clothes poles set in a square. There was a further rough and overgrown patch of ground at the bottom of the garden where it met the six feet high ranch-style wooden fence. The wooden spars were rotten, never having seen a coat of creosote since Brian had taken up residence five years earlier. I didn't put much faith in the wooden spars stopping a bullet. A pea shooter could have punctured a hole in it.

I couldn't get a proper look through the gaps, so I stretched up on my tiptoes and popped my head above the fence. At that precise moment, Brian S. McNutt popped his head up from the other side. His left hand gripped the top spar in readiness to climb over, in his right hand was a handgun.

Our eyes met, inches from each other.

It was evident Brian had climbed out of his rear kitchen window before making his attempted escape. I looked at the gun in Brian's hand, a silver revolver not unlike those used in every cowboy western I had ever seen.

Bill also scrambled up on my left side to see the barrel of a gun pointed right between his eyes. Those terror filled eyes. My eyes nearly popped out of my head. In unison, we did what all big, brave police officers, facing a gun with nothing but a wooden baton in our pockets, would do.

We dropped to the ground and ran away.

Barbeque Bill had a slight start on me, but I had faster springier muscles, and within twenty yards I was pounding away from the back fence of Brian S. McNutt's house faster than Linford Christie when he broke the British record for the 100 metres.

I swear that in that first thirty yards I would have outrun a cheetah. I didn't even look back until we reached our car. It was only then I realised Brian wasn't chasing us and we weren't being shot at.

There was no sign of Brian S. McNutt.

Still gasping for breath I heard Sergeant Brown on the radio, "I now have a positive ID. Brian S. McNutt is at his front window looking out at us."

Brian, it appeared, had got as big a fright seeing us as we did seeing him. He'd slipped out the back window, made to climb his fence and came face to face with Barbeque Bill and me. Surprised, he had taken flight and darted back through his rear kitchen window into his home.

Barbeque Bill and I edged our way back to the rear of Brian S. McNutt's flat.

We took up a position where we could observe as much as we could but also get a head start should we need to run away. From our position, we could see up the side of the house to the main road. Flashing lights of several police vehicles gave the surrounding buildings an unusual blue flickering like we were on the set of some American TV cop programme when all the action has finished, and the lights were needless.

We could also see into the rear kitchen of Brian's flat and the tension in our bodies increased when he appeared at the window, straining to see if there were cops still out there. Then he disappeared back into the flat, only to repeat the scrutiny of his backyard a few minutes later. Each time he did so more adrenaline pumped through our veins, preparing us for our flight response - we had no intention of entering into a battle. You don't take a stupid little wooden baton to a gun fight.

For about an hour we remained, geared up and ready to run, watching the back of Brian's flat and occasionally seeing him appear at the kitchen window. Each time I reported the sighting to the Control Room Inspector unaware, that the pitch of my voice kept getting higher and higher. By the end of the hour, I sounded like I was a seven-year-old girl after being given a horse for her birthday.

We were in a stand-off situation.

We were there to wait it out. Unless Brian S.

McNutt changed the status quo and forced our hand, we were in for a long night.

Then something bizarre happened.

A small blue Vauxhall Viva pulled up outside the house. It was a two-door unmarked police car used by the local CID.

Out stepped Detective Inspector Kamikaze Mac-Kenzie, rather unsteady on his feet. He was wearing a tuxedo and black bow tie. Even from the back garden, we could tell he had had a few libations; we could almost smell it. He straightened up his tuxedo and walked up to Brian S. McNutt's door and, without knocking, opened it up and went straight in.

Bill and I gave each other an incredulous look before turning back desperate to know what would happen next?

A minute later Detective Inspector Kamikaze MacKenzie exited the flat holding Brian S. McNutt by the collar. He marched him across to one of the police vans and threw him into the rear.

No one breathed a word; we were all stunned by what we had seen. Detective Inspector 'Kamikaze' Mac-Kenzie had gone against procedures, he had ignored all common sense and by-passed the normal practices.

We should have had a fully briefed and deployed firearms team in place before opening a safe line of communication between Brian and a trained negotiator. All appropriate advisors should have been in place, a firearms tactical advisor, a senior negotiator, a public order team perhaps and even the dog section should have been there in readiness.

A senior officer should have taken the role of 'gold commander,' identifying himself as having full responsibility for the operation. No one should have taken any action without his express authority.

Instead, a rather drunk detective inspector risked his life in the most unorthodox way.

Had his actions not succeeded they might have demoted or even sacked him. Instead, he staggered back to the unmarked Vauxhall Viva climbed in and with a crunch of the gears and a few unnecessary revs of the engine he drove off with nothing other than confirmation he had the right nickname.

It was times like that, despite the obvious danger, I was thankful I had chosen such an interesting and exciting career.

We found Brian's girlfriend in the bedroom, sound asleep with her son.

The gunshot seen and heard by Sergeant Brown was Brian shooting the television, he didn't like the *'Old Grey Whistle Test.'*

The flat became a crime scene.

We bundled Brian's girlfriend and two-year-old son off to a nearby relative and secured the flat to await the morning when the scene of crime officers would attend to examine the flat for evidence.

Sergeant Brown instructed me to guard the flat to prevent any unauthorised entry.

Despite the flat being secured by lock and key, the duty inspector thought it prudent to leave officers outside to ensure that the chain of evidence remained uncompromised.

I was still buzzing, adrenaline had flooded my system for two hours, and I couldn't have been any edgier if I had drunk fourteen cups of coffee and eaten a cash-and-carry sized bag of gummy bears.

They gave me a fresh out of the wrapper rookie cop to keep me company.

A tall, ginger-haired young lad. He had just started his first night shift and had missed all the excitement. He had an unnatural deathly pale about him. I wondered if he had a pulse.

I knew we would be at the scene for the next eight hours. I thought it would be good to get to know my companion, so I sparked up a conversation - it helps pass the time.

"What's your name and where do you come from?" I said in my best Cilla Black, *Blind Date* voice.

"Neil."

"What's your favourite film?"

"I don't really watch films."

"What would be in your top ten desert island discs then?"

"I'm not really into music."

"What would you say is the funniest sitcom that has ever been on the telly?"

"I don't really watch television."

"Football team?"

"I'm not really into football."

"What is the most inspiring book you have ever read?"

"I don't really read books."

"Favourite holiday destination?"

"We always just go to her mum's cottage in Wales."

"Who would be your dream date?"

"I'm married."

"Did you see the news tonight?"

"I don't really watch the news."

"Do you play any sport?"

"I'm not really into sport."

"For goodness' sake Neil, you don't do much do you? You don't watch films, don't listen to music, don't watch telly, either for the comedy or the news. You don't play sports, you have no thoughts about the opposite sex, you don't read books, and you go to the same cottage every year on holiday with your in-laws. What on earth do you do?"

"I told you," he said in all seriousness, "I'm married."

Still pumped with adrenaline my brain buzzed, in need of stimulus. Neil sat quiet, staring out the window.

"What are you thinking about?"

"Nothing."

"Nothing? We always have thoughts going through our head; everybody has to be thinking of something. Even when we sleep our brains continue to process information, you must have been thinking of something."

"No, not really."

I waited. Just sat in silence.

Thinking thoughts.

Bored.

Half an hour passed.

"What are you thinking about now Neil?"

"Em. Nothing really."

"You must have been thinking about something, what was the last thing that went through your head?"

"...Nothing,"

"I think you will make a good traffic officer," I said (which I think he took as a compliment).

"I spy with my little eye, something beginning with B," I said, and wondered how long it would take for him to guess the B referred to him.
I knew then it would be a long night.

It was at times like that I wondered why I had ever joined the job. I wondered why Neil had joined the police. I wondered why anyone wants to join the police?

GIVE A MAN A FISH AND YOU FEED HIM FOR A DAY.

Give a man a uniform and he won't need dinner because he will out dealing with emergency calls.

CHAPTER 1

EVER SINCE I WAS A WEE BOY

Oh, my god! What have I done?

I opened the door to find a pot bellied, unsmiling police sergeant in full uniform standing on our doorstep.

"I'm Sergeant Bruxton, I'm here to do your home visit," said Sergeant Bruxton. His voice gruff and his eyes bore into me like he wanted to slap me on the face.

In days of old, when prospective police officers had passed all the various checks needed, the final stage in the process was a home visit from a local sergeant. The sergeant would, in theory, identify those who were perhaps not suitable because of intemperate personal circumstances.

Were they living in a cesspit?

Don't get me wrong; it was okay to live somewhere that was ramshackle and rundown. It just raised questions if **you** were the reason the place was a shithole.

I invited him in, and he followed me through to our good room.

I say 'good room' as if we had several to choose from.

Apart from the 'good room', there was only the kitchen, the dining room or my bedroom.

The kitchen I dismissed as too uncomfortable and we had just had our dinner - fried fish. Probably best to avoid the lingering aroma. The dining room was not so much a dining room as a games room, and the dining room table was being used to support a quarter size, snooker table. I thought it prudent not to alert him to my misspent youth.

My bedroom wasn't an option. I shared a tiny room with my two brothers, three teenage boys squashed into the one room, sweating and farting - if you thought the smell from the fish was bad!

So I took Sergeant Bruxton through to our good room, offered him a seat in my father's comfortable armchair while I sat, as upright as I could, on our floral green couch and prepared for a barrage of probing questions. Daunted by his dour expression, I wondered if I would make it through this final hurdle in my quest to join the police.

I say 'quest' as if I always wanted to join the police; In fact, I wasn't sure what I wanted to do with my life, I'm not even sure what I want to do with my life now.

If I had given it some thought, why would I want to don a uniform and plod the streets, morning noon and night, rain, snow or hail? Why would any sane person want to deal with road accidents, deaths, fights, murders, floods, fires, frauds, and forgeries? Why on earth would anyone make themselves the target so much unwarranted verbal and sometimes physical abuse?

The truth is, I didn't know what I was letting my-self in for. I had no idea what it would be like. I hadn't thought it through. I just thought it might be a good idea to get out of cleaning windows for the winter.

"Why do you want to join the police?" he asked.

"Well it'll keep me off the streets, I suppose."

Sergeant Bruxton gave me a withering look. I thought I better say something else.

"Ever since I was a wee boy, I always wanted to join the police," I said, wide-eyed and innocent.
My mother's head popped around the door, smiling. In her usual pleasant manner, she asked Sergeant Bruxton, "Would you like some tea?"

"No thank you," he said. (I later learned that Sergeant Bruxton preferred copious amounts of 'rum and coke' and he would definitely have had one or two of those, if offered).

I took his refusal of a cuppa to be a bad sign, today would be a bad day. He took out his notebook and made a few notes. I bumbled my way through his questions, cringing at myself for not having thought anything about what I would say in this situation. I was unprepared, and it showed.

"What do you think are the main challenges facing the police at the moment?"

"Er, um, I don't know."

"What effect do you think the Scarman report will have on policing?"

"There is a scare man report?"

"The Lord Scarman report, his investigation following the Brixton riots?"

"Er, Um, Bricks and riots... where about?"

Then my Dad saved the day; he walked into the room, unaware that Sergeant. Bruxton was there.

"Oh, hello Bill," he said smiling.

"Oh, hi Alex," said Sergeant. Bruxton and his

rather stern expression loosened and turned into a cheery smile.

It turned out that, many years ago, my Dad had worked with Sergeant. Bruxton at an engineering firm.

'It's not what you know, it's who you know,' couldn't be truer.

I found that a lot of proverbs turned out to be true. Like, 'the best things in life are free,' - a shoplifter told me that.

So why did I want to join the police?

Some people have no choice; they are just expected to make the police their vocation. They come from a long line of police officers, like father like daughter, like grandson. Those people know of nothing else and would not even consider another occupation.

Born into the family firm. Like circus performers, most of them grew up with it in their blood. The big difference between the circus and the polis, however, is that in the police the lions aren't tame, there is no safety net, and there is a lot more blood.

There were many officers I came across whose mother or father had been or still were, in the police. I think those officers held a slight advantage. It must be a benefit to have a mentor, a family member or even just a friend who is keen for them to do well.

From the start, they have a better understanding of how things work. Their mother or father's encouragement and guidance will help them rise through the ranks, often surpassing the promotions and achievements of their parent(s). So not a bad thing to join the police if your dad was a sergeant or inspector or superintendent; unless your dad is a twat (or worse you are). Then there are those who always wanted to join the

Police.

They feel in their hearts they will don a uniform and serve. Ambition achieved the moment they successfully pass through their probation. Policing, for them, is a mission. An undertaking not dissimilar to the divine call a minister might experience from his God. The people who 'always wanted to be a policeman, ever since they were a wee boy (or girl).'

Doing something other than joining the police would be as alien to them as a Rangers supporter wearing green knickers or a Celtic supporter wearing any knickers.

Such officers walk down the street with a skip in their step and a smile on their face. They get on with the job because they love it. Even when the work is a strain, and they get tired, or frustrated or angry, they still adore getting out of their beds, and will proudly put on their uniform to head off and carry out their chosen trade. These people are the lifeblood of the police. They work hard and long. They are much appreciated but often given little recognition in the way of promotion (you know who you are and I salute you).

There are some for whom the police is a secondary career.

Those who served a few short years in the Army, Navy or Royal Air Force and are still too young to retire. They will naturally gravitate towards another disciplined service.

The change from an armed force to the police force you would think would be smooth. It is not. The gun swapped for a pen, and then like many others in that situation, they find that the paperwork can be purgatory. *(What do you mean we don't get to shoot people anymore?)*

There are also those who gravitate towards joining the police having experienced the job from the inside.

Whether working in the role of an office clerk or analyst or a mechanic, they come to realise that they could do the job of a police officer just as well as anyone.

Their entry is a smooth transition. Experienced police civilians know what to expect. They know the systems, the people, and the job. They evolve from a civilian to a police officer and welcome the better pay and pension. Then a few months later they go right back to doing the civilian role they had before because of cutbacks the bosses dispensed with their original position. Who better qualified to fill the vacant job than the one who was doing it for half the wages before?

There were a miscellany of miscreants too.

The boy who liked to pull the wings off a butter-fly - destined to be a report checker. The pervert - covert surveillance officer. The skiver - they are hard to find. The victim of bullying - complaints and dis-cipline. People with a clear conscience - those with a bad memory. The outstanding in their field - those that look like scarecrows. 'Fine' folk - traffic department.

Last (and probably least) there are the likes of me.

What made me join the police?

It was my destiny.

November 1983; winter was biting. In London 6,800 gold bars worth £26 million had disappeared in the Brink's-Mat robbery, Aberdeen was romping to an-other league title under Alex Ferguson, having already won the Scottish Cup, the European Cup Winners' Cup, and European Super Cup that year. It was a time when we had the best of music, Madness, Culture Club, Bob Marley, The Eurythmics and 'Every Breath You Take' by The Police was riding high in the charts.

I had been out cleaning windows, and to avoid frostbitten fingers I'd popped into the local pub. I had earned enough money to buy a pint of beer; destiny had drawn me to the pub where Rab, an old schoolmate, was sitting on a stool at the bar.

"What you up to these days, Rab?"

"I've applied for the police."

"How much does a police officer get?"

"About one hundred pounds a week.

Rab gave me the idea.

The next day I filled in an application and it sent off. I had a home visit by Sergeant Bruxton and three weeks later I was standing on the Parade Square at The Scottish Police College at Tulliallan, sporting a tunic, hat, and spit polished boots. The drill sergeant roaring at me for turning left instead of right.

Oh, my god! What have I done?

CHAPTER 2

PASSING OUT CHARADE

The Scottish Police College is in the middle of Scotland, equidistant from Edinburgh in the East and Glasgow in the West. Similarly equidistant from Aberdeen to the North and Dumfries to the South.

It couldn't be better placed to suit the training needs for all of Scotland's newly appointed police officers. It is situated in ninety acres of parkland on the northern outskirts of Kincardine. The 18th-century Tulliallan Castle, built by an admiral in Lord Nelson's cabinet, was paid for from the spoils of war. It is at the heart of the Scottish Police College, which extends out into halls, classrooms, and sleeping accommodation.

There are four classifications of prisons in the UK: A, B, C and D. Category D are open prisons for non-violent offenders. To put that into perspective, the Scottish Police College is a category B.

I learned a great deal at Tulliallan: how to fool the breathalyser, how to trick someone into to pressing my uniform and how to deal with a bastard sergeant. I'll explain later.

Kincardine is famous for one thing, the Kincardine Bridge.

It is an ugly little town that slowly urbanised, spreading outwards, abandoning older properties for newer builds with no concern for the haphazard way the town formed. It was a place where people drove into and, just as quickly, out again.

In the 1960's developers took it a step further by building three high-rise buildings. A trio of concrete monstrosities nobody liked. So the council gave them a makeover and painted them pink - if Barbie Doll did tower blocks!

It must have been like living in a packet of bubblegum. They were eyesores on a face already scarred with pock marks and pimples.

It is a surprise that the Scottish Police College is pleasant to look at, an oasis of beauty in the drab surroundings. Hidden from the road by a belt of forest, passing drivers would never guess that an imposing castle and well-kept grounds are concealed within.
For a recruit, the Scottish Police College can be a somewhat forbidding place. I recoil from spiders, get dizzy at heights, and run away from jellyfish but as soon as I arrived at the Scottish Police College, it topped the my list of scary things. I was young, naïve and felt like a pathetic milksop compared to my brave fellow recruits.

We had to share dormitories. Those dormitories have since been done away with in preference for single occupancy rooms, and it is a much less frightening place these days.

I was one of four new starts from my force intake. The three others were Hoddit, Doddit, and Bruce. I was the only one of the four to last the full thirty years in the job. Hoddit, Doddit, and Bruce all left to follow other pursuits.

Our training department gave the four of us

a forgettable one-week induction course before they parcelled us off to the Scottish Police College. The only thing I remember was the training sergeant issuing us with our shoulder numbers. My identity for the next thirty years would be a three digit number. I recall thinking *'these numbers might come in handy if we ever got lost, they would be able to match where we came from and put us back.'*

On a Monday morning in December, a day so cold I wouldn't touch my willie in case it fell off, I arrived at the Scottish Police College. In the main hallway I was issued with an identification badge and a lanyard to hang it on. I was warned, by the unsmiling Sergeant MacStern, not to lose the lanyard and to wear the identification where it was visible at all times. He made it sound like I would be shot as an intruder if I was caught without it. From there I was ushered into a dormitory with a dozen other recruits. A mixed bag of people who had come from all walks of life. My distorted memory of the place was that it was like something from an Oliver Twist film. A big dormitory full of bully boys and horsehair blankets.

Quietly I unpacked my stuff beside my bed and was considering stuffing it all back in and walking out when the familiar face of Doddit walked in. All eyes turned to Doddit, and several did a double take, then blinked to ensure their eyes weren't playing tricks on them. Doddit is a remarkably ugly big guy; he looks like the love child of Mrs Shrek and Frankenstein.

Doddit had been an amateur boxer. At six foot, eight inches in height and as wide as an American fridge he was quite a sight. His battered face was a testament to his reasons for giving up boxing. His sheer size and pugilistic phizog made a rather intimidating appearance. When first introduced to Doddit, on our induction course, my gut instinct had been *'don't get on the wrong side of him.'* I had remained wary and obsequiously polite. In my new found circumstances it was different, I was ever so glad to see a familiar face, even one as hideous as his. I smiled at him, and he crossed to my bunk and engaged me in friendly banter. The ugly big bruiser of a man was talking to me. *All the other bully boys had better watch out.*

Hoddit and Bruce arrived soon after and despite only having met these guys a week before we were chatting away like old friends. Together we settled into our new life learning the law, police powers and how we should put them into practice.

My gut instinct not to get on the wrong side of Doddit was a wise precaution as proved when he fell afoul of a slight but plucky Glaswegian called Nigel. I say plucky - I mean stupid.

Nigel had the top bunk above Doddit. On the first night, we were all lying in bed, some of us reading, some of us chatting when the duty sergeant came in with the news that it was time for lights out. I was intrigued when Nigel climbed out of his bunk and went down to his knees clasping his hands together in prayer. He closed his eyes tight shut, and I saw his lips move as he recited his silent plea for forgiveness.

All eyes turned towards him; there were many a querying look between us, I am fairly certain that the only time the rest of us recruits went down on our knees was to pick up money.

My eyes landed on Doddit who was now lying on his bed at the same level as Nigel's head. Doddit gave

Malky McEwan

me a mischievous look as he manoeuvred himself so
that his big hairy arse poked out from under his covers
- inches from Nigel's face. This sight was enough to
send suppressed sniggers around the dorm, but it was
nothing to the explosion of laughter that erupted when
Doddit let one rip. A fart exploded from his big hairy
arse right in Nigel's face.

Nigel never put himself in such a kneeling position again but from then on Doddit considered it up-
roarious to fart just as Nigel climbed onto the bunk
above him. Some might say it was an innocuous
thing to fall out about, but Nigel had a quick temper
and didn't take kindly to Doddit's rancid vapours. He
never forgave him for interrupting his dedication mid-
prayer.

Doddit got on his nerves, metaphorically he
scraped his nails down Nigel's irritometer (I made that
device up) even more by calling him 'Nigella.'

"Hey, Nigella."

"Don't call me Nigella."

Fffffffrrrrrrrrppppp.

"Take that Nigella. He, he, he."

The farting continued for several days. Nigel, to
his credit, squared up to the big ugly ex-boxer. A brave
thing to do for someone half his height and half his
weight, but face up to him he did. Nigel objected to his
mistreatment.

"If you fart at me again I will punch your lights
out."

Doddit smiled, then turned and farted in his direction again.

Fffffffrrrrrrrrppppp.

The plucky Glaswegian threw caution to the

wind. He attacked Doddit with a flurry, his skinny arms flailing like a broken windmill.

Doddit remained calm. His boxing training had prepared him for this situation. As soon as the plucky Glaswegian stepped into range, Doddit dispatched him ten yards backwards along the floor. A single jab to the face being all that he required.

The dorm went silent.

There was a moment as Nigel lay immobile on the floor when everyone assumed that Doddit had killed him. Nigel lay motionless, dead-eyes staring at the ceiling.

Glaswegians, however, are made of sturdy stuff, it would appear. Nigel twitched, then rolled over, gathered his senses and stood up. He looked at Doddit, got angry again and ran straight back at him, arms flailing. The plucky Glaswegian was once more dispatched backwards along the floor at which point we all stepped in and prevented any further assaults.

Good training, I expect, for the job we had signed up to do.

Hoddit was the opposite from Doddit, a brighter than average cop, lean physique and handsome. Everyone assumed he was going places. Even from such an early stage in our service Hoddit impressed with his effortless ability to learn stuff. While we all had to cram like mad, re-read our material and study on the weekends, Hoddit could read a book in the time it took him to do a poo and then remember it all.

His ability to retain information was evident in the classroom. When asked a question, Hoddit would shoot his hand up even before the training sergeants had finished the question. Nobody else put their hand up. Sergeant MacStern looked round the lecture theatre waiting for someone else to stick their hand up, but after a while, he would have to resort to asking Hoddit,

"Okay PC Hoddit, what is the answer?"

"Sir, Hamesucken is the violent and premeditated attack on a person in their home."

After a while, my confidence grew, and eager to please I too would put my hand up. Sergeant Mac-Stern now had a choice between myself and Hoddit. He would still look at everyone in the room, frustrated that no-one else tried to answer the questions. By the third week, he showed his impatience. He badgered us, "Come on, at least make an effort. There are only ever two hands that go up."

Then he asked his next question, "Other than to enforce an arrest warrant, under what circumstances can a police officer force entry to premises?" Sergeant MacStern asked us.

Hoddit shot his hand up straight away. I remembered that, in common law, the police could also force entry to premises to quell a disturbance, so I too put my hand up in the air. Hoddit and I were the only ones with our hands up. Sergeant MacStern looked around the room at everyone else, waiting for someone other than Hoddit and me to put their hands up. No one did. He loathed to choose Hoddit or me again.

"Come on," he said frustrated with the lack of hands in the air, "I want to see more hands up than this!"

Hoddit and I looked at each other. We couldn't help it. It was like we read each other's minds. We looked back at Sergeant MacStern, and in unison, we both raised up our other hand as well.

I burst out laughing and couldn't stop; everyone

else joined in. After five minutes heehawing the class started to quiet down, not me. I just kept going. Raising two hands was the funniest thing imaginable. Even, the scowl I received from Sergeant MacStern wasn't enough to get me to stop. It was just too funny. I had to excuse myself from the room before the scowling Sergeant McStern threw me out.

When I returned, I tried my best to remain stony faced and not look at Hoddit in case I burst out laughing again. The topic had moved on to manslaughter.

"Why is murder called a homicide?" Asked one of the students of Sergeant MacStern.

Sergeant MacStern looked blank. Hoddit put up his hand and answered for him.

"Sarge, homicide comes from Latin, homo meaning man and cida meaning to kill. There are other derivatives from the French such as infanticide - the killing of a child, fratricide - the killing of your brother, and matricide the killing of your mother."

Hoddit folded his arms and gave Sergeant McStern a smile so smug I could see the steam coming out of Sergeant McStern's ears.

"What do you call it when a sergeant kills his student?" MacStern asked, glowering at Hoddit.

I couldn't help myself, "Would that be insecticide, sarge?"

Bruce was entirely different from Doddit and Hoddit. He wasn't a boxer but could handle himself. He didn't have the physique of a boxer - more a whippet. Bruce liked to use the element of surprise and get his retaliation in first. He wasn't that good-looking or as smart as Hoddit, but he was worldly-wise and could talk his way into or out of anything.

Bruce had been in the Merchant Navy before joining the police. He enthralled me with his many stories of adventure. He had travelled all over the globe and had many great tales to tell. As a child, I had only ever been to Butlin's holiday camp, so his tales about all the exotic places he had seen around the world fascinated me.

We became drinking buddies and made the best of our time at the Scottish Police College. Perhaps Bruce and I got up to a little too much nonsense. When I think back, we were lucky not to be given our marching orders.

It is fair to say that Bruce was a bad influence. Whenever he got fed up studying at night, he would chap my bunk and suggest we go to the pub as he had a story to tell me. It didn't take much persuasion for me to fold up my study materials and follow him out of the dormitory.

"I've got a story for you," Bruce would say, and I'd be up and out of my chair quicker than Usain Bolt from the starting blocks.

We'd make our way to the bar, buy a couple of beers and settle into our chairs. Bruce would then regale me with tales of his travels. Faraway places, full of mystique and adventure. He entertained me with the account of his voyages and experiences in exotic locations all over the world. One night he produced a photograph from his wallet. He showed me a picture of a blonde haired, olive skinned young lady in a colourful dress squinting at the camera from the sun.

"This is Jennifer," he explained. "We got engaged in Sydney about three years ago."

"Congratulations," I said. I was totally unaware

that Bruce had a girl, far less was engaged.

He then produced another photograph, this time of a petite Asian female with long jet black hair and shining white teeth.

"This is Jessi, she and I got engaged about two years ago."

Jessi looked pretty as she smiled at the camera posing in front of the Chhatrapati Shivaji Terminus in Mumbai.

"You are engaged to two girls?"

"Not just two," Bruce said grinning like a lemon shark.

The next photograph showed Bruce with his arms around a tall, and gorgeous Brazilian called Gabriella, it was an idyllic-looking picture of the two of them with the statue of 'Christ the Redeemer' in the far background. He was also engaged to Gabriella. in all, he had seven pictures of his various fiancées from around the world, each one more gorgeous than the next. I almost quit and signed up for the Merchant Navy there and then.

Once I settled in, the Scottish Police College turned out to be not that bad. We had numerous newly promoted and enthusiastic training sergeants who were not at all intimidating. Their main purpose was to help us new recruits get through our training and ensure that we prepared for life out on the street. I found them to be extremely obliging and ready to lend a hand, especially when it came to showing me how to put the creases into my parade tunic and trousers. A task I could never master. I stood over the iron and waited for one of them to come by, which they did several times a night, and asked, "How on earth do you get such sharp creases in your trousers?"

The training sergeant kindly took the iron from me and proceeded to give me a lesson in ironing. My lack of ability in this task was startling. The next night I would ask again. Because the sergeants were all on a rota, I had a different sergeant to ask every week. I got to about week seven without so much as pressing a single pair of trousers. Sergeant McGrain was particularly 'helpful,' he pressed my tunic, ironed my trousers and applied spit and polish to my shoes on at least a dozen occasions.

The exception was Sergeant MacStern; Sergeant MacStern wasn't so nice. His main purpose, it seemed, was to bully as many of us into resigning as he could. During one lecture he stopped talking and focussed on a wispy looking Fifer, I think his name was Tony. Mac-Stern just stared at him. Two or three minutes went by; Tony's face reddened, and he wriggled uncomfortably in his seat. MacStern roared at him, "Fekkin sit up straight you little shit!"

Tony wilted, tears welled up in his eyes.

The rest of us wriggled in our seats so we were sat up straight. but avoided looking Sergeant MacStern in the eye.

We were pretty cowardly for not sticking up for Tony. MacStern had a reputation, and we twiddled our thumbs and looked away. He wasn't one to be crossed. We had all been on the end of his scowls, and there were stories of him roaming around the college at night trying to catch out us young probationers. He reported anyone he even thought of as being up to no good.

Tony disappeared that night, never to come back. Bullied into leaving. There were several others who considered leaving because of MacStern and his bully-boy tactics. Macstern's favourite saying was, "If you can't take it from me then won't survive out there."

MacStern was an overly officious, nagging shrew-like person. A man who abused his power. Even after chewing out someone he never left it at that, he still reported the least little thing to the commandant, it was his hobby. We would have preferred he collect stamps.

Having McStern as an instructor on our course was purgatory. It wasn't until the last week of the course that MacStern ended up getting his just desserts. I'll tell you about that in a moment.

A great deal of effort also went into getting us fit. The exercise wasn't quite in the same league as the Royal Marines induction course, but it was a little more exerting than my previous exercise regimen (bending down and tying my shoelaces). Daily, we had to go running through the woods.

I don't like running, (other than to catch up with an ice cream van) so, for me, our daily runs were a gruelling embarrassment. Our P.E. instructor was a stick insect, weighing in at slightly less than anorexic cheerleader. Like a meatball on the end of a pair of chopsticks. He could run all day without so much as working up a sweat. *Forrest Gump* wasn't due to come to our screens for another ten years, but our P.E. instructor would have put him to shame.

At the start of a three-mile run, he would lead the way out into the woods. As our group stretched out, he would then run to the back of the line and give me encouragement to keep up with the rest of the recruits. Not once did I hear the chimes of 'O Sole Mio' promising an ice-cream cone, all I heard was the P.E. instructor shouting, "Hurry up McEwan." He would then jog back to the front and repeat this five or six times during the run. We might have covered three miles, but he would have run double that and still didn't have a lick of sweat on him. I just needed to look at a gym, and my brow would gush with sweat. I could break into a sweat sitting in the classroom just thinking about running.

If we weren't running, or marching up and down on the Parade Square, then we were stuck in a classroom or lecture theatre. Ten weeks at Tulliallan Police College was supposed to prepare me for what was to come. And what to come was sometimes a surprise.

I thought I knew what a murder was, as it turns out there is more to it than you think. The definition of Murder is the taking of life by intent, or by a reckless disregard for the consequences of your actions. If there is no intent or reckless disregard, then the crime is 'culpable homicide' a lesser charge with a lesser penalty. Not everyone is successful, try and fail to kill someone then the charge is 'attempted murder.' People found guilty of attempted murder end up getting a lesser sentence. The actions might be identical, but if you cock it up, you will spend less time in jail.

I also learned what a 'breach of the peace' was. In a nutshell: *A breach of the peace is the common law crime of causing a bloody nuisance of yourself.*

It is an extremely useful crime to fall back on when dealing with obnoxious members of the public. Expertly taught to us by Sergeant Dick who, in the middle of his lesson, had to pause when Sergeant MacAskill entered the lecture theatre and shouted, "Sergeant Dick."

"Yes."

"You are well named."

"Pardon."

"You heard me. Dick."

"This is not the time or the place."

"This is not the time or the place," Sergeant MacAskill mimicked in a high-pitched squeaky voice full of mockery.

"Get out of my class."

"Will I fek. You can't tell me what to do Dickhead."

The two squared up to each other. Both sergeants' got louder and louder until they ended up bawling and shouting. Nose to nose, swearing and gesticulating offensively.

Abruptly they stopped. Sergeant MacAskill turned and walked out.

Sergeant Dick turned towards us and calmly asked if what we saw constituted a breach of the peace.

It was a complete setup.

Their antics provoked a good discussion. We disagreed on the exact point where Sergeant MacAskill had caused a bloody nuisance of himself, which I think was actually the point of the demonstration. The law is one big grey area and not straightforward as you might think. It is often open to interpretation.

At one time bawling, shouting cursing and swearing at a police officer was a perfectly good reason for locking someone up. Then a judge decided that a police officer shouldn't consider that to be a bloody nuisance, and it became okay to verbally abuse a police officer. Then some other dithery old fool, in a stupid wig thought there should also be a public element to a breach of the peace. That decision complicated things all the more. Of course, there is a public element to it. Did the dithery old fool think we went about arresting people for being a bloody nuisance on their own? The law is difficult enough to get right without them interpreting it differently all the time, but there was even more to learn. I also learned the secret of how to cheat the breathalyser.

Every Thursday night we trooped off to the local pub to wind down. Occasionally when returning from the pub, we would sneak through the corridors to the 'Camic' room. The 'Camic' room was where they kept the breathalyser machine. The police use the breathalyser machine, in real life, to establish whether or not someone is fit to drive. The machine measures two separate breaths and provides a reading indicating how much alcohol is in your system. If you fail a roadside breath test, you are arrested, cuffed and taken back to a police station. Once the custody sergeant enters your details into the computer, you are then required to blow into one of these machines.

It was here that I learned the secret. The knack of tricking the machine into reducing the amount of breath alcohol it would record. One night a group of nine of us went out to the pub. We had the same amount to drink during the night. All nine of us returned to the Police College and sneaked along to the breathalyser room. The highest reading was from a surprisingly sober-sounding Shetlander. He blew a count that was 135 microgrammes of alcohol per 100 millilitres of breath. He was 100 microgrammes of alcohol over the legal limit to drive.

There were various other readings all the way

down to just under a hundred. Not a single was fit to drive. Then it was my turn. I took a deep breath and exhaled into the machine. The result was a surprise to everyone. I had just as much alcohol as they had, but I blew a count of thirty-four. A reading exactly one under the legal limit. My fellow students looked as if they had been smacked in the face with a wet cloth.

Yes, I knew how to cheat it, my little secret worked.

Not that I would consider drinking and driving. In any case, the law In Scotland changed in 2014, and the limit was, rightly, reduced to twenty-two micro-grammes. Nobody can cheat it that much. So if you want to avoid getting charged for drunk driving - take a taxi.

Our penultimate week of our ten-week course marked quite a change in all of us. We now knew a little about the law, a little about how to apply that law and even I could press a pair of trousers.

As was the tradition; we took our training ser-geants out for a night out. Keen to show our appreci-ation for the hard work and effort that they had put in to get us up to speed both in the classroom and out in the woods, it was time to celebrate. We decided on a trip to the glorious pubs in Kirkcaldy, Fife and then to round it off with a visit to, the now demolished, *Jackie O's* dance hall and nightclub on the esplanade.

Much to our disdain, Sergeant MacStern decided that he would come along too.

The first pub cheered us up. Likewise the second, until MacStern came and sat beside Bruce and me at our table. I groaned under my breath. Nothing would spoil my night more than having to spend time with Sergeant MacStern.

"So you two think you will be cops then?" Mac-Stern looked at us, mocking, "I give you both a year before you are out on your ear," he laughed at his rhyming put down.

"What makes you think that?" I plucked up the courage to challenge him but probably asked the wrong question.

"I just know," MacStern glowered at me, "you have no stamina, no staying power. You have to be tough to be a police officer; you have to be mentally strong."

Bruce chipped in, "So you reckon you are tougher than us?"

MacStern laughed, "Hah, hah, I've wiped the floor with better girls than you two."

Meanwhile, Bruce finished his pint and, to my surprise, asked MacStern if he wanted a drink, he did, so Bruce headed off to the bar.

MacStern told me stories about the things he had dealt with on the street, "... you would have pissed your pants if you had come across the things I have seen."

In due course, Bruce returned to the table with a tray of drinks. A pint of lager for each of us and three double Tequilas in shot glasses. Bruce picked up his Tequila and downed it in one go. He then looked MacStern in the eyes challenging him to do the same. MacStern picked up his glass and he too downed it in one. I rolled my eyes; not a fan of Tequila but, what the hell, I too downed my glass in one go.

My Tequila tasted like water. I was just about to say something when Bruce gave me a conspiratorial wink. Something twigged in my brain.

"My round," I said and made a beeline for the bar, "a double shot of Tequila and two shots of water please."

Bruce and I downed our water in one go. MacStern followed suit with his Tequila, determined that he would not be outdone by two young probationers. By the time we headed off to the next pub, MacStern was looking decidedly unsteady on his feet.

In the next bar, others joined in buying MacStern Tequila, and a cheer went up from all of us when each tray of shots arrived at our table. MacStern, defiantly continued to throw the Tequila down the back of his throat. We did likewise with our water. An hour later we decided to move on to the next pub in our crawl, MacStern found that his legs wouldn't work. He tried to stand up and couldn't. He collapsed to the floor like a gibbering wreck.

"Right, Malky, you get one side, and I'll get the other," said Bruce.

"What do you mean, can't we just leave him?" I replied, somewhat puzzled.

"Oh, no," replied Bruce, "he is still one of us, and we need to make sure he is safe."

Reluctantly, I assisted Bruce in dragging the inebriated Sergeant MacStern out of the pub. We were just across the road from the train station. MacStern was babbling nonsense and still couldn't use his legs. With his arms round our necks, we hauled him across to the ticket office.

"Wait here," said Bruce, and he went to look at the timetable, while I propped the rubbery MacStern up against the wall.

"This way," Bruce indicated when he returned, and together we manhandled MacStern onto a waiting train. We plopped MacStern on a seat, and his head flopped against the window. I sat down beside Mac-Stern and expected Bruce to sit opposite.

Bruce grabbed me by my collar and yanked me to my feet.

"Come on, we have *Jackie O's* to go to," as he marched me off the train.

No sooner had we stepped off the train the doors closed behind us, and the train took off. We saw Mac-Stern's face still pressed up against the window as the train trundled past but MacStern was oblivious, out for the count.

"Do you think he will be all right at the other end?" I asked Bruce.

"I hope so," replied Bruce, "considering this is the 10:13 train to Inverness we've put him on, he'll have three hours to sober up before he gets there."

For his ingenuity, we rewarded Bruce with free beer for the rest of the night.

So that was Hoddit, Doddit, and Bruce. What about me?

Well, I won the 'Baton of Honour.'

The 'Baton of Honour' is the highest award a student at the Scottish Police College can achieve. It is presented to the student who has shown the highest degree of professional and academic ability. The officer receiving this award will have displayed leadership, personality, and strength of character. He or she is presented with a commemorative baton to keep and has their name inscribed upon an honour board within the college that stands in tribute to the most excellent student.

The board dates back to 1954, and the list of names is impressive. Many of the recipients have gone on to become senior officers, including several that have attained the rank of Chief Constable. There have been further honours in public life for those awarded the 'Baton of Honour'; some have earned a CBE, OBE, and even an MBE.

I am not saying I was actually awarded the 'Baton of Honour.' I won it, though. The award went to a hard-working Taysider. On the night before the award ceremony, I played three card brag with him. On the last hand of the evening, he put the 'Baton of Honour' up as the ante. Sitting with three kings in his hands it, seemed a sure bet. Unfortunately, he lost to my three aces. The next day he was presented with his trophy, but he never passed it on. Hardly honourable!

So that was how I spent my time at the Scottish Police College. However, it was my last night I'd like to forget most.

On my last night there, the night before our passing out parade, we went to the pub, intent on celebrating our survival of everything Tulliallan Police College had thrown at us.

As the night went on our numbers dwindled until only the stalwarts were left. When the pub closed Bruce, and I staggered our way back to the college.

Back at the college, Bruce showed me the half bottle of whisky he had stashed, and he persuaded me to sneak off and finish it with him.

Bruce and I made our way to the Castle (the section of the college that was the domain of the senior college staff and out of bounds for us during the day - far less during the middle of the night). We found two comfortable leather armchairs in the officer's library. To this day I am not entirely sure how we didn't get caught. I certainly made enough noise, trying to suppress laughter as Bruce related his life exploits. We finished every last drop from the bottle.

Now I reckon it might have been a good idea to have tottered to our beds, but Bruce declared he was hungry. I was a little peckish myself.

We had a 'Hogwarts moment.'

Under the influence of my 'invisible cloak' of alcohol and Bruce's first-rate persuasion, we tiptoed our way to the college kitchens and made ourselves a delicious sandwich from the bread, ham, and cheese we found.

Then Bruce came up with his great idea.

"Come with me," he said, "I have a great idea!"

I followed him out of a window and round the back of the college to the Parade Square. We ducked in and out of the bushes and arrived at the flagpole. The podium for the flagpole was where the senior officers stood and saluted the students as they marched past on their 'passing out parade'. A parade that would involve myself in less than five hours time, a fact which the copious amount of alcohol I had drunk had made me oblivious to.

Bruce produced a picture from his pocket. It was a picture of Sergeant McStern saluting, just the top half of his body. It looked like he had cut it out of a magazine or something. He had typed a caption below the picture that read *'I'm the real boss'*. Bruce got me to clasp my hands together and lift him as high up the flagpole as he could. He then taped the picture to the flagpole. He dropped back down to the ground, and we looked up at the picture - well out of reach and burst out laughing.

"Now when we pass by this flagpole in the morning," Bruce explained, "you will know that all the senior officers are standing on the podium with that picture behind them, they won't see it until they turn around to leave. I bet you can't march past without laughing."

I woke the next morning to the sound of 'Reveille' and slowly realised that it was just the ringing in my head. No amount of teeth brushing could remove the stench of alcohol from my breath. The thought of standing on parade, marching up and down filled me with dread. However, it was my passing out parade, and I intended to pass out (although I hoped not literally).

We all scurried about making last minute preparations to our uniform. Parade boots given their last spit and polish, we brushed our tunics, and patted sticky tape all over to get them as free from dust specks as humanly possible. We assembled on the Parade Square stood rigidly to attention as the daily marching routine dictated. We then carried out various manoeuvres up and down the Parade Square in perfect unison, a routine we had practised almost to perfection.

On the final part of the routine, we had to march past the senior officers standing under the flagpole. As we approached the podium, the drill instructor shouted out, "EYES... RIGHT."

Our entire squadron turned our heads and saluted the senior officers. The college commandant turned to his aide and asked, "Who the hell is that laughing?"

Bruce and I were both giggling at opposite ends

of the parade, and thus no-one was quite sure from where the giggles were coming.

Bruce and I made a quick exit as soon as we were 'stood down' by the Parade Sergeant. Time for us to head back to force, join a shift and be the unfortunate recipient of many a practical joke.

The last I heard of Sergeant McStern was that he was posted to Inverness - life can often be full of karma.

CHAPTER 3

HOW TO CATCH A HOUSEBREAKER

Doddit, Hoddit, Bruce and I all went back to our force where we were all posted to different stations.

Doddit completed the rest of his stint at The Scottish Police College without further use of his fists. Posted to a station on the opposite side of our force area from me. I had no contact with him, other than when we met up on the occasional training course.

Doddit was the type to project himself as having no fear. His boxing training and his size ensured he carried out his duties confident that no-one could beat him in a fight. Looking the part is half the battle but looking the part, being fearless and capable of backing that up with swift and decisive action is as good as it gets.

Officers who worked with Doddit would extol his virtues. On a Friday or Saturday night if you were to walk into a bar brawl I would imagine it was always better to walk into it with a six foot eight inch tall, muscular and confident ex-boxer behind you. Arresting angry men with Doddit was a pleasure. No matter how big and angry they were Doddit would soon knock it out of them. They would be on the ground in handcuffs before they knew it.

One night Doddit was on patrol outside a local

nightclub when a group of four youths, smashed on high-voltage cider, caused a bloody nuisance of themselves. When Doddit and his colleague intervened, the four youths turned their anger towards the police. Whether it was the drink or just sheer bravado, they took on the formidable-looking Doddit. All four approached him arms flailing in unison, determined to take the 'big cop' down.

Doddit, happy to keep his arms by his side, calmy danced around their drunken efforts to punch him. Dodging punches was something he could do well. He had trained for many years to avoid taking a punch and avoiding taking a punch from a drunk man was pretty damn easy for him. Avoiding taking a punch from four drunk males was harder, but he showed just how skilled a boxer he was. He did it with aplomb. He floated in between and around their drunken efforts, and within a minute or two he had the crowd cheering him on. They were on his side, laughing and goading the tiring drunken youths. In the end, he grabbed two at a time by their collars and marched them to the prison van that had arrived. All four spent a night in the cells wondering what happened.

With such stories of his boxing prowess circulating, the bosses considered that Doddit could well look after himself. They moved him to a smaller station even before he had finished his probation. His new area was well known as a violent and dangerous place. It was a tiny police office and only had a few police officers. It meant that often he would cover shifts working on his own. Nobody had any fears that Doddit wouldn't be able to handle himself. They had put him there to sort the locals out.

The powers that be posted Hoddit to a big station, and he quickly got a good reputation. An intelligent officer who would go far. When we met up on training courses, I was always pleased to catch up with them.

Bruce seemed content with his life, and his natural ability to wangle his way out of anything would see him through his probation no problem.

They posted me to my hometown. A medium-sized place that once relied upon trade through its port. The river feeding the port silted up and the ever-increasing amount of sediment made it impassable for larger vessels. The town's industry suffocated along with the river. The once thriving docks long since ceased to exist. A brewing industry flourished for a while, but bigger players elsewhere caused the local industry to decline. The population went from living on the spoils of making beer to drinking beer and spoiling their lives.

A tough wee town, full of hard men and harder women. Once described by a cynical old cop as a place where all the men walked with limps, and all the women had big boobs and even bigger beer bellies. Not the best place in the world, but it was my hometown, and I have to say, I can still tolerate the place.

My first shift was a back shift, starting at two in the afternoon. I walked into the office nice and early hoping to get shown around, allocated a locker, and eased into the start of my new career. For me, this was the day that real policing began. Everything until that point I had learned from a book or from sitting in a classroom. I was keen to get started but was more than a little apprehensive - I didn't feel like a cocky little upstart on the inside. My Mum didn't help to ease any of my angst, who I confided in before I left for work, "Mum, I am worried that I might not be clever enough to do the job."

"Don't be so stupid!" she said as she saw me out the door.

I headed off on the long walk to my new police station, stomach churning all the way. The second I entered the office a cop grabbed me by the arm and said, "You must be the new start. Come with me."

Constable Gordon Hop-A-Long rushed out of the front door pulling me with him. He ran along the street, and I obediently followed. As I ran after him, I noticed that he had a gammy leg. Hop-A-Long it would appear was appropriately named. His gait, while making haste, was more of a hop, run, and skip. He ran fifty yards as fast as his hop, run and skip could take him. I tagged along behind at an easy trot.

"Where are we going?" I asked.

Hop-A-Long was already out of breath. He looked at me, gulped in some air and waved his hand for me to follow him. We turned left and ran halfway down the next street where he stopped at a small knick-knack shop. The type of shop that opens one week and closes down the next. Some are lucky to last a little longer if the family funds can stretch to having a wife or daughter sit in a shop all week long and pose for a couple of curious customers. Those curious customers pop in, look at the tat on offer and make a quick exit when they espy the inflated prices.

We entered the shop and a middle-aged lady, plastered in make-up, pointed to a straggly looking youth, "It's him!" she screamed.

I looked around and wondered who else it could

have been as he was the only other person in the shop. Hop-A-Long caught his breath and took charge. He took the youth by the arm and ushered him outside. There simply wasn't enough room for the four of us in the shop. He told me to wait outside with the straggly looking youth as he headed back in to speak to the middle-aged woman to find out what had happened.

The youth looked at me nervously, I looked back at the youth, just as nervous. I was probably even more nervous, totally wet behind the ears and not certain what I would have done if the youth had walked off. I hadn't even started my shift, and here I was in full uniform feeling as if everyone was looking at me (and they are) with a 'prisoner' although at that point we hadn't arrested him. The straggly looking youth stood there looking at the ground. I stood watching him. The pair of us looked as forlorn as each other.

My shoplifter had no idea I just started. He didn't know that I was as nervous as him. He didn't know I hadn't a clue. All he saw was a broad-shouldered, ugly looking policeman in full uniform, polished shoes, tunic pressed in the right places, wearing a black-and-white checkered hat. It did not even cross his mind to run away.

It was my first lesson in policing. If you listen to politicians, half the time they talk without actually saying anything. It is not what they say; it is the way they say it. With policing, how people react to you is often to do with how you look and act. I might have known nothing, I certainly hadn't dealt with anything until then, but all that boy saw was the uniform. The straggly teenager saw a person of authority, with the power to hold him there for as long as deemed necessary. He did not see beneath the uniform to the nervous young cop I was; he wasn't to know I had just started that day.

'Looking the part is half the battle,' was a favourite saying of one of my most respected colleagues. I heard him say it many a time. To be a good police officer you need to look like a good police officer. You need not be tall or strong. You just need to be well turned-out, project a good image and be confident in what you do. Later in my service, my advice to any recruit was, 'be smart and wear your hat.' Maybe I should have expanded on that;

'Don't be scruff or you'll look duff.'

'No hat? Then you're a prat.'

'Dress like a tart - unwelcome fart.'

Constable Hop-A-Long eventually emerged from the shop. He had obtained a statement from the make-up plastered, middle-aged shop-owner. He turned to the youth and had him empty his pockets. The one and the only thing the youth had in his possession was a mini, vintage, cut glass, knick-knack dish. The underside bore a handwritten price tag of £2. Hop-A-Long handed me the dish and announced that I had my first case. A shoplifter.

So it was on my second day, back at the station, before I attended my first shift briefing. Before starting duty, we all came together in the briefing room where our sergeant would bring us up to speed on what had been going on, what crimes had been committed, etc. He then allocated us the beats we were to patrol and dished out any work needing done. I was keen to make a good first impression so attended nice and early for work. I changed into my full uniform in the locker room and made my way to the briefing room next door. A dozen plastic chairs were lined up in an irregular pattern facing the desk at the back of the room. I was the first cop into the briefing room and was a little surprised to see my shift sergeant sitting behind the desk already. Sergeant Charming was studiously examining a great big log-book and referring to several printed sheets of paper. He took notes in an A4 sized notebook. He looked up for a moment and told me to take a seat.

The chairs were set out in three rows. I didn't want it to look like I wasn't keen so avoided the back row but I was still at the biting nails stage, anxious enough not to want to sit in the front row, in the line-of-fire. I sat right in the middle of the middle row. Sergeant Charming continued to pore over the big log-book in front of him, I didn't want to disturb him, and he seemed focused on what he was doing, so we sat in silence. I waited for the rest of my shift members to appear.

After sitting quietly for fifteen minutes, the door to the briefing room swung open and in walked John. I looked around to smile and nod at my new colleague in as friendly a manner as I could muster; I wanted to give the impression of being confident and cool but approachable. I couldn't believe what I saw. My eyes bulged out of my head in surprise.

John was a big guy, six feet four, maybe seventeen stone. He looked formidable in his collared white shirt, black tie, and buttoned up tunic but that was not what surprised me. My astonishment was that he was not wearing any trousers. He marched in sporting nothing underneath other than his boxer shorts, black socks, and Doc Martin boots. I looked up to see Sergeant Charming's reaction, but he still had his head down behind his desk scrutinising his log-book.

John came and sat to my left, smiled at me, took out his notebook and a pencil and made ready to take notes. I didn't know where to look; I was too stunned to make any comment to him regarding his state of undress. I sat there confused, after a few seconds I heard the door squeak open again, and I looked around once more, this time, to see Herbert enter the briefing room. Herbert was a slim, fresh-faced cop. He was the same age and service as John, but because Herbert always had a cheeky grin on his face, he looked a lot younger. He strolled in, gave me a big smile, and came and sat to my right. This time, I wondered if I was seeing things, for Herbert, like John wasn't wearing any trousers. They had on their tunics but their legs were bare. Herbert theatrically crossed his naked legs as soon as he sat down. Sergeant Charming still didn't look up from his log-book.

'What on earth was going on?' I thought to myself as I struggled to grasp what I was seeing.

The door squeaked open again, and this time, the rest of my shift plodded in. Every single one dressed in a shirt, tie, and tunic but missing their trousers. Boxer shorts, black socks, and black boots were all they wore on their lower half. My consternation grew, bewildered by the bizarrely dressed people around me.

Was I going insane? Was this really happening?

I looked up at Sergeant Charming and wondered what on earth was he going to say when he eventually looked up from his logbook and saw all his shift, apart from me, only half dressed?

Sergeant Charming sat for a minute more eyes glued to his log-book and taking the occasional note on his A4 notepad. Then he coughed a little to indicate to the group that the briefing was about to start. The quiet mumbles being passed around between the shift ceased, and we all paid him our full attention. Sergeant Charming looked up scanned the room taking in that everyone, but his new probationer had attended his briefing today minus their trousers. His eyes settled on me.

"Malcolm, why are you wearing your trousers?"

I went bright red and couldn't think of a single thing to say. Some form of gurgling came from my mouth, but it was incomprehensible. I sat there flabbergasted. It was only when Sergeant Charming stood up from behind his desk I could see that he too was trouserless.

This gave the game away. The rest of my new shift could no longer hold it in, all burst into raucous laughter, and it was then I realised that I was the butt of a practical joke. The first of many.

Later, once they put on their trousers and the hilarity subsided, Sergeant Charming introduced me to my new colleagues and my first tutor, 'Officer Dan Dribble.' Officer Dribble looked me up and down, grunted and nodded. I wasn't sure if he approved of me or not. He was quite a strange-looking character. He was six foot tall and had a solid square face and tired eyes. Despite shaving first thing in the morning his beard grew so quickly that, by the time he had finished breakfast, he already had stubble. It gave him a dark and desperate look. Often he appeared with shaving cuts, especially on the early shifts. He would come in with bits of toilet paper stuck to the cuts on his face in his hit-and-miss attempts to stem the bleeding.

Constable Dan Dribble was nearing the end of his service. As I got to know the other characters on my shift, they told me stories about Dan. I wasn't sure if they were wholly true or not, but there certainly seemed to be a degree of fact about them. I learned that Officer Dribble was the son of a senior police officer, a superintendent no less. Dan was therefore expected to do well, but it was clear from the outset he perhaps wasn't as quick thinking as his father. His slowness on the uptake they explained in one of two ways. The first being that not long after he started as a cop he got into a fight with a gang of youths. These youths knocked him to the ground and kicked him several vicious blows to his head. It was a notion that Dan never fully recovered from that kicking. The second reason put forward surmised 'that is just the way he is.'

Dan had been an unimpressive recruit during his probation. So much so that his training sergeant approached his father, the Superintendent, and gave him the bad news. Dan isn't good enough. He failed his exams, is slow on the uptake when it came dealing with anything other than the most simple of matters. He just isn't up to scratch. They would have to let his son go.

Dan's father wasn't too happy, nepotism crept in and he 'asked' that they extend Dan's probation for six months. During that time he would work with him and bring him up to speed. If he still wasn't good enough to be a police officer after that time, then they could let him go. Not wanting to make any enemy of his boss, the sergeant agreed to this remedial training arrangement.

After six months the reports on Officer Dribble showed that he still wasn't suited to life as a police officer. One thing at a time was about as much as he could cope with and in a busy station where calls came in thick and fast. Dan was just about muddling through and no more. Not that he was lazy or not keen enough. He simply dawdled along at a pace where he could do one thing at a time and no more. All police officers have to juggle numerous cases and demands on their time. Dan could only take on one thing at a time and slowly follow it through to a conclusion. The training sergeant made a return journey to Superintendent Dribble's office with the regrettable news.

"I'm sorry, sir. We have given Dan another six months as you requested. He still isn't coping, and he hasn't reached the standard required to get through his probation."

Dan's dad, the Superintendent, gave the training sergeant a stern look.

"Well, there is nothing you can do about it now," he said, "the regulations clearly state that a Constable's probation is to last two years. Dan has been in for two years and six months and is thus no longer in his probation. You will just have to keep him."

That, as the story goes, is how Dan Dribble remained a police officer despite not quite making the mark.

It turned out, however, that Dan was about as ideal a tutor cop as you could get. At least for the first two months of my service, anyway. He was slow and methodical. We took on one task at a time and followed it through to a conclusion. It was a good way to learn. Dan explained every step of the process as we went through it. He checked everything I did and gave me a good initial grounding.

Unfortunately, Officer Dribble had a few idio-syncrasies. His driving, for one, was most definitely not the best. I didn't sit my police driving test until later in my probation, so Dan drove everywhere. Ser-geant Charming always allocated Dan the 'big van.' The van was the oldest most decrepit vehicle at the sta-tion. Before going anywhere, Dan went through an end-less series of checks before driving off. He would drive everywhere we went at fifteen miles per hour in fourth gear. The poor decrepit old van rattled like it was full of bones.

The only time Dan wasn't in fourth gear was when we on our way to an emergency call. After a while, I came to dread the announcement over the radio directing us to a '999' incident. Officer Dribble would stop the van. Cautiously, he would activate the blue lights and the siren. The blues and twos broadcast-ing his intention to other road users we were in a hurry, there was an emergency somewhere, and we needed them to get out of the way. This police van needed to get there as quickly as possible.

Dan would then engage first gear, drive off and rev the beleaguered engine until it screamed in protest. Only then would he change to second gear. No matter what the emergency or how far away it was, Dan never put the van into a higher gear than second. The siren would blare, and the lights would flash. The engine would scream with dissent, but the van was incapable of going any faster than fifteen miles per hour in second gear. Cars in front of us would slow down, pull to the side and let us pass. Then they would nip in behind and follow us at a slower speed than they were travelling in the first place. I would sit in the passenger seat, cringe and hide my face.

It turned out that Officer Dribble hadn't passed his police driving exam. In his early days, every officer had to go on a two-week training course before being allowed to drive a general police duties vehicle. Officer Dribble failed his general police duties driving course three times. Sent back to his station to walk the beat, the only time he got into a car was as a passenger. After a few years, his sergeant became a little fed up having to cater for Dan and his inability to drive so he requested a temporary authorisation for him. Dan remained temporarily authorised to drive general police patrol vehicles right until he only had two years service to go.

After twenty-eight years as a temporary authorised driver, Officer Dribble crashed the police van. I saw it happen. By that time I had moved to another station and was off duty. I was driving through the town and fell in behind a police van driving at fifteen miles per hour. I guessed it might have been Dan. He came to a T junction, looked left and saw a car approaching, he looked right and saw another car approaching, he looked left again and saw that the car was almost at the T junction. Then he pulled straight out in front of both cars. The drivers couldn't do anything, they crashed into Dan's van, powerless to take avoiding action.

I stopped and was about to get out and check that everyone was all right. Dan stunned me by getting out of his van first. He was okay by the look of him but his brow furrowed and his eyes blazed. Next thing I knew he was shouting at the car drivers, remonstrating with them as if it was their fault. I decided that it was probably not a good idea to be a witness, so I drove on.

After an accident investigation the bosses real-ised that Dan only had a temporary authorisation. He had been driving on it for over two decades. They promptly took his temporary authorisation from him, and Dan went back to walking the beat. For the remain-der of his police service, Dan got the job of delivering citations on foot.

After a few months working with Dan, I got a bit weighed down. Going to incidents similar to ones we had dealt with before became laborious. Dan did one thing at an interminably slow speed. It was frustrating because Dan took so long to deal with everything.

On one occasion we went to a house to deal with a neighbour dispute. Invited in we sat down on a comfy sofa in a nice comfy house. We listened to the com-plaint from the middle-aged couple. The wife droned on about how bad their neighbour was and recounted every little thing that had happened since they had moved in four years previous. I tried to get her to hurry up and get her to the point of the latest call. Dan, how-ever, contented himself on the comfy sofa, in her warm house and listened to her full unabridged version of events. The wife was more than happy to drone on and on.

Eventually, she finished her story. Only then did Dan take out his notebook and inform her he would have to note all that down. Dan's writing was akin to writing with a chisel on stone. His pen scratched out each word like he was engraving the Ten Command-ments. The story had to be repeated slowly, so utterly slowly. Dan inscribed each word to his notebook in classical lettering. I sat and agonised over the time it took. My presence in the room became in body only. I settled my gaze on the muted television and fell into a daydream. The minutes slowly passed.

"Excuse me?"

"Excuse me, excuse me?"

"Hello?"

Poked out of my daydream as the middle-aged homeowner grabbed my attention. I looked at her sheepishly, but instead of making a comment about me, she pointed at Officer Dribble. Dan was still on the sofa, notebook on his lap, the pen in his hand. His head, however, had slumped forward and a big dribble of saliva fell from his mouth and landed squarely on his notebook. He had fallen asleep halfway through writing this poor woman's statement.

On another occasion, Dan and I left our night shift briefing and headed off to execute an arrest warrant. Dan was eager to get there as the warrant was for Harry Haslam, an old adversary of his. We arrived at the home of Harry Haslam, a mid terraced council house in the less salubrious part of town. The lights were all off downstairs, but a light coming from the upstairs bedroom suggested there might be someone at home.

Dan marched up to the front door and banged loudly and repeatedly. He made his presence clear to anyone inside. After a moment the bedroom window opened, and Harry Haslam popped his head out. "What the fuck do you want!" he shouted.

Dan looked up, stepped backward so he could see him better and tripped over a row of angled bricks sticking out of the ground that designated the separation between the path and the raised flowerbeds. Dan fell backward and landed on a rose bush squishing it beneath his large frame.

"You've just destroyed my fucking rose bush!" shouted Harry Haslam with indignation.

Dan looked up from where he lay on the ground. "You're under arrest!" he shouted back.

"Fuck off!" was Harry's response, and he ducked his head back into his bedroom and shut his window.

Dan extricated himself from the flowerbed and in a fury made his way to the front door. Bending down at the letter-box he opened it up and shouted, "You're charged, you're charged, you're charged. Open the door. You're charged."

I couldn't help but chuckle to myself but after a minute watching this surreal scene, I went up to the door and tried the handle. It was unlocked. I opened it and marched upstairs, closely followed by Dan. We arrested Harry Haslam on his warrant. There was a brief struggle before Harry submitted to handcuffs and we escorted him from his house.

We arrived back at the station with our prisoner, and Harry bombarded the custody sergeant with complaints.

"They can't just barge into my house," he moaned.

Sergeant Gaberston looked at us, and we showed him the warrant.

"This is a 'means' warrant," he said, "this doesn't carry any powers of entry."

Dan (in what was an unusually quick piece of thinking for him) replied, "We are also charging him with a breach of the peace for swearing at me sergeant."

Officers are empowered by law to enter any premises to quell an ongoing disturbance.

The additional charge satisfied Sergeant Gaberston, and Harry was lodged in a cell before his appearance at court the next day.

Our night-shift week ran from Monday to Sunday. We had two days to recover before starting our back shifts on Wednesday. After a tiring week of night shifts, I'd felt like a zombie. I slept most of the day on Monday, and thus we only had the Tuesday off before we were back to work on Wednesday.

Others on my shift had their routine to deal with it.

John would stay up all day on Monday so by his bedtime he would be completely exhausted. He'd sleep all night and pretty much be back to normal the next day. I tried John's method but by teatime, after feeling grumpy and sloth-like, I succumbed to a comfortable couch and missed the rest of the evening. I'd be wide awake about two in the morning and struggle to get back over asleep.

Herbert recommended going to bed later and later every day for the full week. His theory being that on Monday it was easier to stay up all day and go to bed at the normal time. I tried Herbert's method and found that staying up later every day is boring. You sit around waiting to go to bed. Then getting out of bed in the evening and going straight to work made me feel like I had missed the best part of the day.

One day in the canteen we were talking about our night shift recovery routines when John and Herbert (and the rest of the shift) urged me to ask Officer Dribble what his Monday off the night-shift routine was. There was something conniving about their urging that made me think they were up to something. I tried to get them to tell me, but they urged me to find out for myself.

I had been working with Officer Dribble for over two months by that time. Whenever I complained about anything on the night shift, he always replied, "Never mind. Monday night is bath night."

"I'm tired," I would say about six in the morning"

"Never mind. Monday night is bath night."

"I'm cold."

"Never mind. Monday night is bath night."

"I'm wet."

"Never mind. Monday night is bath night."

"I'm tired, I'm cold, and I'm wet."

"Never mind. Monday night is bath night."

Eventually, I became curious enough to ask him, "What exactly do you mean by 'Monday night is bath night'?"

Dan looked me up and down before replying, "It's the best way to recover from the night shifts."

"Having a bath?"

"Aye. But first I buy six cans of beer. Then after dinner I fill the bath and lie in it, drink my beer until all six cans have been drunk," he paused before adding, "then I make love to the wife and after that, I sleep like a log."

From then on whenever he said, "Never mind. Monday night is bath night," he would give me a great big sleazy grin.

So it was Officer Dribble who first taught me how to be a cop. He taught me how to write a statement, how to prepare a report, how to label a production and all the other duties required of a police officer. He even taught me how to catch housebreakers.

One night the alarm went off at the local rugby club. Dan and I were quickly on the scene and found the side door forced open. Due to not seeing anyone running away, we were certain the culprit or culprits were still inside.

Dan whispered in my ear, "Once I give you the signal... start barking like a dog."

Before I could query 'why?' he strode up to the broken door and shouted, "Right! It's the Police. If you don't come out now, I will send the dog in."

And at that, he pointed at me in a clear sign I was to start barking.

So I did.

I made my bestest impression of an angry and hungry Alsatian.

"Woof, Grrr, woof woof, howl, grrr grrr!"

And that is how we caught our thieves.

It turned out the two thieves had climbed onto the roof where they lay unobserved in complete darkness. We were oblivious to their presence and oblivious to the fact that from their vantage point they were watching our every move. When I barked, the sight of a uniformed cop pretending to be a dog was too much for them, and they both chuckled, struggling to contain their laughter. They couldn't help themselves.

We overheard them and persuaded them to come down before we called for a real dog and sent it up.

I enjoyed catching the bad guys, not so much getting pranks played on me in the mortuary - as was soon to happen.

CHAPTER 4

IT'S COLD IN HERE

Sergeant Charmer appreciated that people could only work with Officer Dribble for so long. As the months rolled in, he paired with others on my shift. I tried not to show that I was getting a bit frustrated working with Officer Dribble, but it wasn't easy. The occasional pairing with others on my group was a welcome relief. We had some entertaining personalities on the shift; in particular, John.

John was a good guy. A quick-witted comedian who could control any situation with an acerbic comment that put our clientele firmly in their place. On the odd occasion Sergeant Charmer announced I was to work with John instead of Desperate Dan I had to suppress a smile. John never failed to amuse. Everyone liked to work with him. When calls allowed, he entertained us with jokes and stories. When we were busy, he dealt with matters quickly and efficiently. His ability to run rings round our regulars with his rapier-like wit was a joy to behold. He could diffuse almost any situation with his humour and bring even the angriest man around to our side. On the odd occasion when they were just too drunk or too thrawn, John used his superior intellect to cut them down to size. Everyone in hearing distance left in no doubt as to their pettiness and stupidity. Yes, John was great to work with, and we left the briefing room with a skip in our step when we got paired up with him. There was one exception to that rule; nobody liked to work with John on the night shift. I soon found out why.

The night-shift week came around, and Officer Dribble had taken it off as part of his annual leave entitlement. John slotted into the tutor role. He grabbed the keys for the best car at the station, a two-year-old, marked, Ford Sierra. Not that it was anything special, just a basic model, but it was the roomiest car we had.

John drove around our beat for an hour, amusing me with his stories and making witty comments about any funny looking locals as we passed. Nearing midnight, just as it was getting quiet, another crew took a report of a housebreaking at the other end of the town. Without blinking an eye, John informed me that the likely suspect would be none other than 'Billy J. McGarvie'. I bowed to his superior knowledge in these matters and assumed that since he knew him to be responsible, we would head straight to Billy J. McGarvie's house and we would arrest him.

John drove through the town and headed out on the main arterial route. We left the town behind, and I presumed that Billy J. McGarvie must live in the next village. John drove into the next village and turned left onto a back road, with a destination clearly in mind. A little further on John turned right and headed up a dirt track.

'Strange place to have a house,' I thought to myself.

But what did I know?

At the end of the dirt track, a great big coal bing

loomed up in front of us. John drove the Ford Sierra round the back of the bing and parked up, so we were facing it. I looked around for signs of a house, but there was nothing there, just blackness. I presumed that this was a ploy. Maybe this was a route that Billy J. McGarvie would take on his road home from his nefarious deeds. Were we going to lie in wait? I looked at John and smiled, pleased that I had guessed what he was planning.

John then adjusted the driver's seat until fully reclined.
"Listen out for any calls on the radio," he instructed, before pulling his hat over his eyes and instantaneously falling asleep.

We weren't lying in wait. John going to sleep was the reason no-one liked to work with him on the nightshift. I sat for the next three hours staring into a black coal bing and listening to John snore like a demented bull. We went nowhere near Billy J. McGarvie, and I too learned to avoid working with John on the night shifts.

As a rite of passage, probationers were often the subject of inappropriate and cruel pranks. These days police officers are cautious about playing tricks on probationers. Today's probationers are a much more savvy bunch. They have university degrees, ambition and know their rights. When I joined, there was no fear that a probationer (I include myself in this) would complain. It was just the accepted practice. No matter how evil the prank, probationers took it as part of the learning process.

I'd heard stories of probationers being sent into graveyards in the dead of night only to run off when a ghostly apparition appeared. That ghostly apparition being the senior cop sporting a white sheet, a mask, and a torch. Not imaginative but executed well it would be the scariest thing ever to happen to some unsuspecting probationer.

My initiation was a simple prank called the 'box.'

My first introduction to the 'box' was on a night-shift. Sergeant Charmer instructed me to walk the town beat and make sure I check the properties. Not long after leaving the office I received a radio message informing me that there was a suspicious character seen at our large Co-operative premises at the top of the town. I wasn't far away, so I hurried along to check the area. The front windows appeared intact, and after reporting this back via my radio, I made my way round the side of the building, through a dark alleyway, to check the rear.

Halfway down the alley, I saw a crate about five-foot by five-foot -square just outside the roller shutters of the goods entrance. That seemed a little strange. I checked the shutters, and they appeared in order. Turning my attention to the crate, I was about to open it up when the lid flew off, and Herbert jumped up like a 'Jack-in-the-box' screaming at the top of his voice.

I nearly had a costly dry cleaning bill.

Two weeks later John had a chat with me, he told me a new probationer had started, and it was my turn to get in the box and surprise him. My colleagues were all scheming and conspiratorial. I felt like I was part of the group, one of them, a trusted colleague playing a part in the shift prank. As we arranged, at 2 a.m., I sneaked down the dark alley to the side door of the Co-operative premises and lodged myself within the crate.

I waited for the sound of feet approaching and pictured myself jumping up like a Jack-in-the-box.

I waited... then I waited some more. I couldn't radio up for an update as they had taken my radio off me 'just in case it gave the game away.'

I waited some more.

Eventually, I realised no-one was coming. Perhaps they had all had to go to a serious incident and had to abandon the prank. The probationer would have been here by now if it had all went to plan. I decided to exit the box and head back to the office to find out what was going on.

I lifted the lid, popped my head up. My entire shift, including Sergeant Charmer, had sneaked up and surrounded the crate. As soon as I popped up, they jumped up around me screaming at the top of their voice.

That time I did fork out on some dry cleaning.

I still considered myself blessed compared to 'Lucky Luke' who was a probationer on another shift. Of course, Lucky Luke wasn't all that lucky. He received the nickname after falling through the ceiling of a house (he had been told to search the attic for stolen property and stepped between the rafters). Despite being a bright kid, he was unlucky on such a frequent basis that the nickname stuck.

My first station had a snooker table in the room where we had our refreshment breaks. It was a strange set up as access to the room was through swing doors leading to a set of five steps down. The room opened out to cater for the snooker table and a seating area with four tables. During our refreshment breaks, we could sit and drink coffee and hit a few balls.

One day I was on my break, playing snooker with Herbert when the swing doors above us crashed open. A locker ended up falling into the hallway above the five steps leading down to the room. The doors swung back to the closed position. Then they swung open again, and Mad Willie MacPherson (a senior cop) came storming in behind the locker. He bent down and lifted the locker so it stood upside down on the top landing before throwing it end over end down the stairs where it came crashing to a stop beside us.

Mad Willie McPherson followed it down. The locker lay flat on its back with the door facing upwards.

"Gentlemen," Mad Willie McPherson addressed us, "I'd like you to meet my new probationer."

At that, Mad Willie McPherson went across to the locker, pulled a key from his pocket and used it to unlock the door and open it.

"I give you 'Lucky Luke.'"

Lucky Luke, looking rather dazed, climbed out of the locker and nodded at us in acknowledgement. I remember wiping the sweat off my brow, glad not to have ended up on Mad Willie McPherson's shift.

Those weren't the only pranks they played on probationers. 'Water bombing' was a favourite of a PC Walter Cram.

Walter was tutoring a new start, PC Johnny 'Tac' Mc-Stone. His nickname 'Tac' was an acronym of 'Totally Arrogant something or other' or it could have been that he was just a little prick. Johnny became a good cop and a jolly good tutor himself, however, he was somewhat of a pain in the backside when he first arrived. The son of a politician, he was the type that knew it all - despite being just in the door. He'd dealt with one breach of the peace case but to listen to him, Sherlock Holmes would come to him for advice. He had a tendency to rub people up the wrong way.

"Can you make tea Tac?" Walter would ask.

"I'm not here to be your skivvy, I'm here to learn the job and be the best police officer you have ever seen," he would reply.

"Every probationer just in the door gets the job of making the tea. We have done it since time immemorial. You are just in the door, and until a newer probationer comes in, you make the tea!"

"I'm not just any new probationer, though, am I?"

PC Cram refrained from slapping Johnny about the head but only just. He hatched a plan to sort him out the bumptious little know-all.

Walter sent his probationer out to walk the town centre. They were night shift, and it was a weeknight, so there wasn't much else going on. Johnny headed off out on foot patrol.

In the meantime, Walter handed out balloons to the rest of the shift. They filled the balloons with water, and they all headed off into the centre of town and took up a position one flight up in a block of flats. They opened the hall window overlooking the road. All they had to do was wait for Johnny to come wandering along and they would drop their water bombs on him.

In due course Johnny wandered into view, sauntering down the road admiring his reflection in the shop windows until he ended up directly below the rest of his shift high above. He was completely unaware. The first water bomb dropped and missed. Johnny looked up, realised he was the target of the prank and proceeded, with some aplomb, to dodge the remaining half dozen water bombs aimed at him.

The joke was on them. Johnny became even more unbearable. Their mission to soak Johnny failed and it only made him all the more smug and arrogant. He swaggered into briefings with a self-satisfied smile and wasn't shy about reminding his older colleagues he was too sprightly to get soaked by dithering old men like them. PC Walter Cram formulated a further plan.

This time, he chose his location with a little more care. There were several tall buildings in the city centre, including the town library. The library had six storeys and access to its roof gotten via a fire escape at the rear. The fire escape came down into a courtyard which people could access via a set of steps along a small vennel. The courtyard would afford no escape except back up through the small vennel.

The next night-shift came along, and Johnny was, once again, sent on foot patrol through the town. This time, PC Cram enlisted the help of six other cops. Each of them armed with a dozen water bombs. The potential onslaught would be devastating. They sneaked their way down the vennel, up the fire escape and positioned themselves up three floors on top of the library.

By arrangement, the office clerk sent a radio message to Johnny.

"PC McStone, can you check the rear of the library, there was a complaint yesterday regarding vandalism to windows in the courtyard at the rear.

"Roger."

Johnny came into sight in the rear courtyard. PC Walter Cram waited until he had crossed to his side. The plan was he would drop his water bombs and as he tried to escape the courtyard, the rest of the troops would drop theirs at the exit as he made his way out.

PC Cram took aim. He dropped his first water bomb, and it plunged down towards his probationer. By pure chance, a second before impact Johnny just looked up. The water bomb smashed into his face. A direct hit. The balloon full of water dropped from three storeys up exploded on contact. Johnny collapsed to the ground and lay there disorientated and prone. Battered by the force of the one water bomb. It was a devastating hit.

The officers, three storeys above, all looked at each other. They had all witnessed this shocking direct hit. There was a worried look on their faces. Had they caused him some damage? What if he had broken his neck or even killed him? Would they all be held responsible? What were they going to do?

They looked at PC Walter Cram for guidance. He looked down at Johnny lying powerless on the ground three storeys below, he then looked at his colleagues and shouted, "FIRE!"

They dropped the rest of the water bombs. Like a Lancaster Bomber dropping its load, the torrent of water bombs exploded on impact. Johnny wasn't so cocky from then on.

The next evening at the start of their shift PC Walter Cram was quick to remind Johnny that, "old age and treachery beats youth and enthusiasm every time!"

There were more pranks played on unsuspecting junior officers in the mortuary than anywhere else.

The mortuary, you would imagine, is a sombre place. A place where police officers take a deferential approach to their work. A place where they show respect for those unfortunate corpses by talking in whispers while they strip and tag the unfortunate dead in an efficient and professional manner. It would seem only right that officers leave all humour and nonsense outside the door of the mortuary. Certainly, you might think that.

The mortuary, whether right or wrong, was often a place where police officers carried out their devious pranks on probationers. I fell afoul of one such prank perpetrated by my older colleagues, John and Herbert.

Our mortuary was at the rear of our main hospital. We met family members at the front entrance and ushered them through the demure surroundings to spend a little time with their recently passed on loved one. A viewing room allowed them to sit and view the departed relative. The mortuary attendant prepared the deceased by removing him or her from the freezer and onto a trolley. He covered the deceased with a shroud (a simple, clean white sheet) and turn the head at an angle before wheeling the trolley into the viewing gallery. Once the family was ready, the mortuary attendant would open the small curtain so they could see their relative. The angle of the head is always facing the viewing window. The bereaved given their opportunity to say goodbye. It is all part of the grieving process.

Out of hours, when the mortuary attendant was at home watching telly or tucked up in bed, we were given the job of doing the viewing. Sometimes we had to do it for identification purposes. The Procurator Fiscal required that we followed a system so that any post-mortem examination was carried out on the correct cadaver.

At the time I was just a naïve young probationer

doing his best to get used to dealing with what was an unfortunate but necessary part of the job. Before the arrival of the family, I got the job of opening up the front door. John and Herbert remained in the rear where they prepared the body for viewing. I had limited experience in a mortuary and can't say it was my favourite part of the job. Preparing dead bodies is not something many of us would want to get used to, is it? Getting the job of preparing the viewing room and ushering the family through, seemed to be the best part of the deal.

I went through to the front door and checked I had the correct keys to open it, in readiness for the imminent arrival of the family. The doctor had refused to certify the cause of death due to lack of medical history, so we asked them to attend to identify the deceased. In such circumstances, a post-mortem might be carried out, and we need to submit a report to the procurator fiscal. The first part of that is to ensure we know who the person on the slab is. Thus two officers have to be present when two relatives view the deceased and confirm that he or she is their dear departed. We then tie a tag to the toe and sign it in confirmation. We don't want the pathologist cutting up the wrong body, do we?

By the time I made my way back through to the viewing room, I had noted that John and Herbert had laid out the deceased on the trolley in the viewing room. The curtains were open. We normally shut these until the family is in place. I made my way up to the window and was about to shut the curtains when I noticed the deceased was facing away from the viewing window. The white sheet covered the rest of the body from the neck down, so all that John and Herbert needed to turn the head to face the viewing window.

I knocked on the glass to alert them of their error; they were in the mortuary behind a curtain where the deceased lay. There was no response, so I knocked that bit harder. The body on the trolley in front of me then moved. The head turned towards me all by itself and shouted, "WHAT IS IT?"

I nearly had another dry cleaning bill.

It was, of course, Herbert under the covers. John came out from behind the door to the mortuary snorting and laughing like a demented boar. Herbert got up and gave John a big high five. Oh, they were so pleased with themselves. To be fair, I was so relieved and their laughter so infectious that I joined in too.

It was all I could do to stop myself laughing again when ten minutes later, I was showing the real deceased to his family.

Afterwards, on the way back to the station, John related the prank his shift had played on him when he was on his probation.

John had arrived at the mortuary to deal with his first dead body. At the time a fresh-faced naïve probationer just like me. His tutor cop informed him that a Boris Grabowski had died earlier in the hospital, the hospital staff conveyed him to the mortuary and then informed the police. John and his tutor were instructed to deal with him.

His tutor busied himself with the necessary book entries and asked John to find Boris. The freezer cabinets had names on them, but none bore the name 'Boris Grabowski.' John informed his tutor he couldn't find Boris. Without looking up from his paperwork, his tutor told him that the hospital staff regularly forgot to mark up the cabinets on the outside and that he should try all the unmarked ones until he found a body.

John went along the rows of cabinets opening each unmarked one in turn. On his third try, he opened an unmarked cabinet and found a body hiding underneath a shroud.

"How can we be sure it is Boris Grabowski?" John asked his tutor.

"Just ask him," was the reply from his tutor, who went back to filling out forms.

John, who had wit in abundance, humoured his tutor, he turned to the corpse and asked, "Are you, Boris Grabowski?"

The corpse pulled down his shroud and stated, "Yup. That's me!"

He had been set up. The previous junior probationer rose from his position within the cabinet laughing and full of glee at their well-worked prank.

That wasn't the end of it. John continued with his story; "About two weeks later a new probationer joined my group, and after much secret discussion I got the role of being the corpse. Before we called the new probationer to the mortuary, I installed myself in the freezer cabinet. At the last second, my tutor handed me a torch stating, "It can get dark in there. Just be patient." I waited."

"I was excited about being in on the prank, but after a few minutes I felt cold and became a little apprehensive just lying there in the dark. I flicked on the torch and looked to my left. There was a corpse covered in a shroud. I then turned the torch beam around and pointed it to my right. Lying on the trolley in the next cabinet was a similar body wrapped in a white sheet.

I panned the torch up the body and realised there was something odd about it. The shroud didn't cover the head. In fact, the head was propped up on its hand and was looking right at me. As soon as the torchlight hit its face, it said, 'Cold in here isn't it?'"

"I screamed until they let me (and the senior cop next to me) out of the freezer."

CHAPTER 5

THE JOB'S FECKED

Despite water balloon bombing, mortuary pranks, and other such nonsense, we still had work to do. There is a lot to learn. Not only did I have to learn the law, but I had to learn how to apply the law in real life situations. Then I had to learn the processes, what the law required me to do when I arrested someone, how to report offences to the Procurator Fiscal, how to deal with missing persons, what to do when I attended a road accident, etc. I listened, I watched, and I learned. My senior colleagues seemed to know everything, and I remained in awe of their experience and ability. In return, they playing on my unsuspecting nature. In the early days of my probation, I was the target of most of the pranks that occurred.

One quiet night shift PC MacDuff, my tutor for the night, decided that we would do road checks. I printed off the road check sheets, got an official looking clipboard, and we set out to cone off a safe area at the side of a main through road. The road check sheets are a record of our activity, and there was a lot of stress from the gaffers to ensure that these we completed these after every check and lodged with the Crime Management Unit in the morning. They would provide verification we were doing some proactive policing. The bosses sold it to us as 'necessary' in case they needed to refer to them at a later date; should there be a complaint about us or, more importantly, evidence of some sort that could link a criminal to a place and time. Hundreds upon thousands of police officers complete these road check sheets every year, millions of pieces of paper filed away in tens of thousands of cupboards - never to see the light of day again.

We stopped every car and spoke to the driver. Depending on who they were and what we suspected, either we checked the vehicle for defects, or we opened the boot to see if there were any stolen goods. There was not a lot of traffic on the roads at two o'clock in the morning. In those days, before we became a twenty-four-hour society, anyone driving on the roads at two in the morning was fair game.

The tactic was quite a dependable way of catching housebreakers (burglars), car thieves and poachers. If you stopped enough cars, you would eventually get lucky. The luckiest cops always stopped the most cars. Of course, if we didn't get lucky and catch a thief there was always the minor traffic offences that would keep us busy. Charging someone with no insurance or even just advising someone about a bald tyre is a good way to make the roads that little safer.

Unbeknownst to me, back at the station, another colleague (PC Weedy Reidy) donned a black jumper and a black balaclava. He then went into my locker and removed the keys to my car. Weedy then took my car and drove it towards our road block. About fifty yards from the roadblock Weedy slowed right down and crawled towards us.

I was standing at the side of the road and saw the

lights of my car approach. I didn't recognise it at first. It was just two headlights coming towards me. Then it slowed right down and crawled towards us. I became a little suspicious and watched it intently. My car edged closer and closer to our roadblock, and as it passed under a lamppost, the street lighting lit it up. I recognised it as a Ford Capri. I should know what a Ford Capri looks like; I owned one. Then I realised it was white, just like my Ford Capri. My suspicions were aroused. Here was a car edging towards us, and it was the same make as my car. It was also white, just like mine. Slowly it came closer and closer until I could make out the registration number. It was mine. I screamed at PC Mac-Duff, "That's my car! Someone has stolen it."

My jumping up and down and screaming alerted Weedy to the fact I had recognised my car, at which point he turned my car around and drove off. I didn't get a good enough look at him to recognise him.

"Quick," shouted PC MacDuff, "get in.

We climbed into our police car, PC MacDuff driving. He put the blue lights on. Despite his initial quick responsiveness in getting into the car that was where his urgency stopped. He then spent an age adjusting his driver's seat to make sure he was comfortable. I shouted at him to hurry.

"Less haste, more speed," he scolded me.

PC MacDuff methodically checked his mirrors and adjusted each wing mirror until he had them positioned to his satisfaction.

"He's getting away!" I screamed.

PC MacDuff just smiled. I should have realised something was up at that point. All the signs it was a prank were there, but I didn't. I just couldn't believe the leisurely manner of him. He signalled to move out before driving off to follow my stolen car.

I was surprised when my 'stolen car' remained in sight. It too was travelling at an equally sedate pace. Still, it didn't click. We followed my car along at about ten miles per hour. I considered getting out and running after it; in the certain knowledge I'd be quicker. Instead I sat there getting increasingly frustrated at my tutor and shouted at him louder and louder.

The slowest car chase in the world continued into a housing scheme. By this time I was ranting. I radioed in shouting for assistance and provided the controller with a running commentary. Every few seconds I provided a further update. The controller (who was in on the joke) requested that I calm down and describe the driver.

My Ford Capri turned into a cul-de-sac, and we followed. I thought we will catch him now. There was no way out. All my tutor had to do was block the road with our police car. PC MacDuff turned into the cul-de-sac and edged his way down. We watched my Ford Capri turn at the dead end and head back towards us. Again I was almost ready to jump out and stand in front of it, hands up like Moses parting the sea, I was invincible, he had stolen my car, and I would stop him.

The driver made his way out of the cul-de-sac. My tutor slowed down. As the cars slowly passed each other, I saw my Ford Capri being driven by a balaclava-clad thief. To add insult, he stuck his tongue out at me.

Fuming mad, I shouted at PC MacDuff to ram my car and was a fraction away from grabbing the steering wheel and wrenching to the right. I don't think PC Mac-Duff could help himself; he burst out laughing. Only then did I realise that something was up.

PC MacDuff engaged in an eight-point turn and as a result lost the pursuit.

On return to the station, there was my car parked in the same spot where I had left it.

"Are you sure it was your car?" PC MacDuff asked, a big dollop of mischief in his voice.

PC Weedy Reidy was inside the station when I entered, and he had a great big grin on his face. I had to concede it was a good prank.

These type of pranks occurred in the days when week-day night shifts were a lot less busy. Back then the pub shut at eleven and people went home. Many people didn't even have a phone in their house. Nowadays everyone in the family has a mobile. They need not move out their beds or even off their chairs in front of the television. They can simply move their right hand, punch three numbers into their mobile and call the police. So they do. You would be surprised how little an irk or minor annoyance can spur people into calling the police. The treble nine system is there for emergencies, yet it is unbelievable what people use it for;

"I'm starving, where is the nearest kebab shop?"

"Is it safe to reheat mushroom risotto?"

"My wife won't have sex with me."

"I've lost my remote control for the telly."

"Can monkeys eat chocolate? "

The easier it is to call the police, the more people decide that they need the interventions of a police officer.

When you call the police today you are put through to some anonymous person in a big call centre who, with a little luck, will direct your call to the appropriate person or department. If you have a non-urgent matter they might note details, create a crime report in line with National Crime Recording Standards (Home Office guidelines to promote accurate and consistent crime recording between police forces). Then they pass it to the duty sergeant. He will have a look at it then allocate it to an officer for enquiry. A day or so later the officer will turn up at your house, do door-to-door enquiry and then mark the crime report as undetected. Thus the damage to your plant when some unknown drunk fell on it the night before will forever go down as an undetected vandalism.

In the good old days, (I'm wearing rose-tinted specs here) we had office clerks in each station who answered the phones, attended the counter and acted as a firewall for the minor matters that people reported. Office clerks were, generally, older cops, who had seen and done everything in the job. They would share front office duties with a civilian assistant who supported them answering calls, carrying out computer checks and the like.

In those early days, the same person calling up about the damage to their plant found themselves speaking to the office clerk who would sympathise and reassure people that we would keep an eye on the area. There would be no time wasted creating unnecessary paperwork or sending an officer to do pointless door-to-door enquiry. The cop on the beat would be free to get on with more serious matters. In two weeks, the plant would have recovered from its encounter with the drunk, and life would carry on as normal.

We had some excellent office clerks in those early days. Crabbit Colin and Wily Willie were polar opposites in their approach but both ended up with the same satisfactory results. They had experience and ability in spades.

Crabbit Colin could be a little abrupt. If you radioed him for a vehicle check, he would moan about being busy but would then go ahead, get it done and pass you the result, anyway. Wily Willie was a little more laid back if you radioed in for a vehicle check he would reply, "Aye, nae bother son."

He would then lean back on his chair, light up his cigar and say to his civilian assistant, "Get that check doll."

Wily Willie also had a wee habit of bringing in a bottle of orange juice on the night-shift. At the start of the night, if you asked him for a wee drink of his juice he would say, "Aye, nae bother son." Later on in the night if you asked him for a wee drink of his juice he would reply, "You don't want to be drinking that juice son," and give you a big a wink.

One day I was going about my business, still learning the job and trying to get my head round a report I was writing when I thought I heard the words, "The job's fecked," whispered over the radio.

I looked around the office, and Wily Willie sat with his feet up smoking his cigar, his civilian assistant, Margaret, continued to fill in some forms or other. Neither of them seemed to have taken any notice, and I presumed that I had misheard. Then the radio sparked into life again and a muffled voice, impossible to identify, stated, "The job's fecked."

This little phrase became a regular occurrence. The Phantom Whisperer would repeat it every so often, much to my amusement.

I heard the phrase whispered over the radio during the quiet times in the middle of the night. A voice disguised so as we could not identify the caller. Everyone on the local channel would hear it, seem to agree with it and nod. The Phantom Whisperer had struck again. Then one Friday night-shift, Chief Superintendent Rattan called into our office.

A Chief Superintendent was an unusual sight at one o'clock in the morning; high-ranking officers tend not to be around after six in the evening. Sometimes the high ranking officer was merely drunk and requiring a lift home from some function or other. However, Chief Superintendent Rattan took it upon himself to call in at various offices in a sober state with the sole intention of catching out his staff.

The initial visit and general pleasantries from Chief Superintendent Rattan on this occasion, belied his devious intent. Sergeant Charmer, Wily Willie and I sat upright and answered his questions in a polite and respectful manner.

Then it all went wrong!

Mid-conversation the Phantom Whisperer, who was completely unaware of Chief Superintendent Rattan's impromptu visit, sent a message over the radio, "The job's fecked," he whispered in his disguised voice.

Chief Superintendent Rattan looked at the radio; he was incensed. Face removed of all pretence at pleasantries; he grabbed the mike. Angrily he shouted down the airwaves, "THIS IS CHIEF SUPERINTENDENT RATTAN TO LAST CALLER, IDENTIFY YOURSELF."

There was silence in the office. We didn't know what would happen. This situation would surely end badly. The silence from the radio was almost deafening as we stared at the little box of electronics in horror. It might only have been four or five seconds, but it seemed like an absolute age. Then the Phantom Whisperer responded. His voice still disguised and still in a whisper, "The job's not that fecked!"

Years later this story had become somewhat apocryphal. A young cop related it with glee one evening and even named the Phantom Whisperer as another young cop called Charlie. I knew Charlie and his reputation for nonsense, but I also knew that the real Phantom Whisperer had retired long before Charlie even joined the job.

Never a dull moment in the police. That can help make it an enjoyable job and less likely for police officers to jump careers as they do in other occupations. There was another reason too.

CHAPTER 6

AN INTRODUCTION TO PC PENFOLD AND ARTHUR SCARGILL

The police service in Scotland is a dynamic organisation. Officers get moved to different stations, some get promoted, new starts come in, and cops and bosses shuffle resources. Some want to go to a new station or move closer to home or even develop themselves in a new post. Sometimes officers change roles against their will, kicking and screaming all the way. However, for them, it is a disciplined service, and ultimately the needs of the organisation come first. Cops get moved on whether or not they want to go.

My first move was to a different group in the same station. I was a little apprehensive; I was happy on my first group and worried that I might not fit in with my new colleagues. I had built up good relationships with my old colleagues, and I didn't know how I would fit in with a new set of people. Most people worry about fitting in when they get moved, I certainly did.

After changing groups I swiftly realised that my new colleagues were a collection of complete and utter nutters. You might think it unfair to brand every one of them as 'heid the baws' simply because they were. The shift had an appalling reputation for having nonsense

and shenanigans, both on and off duty and all of it deserved. At the heart of the nonsense and shenanigans
was PC Penfold.

Contrary to what you might think of the tales
that follow, PC Penfold is one of the sharpest people
you could meet. He is a marvellous social animal, great
company and much loved by his many friends for his
quick wit and generous nature. There have been many
times when he has had me rolling on the floor in tears
with his anecdotes and self-deprecating humour. His
antics are the fodder of many a tale, and there wasn't
a time he didn't have some new and incredulous story
with which to regale.

PC Penfold is no longer in the police. He last
worked in 1985, (although he didn't actually retire
until much later). If you speak to some of his supervisors, they will tell you he didn't work before 1985 either. You would never think to look at him that he was
ever a policeman. Even when he was in uniform, you
would never think he was a policeman, to be fair I am
not sure that even HE thought he was a policeman.

PC Penfold is diminutive in stature, short-
sighted, balding with a body shape that tended towards
the rotund. He had a penchant for beer and any other alcoholic beverage that was available. His mission in life
was to hold an audience and a pint. His quick wit had us
in fits of laughter, but he always directed his acerbic humour at himself. A likeable rogue, with not a malicious
bone in his body. He never planned or orchestrated the
incidents and scrapes he got into. The things that be-
fell him, the things that caused us so much amusement,
were things that just happened to him because that is
who he is.

There are people who are inattentive. If there is a puddle on the road, they inadvertently stand in it and get wet. There are others who are unlucky; they see the puddle, sidestep to avoid it and still get soaked as a car drives through the puddle splashing them. PC Penfold is both inattentive and unlucky. He would jump the puddle to avoid getting wet, then land on a jobby, slip and fall back into the puddle and then get splashed by the passing car.

Every time I meet PC Penfold these days he reminds me I was his probationer, and he taught me all he knows. He tells me if it hadn't been for him, I would never have reached the rank of inspector. You can judge for yourself.

The first day I worked with PC Penfold I had not long passed my police driving course. He threw me the car keys, happy not to have the responsibility of driving. Thus, whenever we worked together, I became his personal chauffeur (to be honest it was safer if he was a passenger). We got into the car, and just as I drove out of the office, a call came in asking for a crew to attend a two-vehicle road accident. PC Penfold looked at me and asked if I knew what I was doing with road accidents. I told him I had dealt with one before and felt confident I could deal with another one.

"Good," he said, "because I've only ever been involved in them."

"But you only own a moped?"

"Aye, I know but I've crashed it three times. I should have paid more attention to what the cops did when they came to deal with those accidents, but it's hard to remember things like that when you are drunk!" he smiled.

There will be more to tell of PC Penfold later.

In America, it was a time when Lionel Ritchie said 'Hello' and Stevie Wonder 'called to say I love you'. But in Britain, 'Two Tribes' went to war.

Halfway through my first year as a police officer a certain Arthur Scargill came along and sealed my fate. Joining the police was only meant to be a stop-gap. My plan was to go back to University after taking a year out. I sometimes wonder where I would be now if I had stuck to my plans but the UK Miner's strike ended up being a deciding factor in my lack of impetus to return to studying.

Scargill led the Miner's Union to industrial action in the face of what he saw as Thatcher's long-term strategy to destroy the mining industry. The government wanted to close unprofitable pits, and Scargill, underneath his ginger comb-over, banged out his protest against any such closures in his distinctive Barnsley accent. Someone once told him if they took 'no' out of the language, he would be rendered silent. Scargill replied, 'no I wouldn't.' He instigated a long and drawn out strike action by the union members.

I was not a political animal. Politics never did, and never would hold any interest for me. The political machinations of Thatcher and her government and the vocal public manoeuvrings of Arthur Scargill made me shrink away. All I saw was a loud, opinionated and inflexible man shout his way across the news in a detestable manner. Unfortunately for him, he was up against the formidable, stubborn and uncompromising Margaret Thatcher. Had two such characters met each other down a dark alley they would both have had fisticuffs. Imagine that, coming across Arthur Scargill and

Margaret Thatcher having a square go in the street. Arrested for disorderly conduct. The preferred mode of transport back to the police office would be a kick up the backside, one yard at a time.

However, the miner's strike did impact upon me. Picketers were out in force at the entrance to the mines and violence spilled over as the so-called 'scabs' arrived to do their work, having taken no part in the strike. It meant me having to get up at four in the morning, to get to work and join a busload of officers sent to the picket line to keep the peace.

We arrived at the mine entrance and organised ourselves into a cordon. Officers either side of the road standing directly in front of the picketers to prevent them from encroaching onto the roadway.

Training was minimal. Safety equipment was non-existent. We stood in our tunics with arms folded facing the striking miners and not without some trepidation. The picketers huddled, en masse, around a good going coal fuelled brazier with only the occasional menacing look at our line-up. We waited on the sound of a bus in the distance, signalling that the 'scabs' were on their way. It was the spur for the picketers to rally to arms. It was our signal to link arms and grip the rear belt of the officer to our right, making our closed cordon complete.

As the bus came into sight, the picketers rushed towards our cordon and began pushing. Any effort to encroach on the roadway and stop the bus from passing the gates to the mine were defended by us holding them back. Occasionally a halfbrick was launched over our heads and scudded off the bus. The brief but frantic struggle was loud and frightening. Striking miners shouted abuse at the workers in the bus. Everyone on the bus hid their faces and cowered below the windows to prevent being seen and to avoid any missiles lobbed at them.

As soon as the bus entered the gates and disappeared out of sight, the picketers ceased their protest. The pushing stopped. The clamour and yelling of abuse mellowed to a murmur. Picketers made their way back to their brazier, happy to have made their point, and we unlinked our arms and chatted amongst ourselves glad to have escaped injury.

After a while, the routine of getting up early and standing in the picket line became the norm. The apprehension had eased a great deal, and in fact, there was quite a bit of chat between the picketers and the police. I recognised a few of the faces, and they smiled and engaged in some teasing. The banter was interrupted for a brief moment as we linked arms to let the bus through. The picketers raised their voices and threw half-bricks at the bus. This routine was sporadically upset when a picketer went too far. If a bus window got smashed, or they targeted a 'scab' at his home, we made every effort to lock-up the perpetrator.

It wasn't just the picketing miners who caused offence, mind you. There was one occasion when an inspector nearly caused a riot.

Inspector McTool was one of those dinosaurs who joined the police in the days when height and a stern countenance were traits seen as a prerequisite for promotion. He was a large man and had a carrot and stick approach to management. He would throw the carrot at you, and when you ducked to avoid it, he would beat you with the stick. His harsh persona, I later realised, was a means for him to hide his ineptitude. I came to understand that many overbearing personality traits displayed by senior officers were simply idiosyncrasies that they used to hide their incompetence. Inspector McTool just wasn't very good at hiding his.

I had been involved in enough scrapes on the front line to know that keeping your temper, remaining calm and dealing with any incidents fairly was, more often than not, the best way to keep the peace. Inspector McTool joined us early one morning to lead the operation. We arrived at the mine, decanted from our bus and mulled around chatting amongst ourselves. We even made the odd cheery comment to the picketers as they engaged us in repartee. Inspector McTool didn't like this. He remonstrated with us to form our cordon (not the best way to instil respect) then he approached some picketers and became objectionable with them. He had no tolerance for them, or us for that matter. The miners were simply standing chatting with us. Inspector McTool wanted a clear divide. The picketers took offence.

'Who the hell did this jumped-up public servant think he was.'

Tensions mounted.

Before long the mood of the place changed. The picketers became louder than normal. We were in position, all lined up much earlier than we ever had before and remained silent. There was no banter. There was, however, a real feeling of malevolence coming from our normally friendly picketers.

Inspector McTool marched up and down our line glowering at us and the picketers in equal measure. His body language aggressive; strutting around like a displeased Gestapo officer. He seemed to be incapable of reading the situation. It was his actions that created this 'them and us' mood.

We heard the bus carrying the strike-breakers in the distance. The moment the picketers saw it they surged forward in a frenzy. Not our usual friendly push and shove. This time, there was no half-hearted pretence at stopping the bus. It was clear they were now determined to stop that bus.

They rushed forward, and Inspector McTool skipped behind our cordon. He wasn't stupid enough to impede the baying crowd. This time, the picketers pushed us back far enough to end up in the middle of the road. The bus, for the first time, had to come to a stop. It sat with the strike-breakers on board wondering if they would get out alive. Bricks, stones, and sticks bounced off the bus. Then the front window smashed, and we were pressed back so far that we backed up against the bus.

At that moment I felt a tap on my shoulder. It was Inspector McTool, and he looked furious. He pointed at a picketer, a stout man in his forties wearing a black duffel coat and black woollen hat.

"ARREST THAT MAN!" he instructed.

I looked at the man I had been ordered to arrest and wondered what he had done. He was in the crowd of picketers making a noise, just like the rest of them, but I could not hear what he was saying. He was just one of a hundred picketers doing the same thing as everyone else. I extricated myself from my position in the cordon and stepped into the fray. My expectation was that Inspector McTool would be behind me, so I turned to ask him what I was to arrest the man for. Inspector

McTool was not there. I could only see the back of his hat as he walked away from the front line.

I made a snap decision to ignore his instruction. It wasn't clear why I was to arrest the man. I had no corroboration to effect the arrest, and I was damn sure Inspector McTool would not provide a statement or be a witness in court. I returned to my position in the cordon and continued pushing back the oncoming protestors.

All that pushing and grunting worked, and we got the bus through, but we took a beating in the process. An ambulance removed several officers with varying degrees of injuries. The rest of us boarded our bus back to the station feeling battered and bruised.

As I was about to get transported back to our station, I noted two other officers with handcuffs on two protesters. The cops were discussing their arrests with the duty sergeant. Both had arrested the men on the instructions of Inspector McTool. Inspector McTool had disappeared. As soon as the pushing and shoving had ceased, he had made good his escape in the first car out of the area.

The duty sergeant radioed Inspector McTool and asked him what he wanted done with his prisoners.

"That's the cops problem," he radioed back.

There was a bit of discussion, and the duty sergeant made the prudent decision to warn the men and send them on their way.

In other parts of the country, there was a lot more violence. In some places, particularly down south, there was a serious evil intent shown towards the strike breakers. An intent that was downright nasty in the way they treated 'scabs.' There were a lot of tensions between some picketers and the police, caused by those who had had a run-in with the police long before the strike began. For some, the strike was just an excuse to revert to type.

I also saw some of those picketers leave mining and join the police. The mining industry was becoming unsustainable, no matter what Arthur Scargill thought or believed. Miners were decent people who just wanted to provide for their families. They were just as happy to don a uniform and earn their corn as put on a helmet, overalls, safety boots and enter a mine.

So for months, I worked extra hours in the firing line. The government was determined to crush the strike and paying us overtime was not a problem. Scargill and his union were fighting a losing battle. For me, the big fat pay packet at the end of each month reduced any resolve to leave the police and return to my course of study or pursue another career. I still didn't know what I wanted to do, but there I was enjoying myself, getting well paid and with no impetus to change. I remained where I was, in the police, earning a decent wage. Thirty years and two months later I left the police, still not knowing what I wanted to do with myself.

Of course, we still had to police the streets.

One beautiful Sunday afternoon in the height of summer I was paired with PC Penfold. We drove around looking out for a reason to stop cars and do self-generated work. Well at least that was what I was doing, PC Penfold was just enjoying the sunshine. We spotted another pair of our colleagues in their car, parked at the side of the road. They too appeared to be on the lookout for driving offences and were watching the passing traffic. I pulled in beside them for a chat. After a while, PC Penfold suggested to us that we all do a bit of gardening. There was general agreement from everyone else (bar me because I hate gardening). I was the junior in service, and they ordered me to do as I was told. So I dutifully followed PC Penfold's directions to his friend's house.

On the way, PC Penfold explained that his pal, Kneely, had started out working as a carpet fitter for a big company. After he had become proficient at carpet fitting, Kneely did 'homers,' jobs on the side. The money was quite good, but he soon realised that he could make twice as much money by also supplying people with the carpet. His friends and family would tell him what they wanted, and he would source the carpet, arrange delivery, then fit it cheaper than they could get it elsewhere. Good carpets make for a happy home, and through word of mouth, Kneely got more business. Kneely eventually branched out on his own and started his own carpet company (well he had a flair for it). Before he knew it, he had built up a chain of stores across Scotland.

PC Penfold directed me to Kneely's house. Well, not so much a house as a mansion. The driveway was about a quarter of a mile long, and the mansion sat in about twelve acres of well-manicured lawn.

The four of us alighted from our vehicles in full uniform and Kneely came out to meet us.

"We are here to do some gardening," PC Penfold announced.

Kneely looked pleased and disappeared for a few minutes before returning with a large plastic bucket full to the brim with bottles of beer and ice. We sat in the sunshine overlooking the manicured lawns and chatted and laughed for a couple of hours. It was a pleasant way to while away a Sunday afternoon on the job.

Then PC Penfold decided that it was time to get on with the gardening. He disappeared around the side of the house and a few minutes later zoomed back round to the front garden sitting on top of a ride on lawnmower. PC Penfold proceeded to race around the already well-manicured lawn. Still in full uniform and full of beer. It was ages before I could stop laughing and wipe the tears from my eyes.

Timed races ensued, and we each took it, in turn, to see how fast we could race a course around some bushes, situated at strategic points on the grass. On my last run, I was sure I would beat the record. However, just before I crossed the finishing line, PC Penfold threw my police hat in front of the mower. I bulldozed right over the top of it, and it came out looking like, well just like it had been run over by a lawn mower.

It fills me with pride to say the police are a much more professional organisation these days. They would neither have the time nor inclination for such non-sense.

CHAPTER 7

PC PENFOLD - PLAYING A ROUND WITH THE CHIEF

PC Penfold introduced me to the Police Sports Club. We paid a monthly subscription to the club direct from our wages. I didn't realise I was a member until a few months into the job when PC Penfold pointed out the deduction on my wage slip.

"Have you joined any of the sports clubs?"

"Sports clubs?"

"That's what you pay your fees for."

"What fees?"

"Look see that deduction on your wage slip that says 'Police Club'?"

"Oh, yes."

"Well, that entitles you to watch the telly and play in the sporting events they put on."

I examined my payslip a little closer. Under the large P.A.Y.E amount were further deductions; Benevolent Fund, Convalescent Homes, Insurance Scheme, National Ins, PMAS, Police Federation, St Georges Fund and Superannuation. I cast my mind back to my first day in the job. The training sergeant had sat us down at a desk, placed various documents in front of us and instructed, "Sign here."

Like everyone else I signed on the dotted lines, and the pay department took care of the rest. I remained a dedicated payee to all these little extras for the rest of my service.

The Sports Club, as I found out, was fantastic value. Not just in the benefits afforded by what they provided but as an extension of the police family it gave me a lot of enjoyable times with a growing circle of good friends.

It was nice to get the occasional day off and attend one of our Sports Club events. There were a lot of choices. I could have joined the football team. Unfortunately, my ability to poach a goal was about the same as my ability to poach an egg. I would stand around for too long with the result of making it too hard. Parts of the fly-fishing section appealed to me; trips away with your mates, picnics in the fresh air and beer in the cooler. It was just a shame it involved fishing. There was the sea fishing section - all the fun of fly-fishing with sea sickness thrown in. Crown green bowls - too young. Basketball - I am only 5 ft 11 and a quarter. Rugby - too scared. Darts - can't count. Cross country - yeah right!

There was nothing else for it but to take up the noble sport of duffing a little white dimpled ball across a manicured field until it plopped into a hole.

The tendency when choosing a sport is to follow the interests of your friends and colleagues. Those colleagues encouraged me to take up golf. PC Penfold, my tutor, and others on the group, only ever played sports that would allow them to smoke or drink while they played. There was no pretence of the alcohol being ancillary to the entertainment. The sport was simply a means of allowing them to do something while they smoked and drank before, during and after. PC Hargreaves swore that he had mastered the art of smoking a fag while swimming, but he needed to get drunk first.

PC Penfold was the origin of many stories. A person who seemed to attract mishap and mayhem wherever he went. He was great to have in your company. A quick-witted social animal who could hold court in any situation. A likeable rogue. The guy you want with you if you like a laugh in the pub. Not the kind of guy you would want influencing a young probationer as his tutor cop.

PC Penfold had a tendency to get himself into scrapes. These being more because of his lack of attention to detail as opposed to any malicious intent. His natural ability to make light of things and his self-deprecating manner meant that he was always forgiven.

It was nearing the end of summer. I had had a busy time, we always did during the summer months, anti-social behaviour was rife, and I welcomed when my day off came, and I could play golf. Thursday was the day of our Force Championships. PC Penfold picked me up in his car, and we headed off to the course.

"Did you bring your golf accessory bag that Gentleman George bought for your birthday?" I asked innocently.

"Ah the banter," he replied.

PC Penfold had a habit of going golfing and turning up at the nineteenth hole with only one sock, despite having started his round wearing the requisite pair, one for either foot. Strange then that he ended up with only one sock.

I had been working with Gentleman George earlier in the week. George was PC Penfold's regular golfing partner and found it such a regular occurrence for PC Penfold to finish his round of golf with one sock he did something about it. He knew PC Penfold's birthday was coming around, so he bought him a golf accessory bag. It was a lovely canvas bag that contained a few tees, a pencil for scoring, a divot repairer and some golf balls. Gentleman George being a good friend, (some would say he was more an appropriate adult and carer) removed the golf tees, the pencil for scoring, the divot repairer, and the golf balls. These were all replaced with a roll of toilet paper and a wee card saying;

'Happy Birthday - no more turning up at the 19th with only one sock.'

PC Penfold drove us into the golf club car park and saw the Chief Constable's car, a top of the range BMW, parked by the clubhouse. PC Penfold stopped his bucket of rust on wheels beside it.

"Be careful when you get out," he warned, "I don't want that BMW scratching my car."

We climbed out and removed our clubs from the boot.

"That's the Chief's car," PC Penfold pointed out, "he normally gets a driver to take him to these events, he must be driving himself."

I nodded in agreement as I struggled to assemble my caddy car.

"Yeah. That means he'll only have the five or six pints when he finishes, I hope I'm not playing with him, he is such a miserable sod when he is not drinking," PC Penfold continued, laughing at his observation.

At that precise point in the conversation, Chief Constable McDandy stood up from behind his car. He had been bending down tying the laces on his golf shoes and had heard every word. He glowered at us and walked off into the clubhouse.

We got ourselves sorted and meekly made our way into the clubhouse to hear the draw. PC Penfold received a further glower from Handy McDandy as we took seats at the back of the lounge. The secretary made the draw, and the last three names called out were, Penfold, McEwan and THE CHIEF.

Despite it being a gloriously warm, sunny day we had a frosty start to our game.

There wasn't a great deal of conversation until the third hole. The three of us were all standing on the green ready to putt. PC Penfold was furthest away. He lined up a difficult fifty-foot putt but struck it with a little too much venom. The ball shot past the hole and the slope caught it giving it more momentum as it veered off the green. PC Penfold's golf ball continued over the fringe of the green and trickled down into a gargantuan bunker. For the first time that day the Chief Constable thawed enough to let out a delighted gasp of laughter. His laughing set me off too and, the ever self-deprecating PC Penfold joined in.

Getting himself out from the bunker was a little harder than PC Penfold imagined. Due to the bunker being so deep, as the Chief Constable and I stood on the green, we couldn't see PC Penfold at all. A spray of sand flew up from the bunker, but no ball. Another spray of sand, then another, every effort he made to extricate the ball from the bunker failed. The ball avoided all attempts at extrication from its sandy spot.

"I hope he has a rake in there," I commented to the Chief.

"I think he is playing with it," he responded with a hearty belly laugh. All grievances about the earlier comments in the car park now forgotten.

After that, the rest of the round was a hoot. The Chief Constable played straight man to PC Penfold's irrelevant humour. Neither of them had any airs or graces, and they giggled their way around the remaining holes at a comfortable two over par per hole.

Considering how much alcohol abuse PC Penfold's body had suffered, he kept surprisingly good health. At that time he was getting to the age where things can and do go wrong. A prostate requires checking; blood pressure needs monitoring and bowel movements are a major topic of conversation. There are of course other matters that speed you to the doctor for a check-up. Thus as we wandered round, PC Penfold related the story about his visits to the doctor earlier in the week.

On the Monday morning PC Penfold had taken a trip to his barber. His turn arrived, and he settled on a chair while his barber got to work. Not that there was much hair left with which to work. His balding pate required only a little tidy up at the sides.

"Uh-oh," said the barber.

"What is it?" enquired PC Penfold.

"You have a little brown mark on your head I haven't seen before, you had better get that checked."

PC Penfold massaged the top of his head and identified a roughened patch. It was about the size of a penny, and he hadn't noticed it before. He shared the concern that his barber had shown him. He left the barbershop and made his way directly to the Health Centre. Turning up at the reception without an appointment, he asked to see his usual doctor.

Doctor Proctor had been PC Penfold's doctor for many years. They had been friends ever since they had met in their local pub twenty-five years previous and ended up getting drunk together. Occasionally they met up by chance and repeated the process. On the last occasion, Doctor Proctor informed PC Penfold he had purchased a dog and offered PC Penfold the job of principle dog walker. He argued that as he worked shifts, he could always find time to take the dog out for a walk before he got home from his doctoring.

"Do you get paid for that?" I asked.

"Of course, I get paid at a rate of £6 per hour."

"That is not bad. At least you get some exercise, and you get paid for it," the Chief Constable commented.

"Yeah, I'm also pretty lucky the dog can't tell the time."

PC Penfold continued his story. He got in to see Doctor Proctor who made a cursory examination of the brown mark on his head, he crossed to the medicine cabinet and got a wet wipe. He then used the wet wipe to rub the mark on PC Penfold's head.

"Have you been painting?" Doctor Proctor enquired.

"Yup, I was creosoting the fence yesterday."

"Well that's you cured," said his doctor as he finished wiping the spot of preservative clean from PC Penfold's bald pate.

The next morning PC Penfold woke from a drunken sleep (he'd celebrated the magical healing of the brown spot on his head). Off he went to do his normal ablutions after which he happened to notice what appeared to be blood in his stool. Concerned once more about his well-being, he phoned the Health Centre to see if he could get an appointment. Luckily there was a space about midday, and once again PC Penfold found himself at the Health Centre being examined by Doctor Proctor, albeit this time he was examining the opposite end.

"What were you drinking last night?" the doctor asked.

"I only had a couple of beers in the pub," PC Penfold answered.

His doctor raised an eyebrow at him, which was sufficient for PC Penfold to come clean.

"... and a bottle of wine when I got home."

"Uh, huh?"

"Oh and I found an old bottle of Pernod, so I had a few of those with blackcurrant when I finished the wine."

"Yes. I thought as much. That's what Pernod and blackcurrant will look like when it comes out," his doctor informed him, "that's you cured again."

PC Penfold left the Health Centre with a skip in his step.

The next morning PC Penfold woke with another hangover (having once again celebrated getting the all clear from his doctor). This time when he went to pee, he noticed that it was a deep red colour. Despite being hung-over, he had the presence of mind to stop mid flow and take a sample in a spare jam jar he had handy.* Once again he phoned the Health Centre and got an appointment. An hour later he was sitting in the waiting room with his jar cupped safely in his hands.

*I'm not sure why he would have such a thing handy - this is his story, not mine.

Doctor Proctor called him into his surgery and, after

listening to PC Penfold's concerns, took the jar from him and held it up to the light at the window.

"What did you have for your dinner last night PC Penfold?"

"Just a salad doctor."

"Did this happen to be a beetroot salad?" the doctor enquired.

"... er yes!"

"Well, that's you cured again. Can I suggest that you lay off the celebrating this time?"

So that was how PC Penfold's doctor cured him of three major illnesses caused by Creosote, Pernod, and Beetroot.

PC Penfold's career, at that point, (I think he won't mind me saying) wasn't going anywhere. Although, you could say that of any point in his service. He didn't have to impress the Chief Constable. Handy McDandy was similarly happy, that occasionally, he could relax in someone's company without there being any agenda. The only plan was to enjoy the day. Chief Constable McDandy was all too fed-up with obsequious 'brown-nosers' and their disingenuous hobnobbing. You may know the type;

"There she was, wheedling her way in with the Assistant Chief Constable,"

"Why was that, was the Chief Constable not there?"

PC Penfold, Handy McDandy and I chatted and laughed our way around the course. The golf being secondary to the hip flask and banter. Chief Constable McDandy got around to asking PC Penfold the all-important question, "So will you manage to get time off to go to the

Scottish Golf Championships if you qualify?"

"I should think so sir – you suspended me three months ago."

How they laughed.

Back at work, I was soon to be involved in one of the most hilarious, rib-tickling moments of my career. A seriously funny situation to find myself in. I can laugh about it now, but it wasn't that funny at the time.

CHAPTER 8

IF YOU WANT TO GET AHEAD, GET A HAT

My training continued.

Opportunities to experience working in different departments arose. Although training for new recruits has changed over the years, it remained that probationers had a day here and there to learn about other specialist roles. One such specialist role being the Traffic Department (now called the Road Policing Unit or R.P.U. - but that title is only ever used by senior management to show they tow the party line - everyone else still uses 'Traffic Department' or the one-word abbreviation 'Traffic').

You would think the best way to scupper a career in the Traffic Department would be to crash a police car. Doing exactly that was of a pre-requisite qualification for our Traffic Department. There was hardly a single driver in there that hadn't written off a car at some stage or other. If they were mad enough to climb back in and drive off at break-neck speed looking for another crash, then the Traffic welcomed them with open arms.

I will tell you later how I wrote off a police car while avoiding running over a cat. So, even although I had fulfilled the pre-requisite qualification (crashing a car) my driving skills were not recognised as proficient. There would be no offer to join the ranks of the Traffic

Department. I couldn't blame them, particularly after my Traffic Department orientation day.

The opportunity to experience a day working in the Traffic Department came along. All probationers did it. It gave us an insight into the department (they'd all book their granny for walking on the cracks on the pavement) and identified those interested in a future move there.

My day with the Traffic Department was a Friday. I had been on a date the night before and hadn't gotten home until late. (You can't blame me, she was gorgeous, and I ended up marrying her). Anyway, I arrived at the Traffic Department and PC Monotone, an older cop, was given the job of looking after me for the day. PC Monotone got these gigs as none of the other traffic cops were keen to work with him due to his monosyllabic conversation style and the unchanging drone of his voice. Also, it was a beautiful hot summer day. Within ten minutes of driving out of Headquarters in this big comfy Range Rover, I was giving a reasonable impersonation of a nodding dog. The tiredness, the heat and the lack of stimulating conversation was enough to send me to sleep.

At lunchtime PC Monotone gently woke me. I apologised profusely for my inability to stay awake that morning, but fortunately for me, PC Monotone seemed unconcerned. I stretched off before making my way to the canteen for lunch.

Lunch was welcome as I had missed breakfast that morning, so I gorged myself on the canteen food. An hour later we were back in the comfy Range Rover. My belly was full, and I was enjoying the sunshine again if not the lack of gay wit and sparkling repartee. I don't know what it was, maybe the tiredness, the heat, the comfy car or just having a full belly but I dozed off again. About five in the afternoon I was again gently woken by PC Monotone and deposited back at Headquarters. I toddled off home finished for the day.

Back at my station, the next day Sergeant Charmer asked me how I had got on. I truthfully told him, "Like a dream sarge, like a dream."

So with no real driving skill to speak of, walking the beat became my forte.

A common complaint from the public is that they do not see police officers walking the beat. Spotting a police uniform on patrol is as rare as the White Rhino and it turns more heads.

The problem is that there are fewer officers available on the front line these days. There are now so many departments and other duties that require officers to staff them that there are fewer available to patrol the streets.

The ubiquitous mobile phone means that the public no longer have to get out of their chairs to phone the police. So they do. The officers that are left covering the streets are far too busy going from call to call to go walking their town centres. It might be what the public want, it might be what the politicians want, it is even something the police might want, but the practicalities make it nigh on impossible.

In the good old days, it was a regular occurrence for officers to be sent out on the beat and patrol the town centre on foot. Not just at weekends when discos were spilling out but every night, no matter the weather.

It wasn't a pleasant task to be night shift in winter and get the job of patrolling the town on foot. It could be bitter cold, or wet, or windy. It was particularly horrible when it was all three. Thus crafty officers used a few tricks to make it more bearable. They knew where to stand in the shelter, in a dry close or under a shop awning. A favourite spot was at the back of the bakers. The warmth of the ovens could take the chill from their bones, and the smell of the freshly baked bread was enough to have them salivating.

Another trick was to call in at the local clothing factory and cadge a cup of tea from the night shift security. It was a regular haunt of officers patrolling the town centre. We knew that we could get in out of the cold, receive a warm welcome and a hot cup of tea. The following could, therefore, have happened to any officer from our station; but it didn't happen to anyone, it happened to lucky old me.

One night PC Hill and I were sent out to walk the town. PC Hill was a gregarious fellow, just a few years older than me. The two of us worked well together, and he was always full of jokes and patter. Neither of us appreciated being sent out to walk the town centre on a quiet night mid week. It was cold, and a constant fine drizzle made it unpleasant to be outside.

We had a quick jaunt through the town, confirmed that no-one was lingering about, then made our way to the local clothing factory security office. There we sat warming ourselves in front of the electric fire, drinking a welcome cup of piping hot tea, provided by the friendly security guards.

Unfortunately for us, the instruction to walk the town centre had come from the ambitious and overly strict Inspector McDuncan. He was so severe Robert Mugabe and Colonel Gaddafi used to phone him up for advice.

Most cops worried about getting caught out by him but PC Hill just laughed it off, I fell in line. The security office was warm and dry. The security officers were chatty, and we remained hidden, happily drinking tea and swapping stories.

Then our radios crackled into life. "Where are you?" It was Inspector McDuncan.

PC Hill sat sprawled in his chair, feet up on a small table in front of him. He remained perfectly calm and radioed back telling Inspector McDuncan, "We are in the High Street checking the property."

There was a pause.

"I'm in the High Street," Inspector McDuncan informed him, "...and I can't see you."

We sat bolt upright! "Er no Inspector we are checking around the back of the High Street, we will join you shortly."

Like sprinters out of the starting block, I followed PC Hill as we ran from the security office as fast as we could. We ran up the lane towards the town centre, crossed through the car park, raced around the Post Office and dodged through a close at the back of the High Street. The close took us out into the bottom of the High Street, yards from where Inspector McDuncan was waiting, folded arms and tapping his foot on the ground.

PC Hill and I stood in front of him desperately trying to hide our breathlessness. Inspector McDuncan looked rather angry, but we felt confident we had ran quickly enough to allay any of his suspicions.

Inspector McDuncan looked us up and down. "You have been hiding somewhere out the road, haven't you?" he challenged.

"No. No. Inspector, we were just checking the rear of the properties," PC Hill, answered.

"You have been sitting somewhere drinking tea haven't you?" Inspector McDuncan challenged again.

"Not us inspector. We like to do our job thoroughly. More properties get broken into round the back, so we like to nose around there." PC Hill replied in as sincere a manner as he could muster.

Surely his earnest explanation would be enough to hoodwink McDuncan.

Inspector McDuncan turned and looked me in the eye.

"You have been sitting in the clothing factory security office drinking tea, haven't you?"

It was more of a statement than a question, but I felt obliged to stick to my senior colleague's story. I couldn't let PC Hill down, so I denied it.

"No, sir."

"Are you sure?"

"Yes, sir."

"Then why have you got a security officer's hat on?"

PC Hill looked at the hat I was wearing and groaned.

We'd been rumbled.

In a rush to get out of the security office, I had grabbed the wrong hat. I took the hat off my head, checked the band and saw there were no black and white checks where they should be. Instead, there was only a yellow band and the clothing factory logo. I winced at the bollocking I was about to receive.

The next day I came into work, got my gear from

my locker and headed through to the briefing room. My entire shift was already there. No sooner had I entered the room they all sang;

"Where did you get that hat?
Where did you get that tile?
Isn't it a nobbly one, and just the proper style?
I should like to have one.
Just the same as that!
Where'er I go, they shout "Hello!
Where did you get that hat?"

Strangely, it was about then I felt accepted, just another one of the boys. Although, I would be hard pushed to be accepted as the hero of the day like PC Penfold - if only they knew what he had really been up to.

CHAPTER 9

NOT A BAD DAYS WORK

As I progressed through my probation, I got the hang of this policing lark. Sure I made a lot of mistakes, but I learned quickly and tried not to make the same mistake twice. Every day was different. I dealt with a large variety of matters, sudden deaths, thefts, poaching and road accidents. I even stood in for a lollipop lady who had phoned in sick. It is quite an eye opener seeing what police officers end up having to do; they do a lot of things to keep the peace or simply because no-one else will.

I didn't realise just how diverse my experience had been in that first year until I returned to the Scottish Police College for my second stint. There were officers from other forces who for their entire first year had patrolled just a few blocks in their city centre. They had dealt with shoplifters during the day and drunkards at night. That seemed to be it. Those who worked in the larger cities expected to end up in some specialised unit dealing with one specific crime. Not quite what I would have chosen. I experienced so many things. I liked the variety but my first surveillance operation was an eye-opener.

A series of fire-raisings in one of our remote villages had our CID scratching their heads ('Arson Attacks'

- as reported in the local paper). The concern that there could be a serious incident was on our bosses minds. What if someone was killed?

The fires always happened during the night. It was a small village with a single road through it and about two hundred houses on either side. It had a woollen mill, a coffee shop that sold pottery, butchers, a convenience store and a small inn that catered for the summer tourist trade.

One night a fire burnt down a shed in an old lady's garden. Nobody could figure out how it started, and the investigation came to nothing. The next night a farmer discovered the front door of his barn ablaze, he only just saved it from being totally gutted. A week later, another fire erupted at the back door of a house. Someone had laid a lot of scrunched up newspapers on the step, then set it on fire, fortunately, it had burned itself out. Police investigations proved fruitless. Then another house was targeted, and this time, the fire took hold. Fire services raced to the scene but by the time they got there the house was pretty much burned to the ground. Luckily the occupants had escaped unhurt.

The last fire galvanised our bosses into action, and they mounted a covert operation to catch the culprit. The evidence pointed to it being someone local, so they decided to surround the village with officers during the night and watch what happened. I found myself seconded to the operation for a week.

I attended a briefing on the first day of my night shift and along with a dozen other cops they transported us to the outskirts of the village where we were dropped off. We then had to make our way, silently, to our various vantage points surrounding the village to keep watch all night. My position was in a small copse of trees that overlooked the back doors of a row of houses. I was quite excited. It was summer, dry and not too cold. I had a flask of coffee with me and some sandwiches. I chose my position carefully, under a tree and hidden by a bush. I could crawl into the bush and lie on my front so that I could see everything but no-one could see me. As I lay there, I scanned the row of houses in front of me. Lights went out as the night enveloped us in darkness. Occasionally, a bathroom light went on for a few minutes and then off again. Keen to be the one to catch the arsonist, I stuck to my task despite being not too uncomfortable. However, by the time the sun rose I was bored.

At 5 a.m., our appointed time, I made my way back through the fields to our rendezvous point. The initial excitement had waned, and I wondered how I would get through the next four nights of this rather tedious operation.

On the second night again nothing happened.

On the third night, desperate to relieve the boredom, I took a book with me and about 4 am, as the sun came up, I managed to read a chapter or two. I was careful to keep it well hidden from the sergeant. It would be embarrassing if caught with a book, so I hid it in a copy of *Playboy*.

On my last night PC Penfold was also put on the surveillance operation. It was his first time on the watch, and he brought a great big holdall with him.

"What have you got with you?" I enquired.

"Just some supplies," PC Penfold winked at me, and when he picked up his holdall to put it in our transport, I heard a distinct clinking sound coming from it.

On being dropped off on the outskirts of the village, PC Penfold headed off to his point. He was positioned on a grassy knoll overlooking the front doors of a cul-de- sac. My instructions were to position myself about one hundred yards further along, so we walked together to his grassy knoll. PC Penfold sat down and opened up his holdall. He produced a sleeping bag, six bottles of beer, a bottle of red wine and a half bottle of brandy together with a bulbous brandy glass. These were laid down beside his sandwiches, crisps, sausage rolls and a selection of cheese and biscuits. He then produced a pack of cards.

"Would you like to stay for some supper and a game of brag?" he asked, with a wink.

I declined, thinking I had better not get caught drinking on the job and made my way to my position in the woods. Just as I was leaving, two older cops arrived and joined PC Penfold for a game of cards, a little drink, and a light supper.

Despite being half the length of the village away, I could still hear the noise from the card school. As the night passed, their noise got louder. I couldn't believe it. Here we were in a covert operation, and they were having a rowdy drinking session! I could even see their torches flashing around as they played and drank.

About three in the morning things quietened down, and I presumed that they had finished for the night. I took a little time out to wander down to make sure things were okay. About fifty yards from the grassy knoll I could hear PC Penfold snoring, long before I could even see him. The light was coming up, and as I got even closer, I could see he was in his sleeping bag and unmistakably sound asleep. I went back to my position in the copse of trees and didn't feel so guilty about reading my book. At least I looked up, now and again, towards the back of the houses that I was supposed to be watching.

At the appointed time I made my way back to the transporter at the far end of the village. I passed the grassy knoll expecting to wake PC Penfold from his sleep, but he wasn't there. I continued back to the van. Everyone was gathered around PC Penfold and congratulating him.

"What on earth happened?" I enquired, desperately curious.

"PC Penfold caught the fire-raiser," the driver informed me.

This pleased everyone, the operation could now be called off. The undetected fire-raisings, which had got us on the watch in the first place, were cleared up by the CID. I could not believe it. PC Penfold had turned up for a covert surveillance operation with a bag that would get any good party started. He played brag, entertained two other cops until the early hours. He then wrapped himself up in a sleeping bag, and when I last saw him, he was dead to the world. How on earth did he catch the fire-raiser? Instead of being vilified for such inappropriate behaviour, he was the hero of the day!

I waited for a quiet moment and asked PC Penfold to confide in me how exactly he managed to catch the fire-raiser.

"I had to get up for a pee son," he winked, "and as I was standing peeing on yonder hill, I saw a lighted paper getting put through a letter-box from the inside. The woman who stayed there appears to have set fire to her own doorstep to deflect any attention away from her. She knew that people were suspecting her."

When good things like that happened to PC Penfold, Karma had a habit of coming along and evening things up.

The next Friday, on his day off, PC Penfold took a trip to the bookies. He remained there for much of the afternoon and bet on a few races. On the last race, he scored a big win. It was time to celebrate. He walked down to the supermarket intending to buy a nice bottle of champagne for him and his wife to share when he got home.

On entering the supermarket, the product placement bargain 'half-price' toilet rolls took his attention. Not one to miss a good offer, PC Penfold picked up the bag of fifteen rolls and on making his way to the checkout saw other bargains. He decided that it made sense to do his weekly shop and thus save himself having to do it over the weekend.

PC Penfold grabbed a trolley and pushed it around the store delighted with the number of bargain 'buy one get one free' offers he found. There were even some excellent wine bargains to be had, and he purchased the obligatory six bottles to qualify for the five percent off on the deal that was running.

By the time he got to the check out his trolley was full, and he had to carry six shopping bags, three in both hands. He trudged off laden down with his groceries and headed back to our office where he had parked his car. Carrying all the shopping turned out to be a harder job than he realised. His six bags of groceries were heavy. He even had to carry the fifteen rolls of toilet paper in his teeth.

After a couple of hundred yards of struggling, he

sat and had a rest. It made sense to him to lighten the load, so he opened a packet of biscuits, munched on those and drank a can of juice. Now he had slightly less to carry. He made his way back to the office by stopping every hundred yards and consuming whatever of his purchases took his fancy.

I happened to be looking out my office window when I saw PC Penfold return. It was hard not to laugh at the sight of him as he struggled with his shopping bags and toilet rolls dangling from his mouth. He made it across the car park to his parking spot. I couldn't help myself, I burst out laughing. It wasn't until PC Penfold reached his car parking spot that the realisation hit him. Only then did he remember that his wife had taken the car that day. As he stared at his 50cc moped, PC Penfold wondered how he would get his six bags of shopping and rolls of toilet paper back to his house.

While PC Penfold had his problems; I had other things about which to worry. In my probation, it was the norm for the junior man to make the tea or coffee. I also learned that it was my job to cook the Christmas dinner (or breakfast if you were early shift). I was going to be on early shift (7 a.m. to 3 p.m.) on Christmas day. So on Christmas Eve, my colleagues all chipped in, and we purchased the finest fare from a quality butchers in readiness for me to cook up a feast the next morning.

On Christmas day I arrived at the office at six thirty, about the same time as our conscientious shift leader Sergeant 'Hardy' McHearty. We waited for the rest of the shift arriving, while some left it to the last minute, normally they were all in ready for the sergeant to give us a briefing dead on the hour. This morning I was the only one to arrive on time.

Andy, the office clerk, arrived five minutes late and apologised to Sergeant McHearty for his tardiness. "Sorry Sergeant, I slept in."

It was another half hour before Brian showed up. He looked rather tired, and he too apologised, "Sorry Sergeant, I slept in."

About nine thirty Sergeant McHearty was getting a little grumpy. We still waited for three further members of the group, and he didn't want me to start breakfast going until we were all there. Then Colin arrived.

"Sorry Sergeant, I slept in."

Colin was duly taken into a closed-door session in the sergeant's office for a few minutes, and after that, he gave me my orders to cook the breakfast. We weren't going to wait for Davy or PC Penfold any longer.

In all my thirty years and two months service, I never slept in once. I always set my alarm last thing before going to bed. If I was due to start at seven in the morning, I set my alarm for six. Without fail, I would wake up exactly one minute before the alarm was due to go off. My internal alarm clock came in handy after I got married. It woke me up one minute before the alarm blared. I'd switch it off alarm before it sounded and woke my wife. The strange thing was that if I didn't set the alarm, I wouldn't wake up. I had to go through the process of setting the alarm clock to arm the biological process in my subconscious mind. My subconscious sleeping brain could set an internal alarm all on its own, and even time it down to sixty seconds before the alarm crackled into life. It's quite a handy skill to have.

Years later, I learned that scientists had studied this phenomenon in others. People swore they could wake up at a certain time just by banging their head on their pillow. They would bang their head six times and then wake at six, seven times if they wanted to wake at seven. The scientists proved that this group of people had a measurable rise in the stress hormone adrenocorticotropin from about an hour and a half before the time they had set their internal alarm clocks. Subjects who woke unexpectedly had no spike. The scientists concluded that the unconscious mind could not only keep track of time while we sleep but also set a biological alarm to jump-start the waking process. The pillow ritual might help set that alarm. For me, it was the actual setting of my bedroom alarm clock that set my internal alarm.

Anyway, by eleven, everyone that had made it into the office had eaten breakfast. The remnants I put on a low heat in the oven in case the last two shift members turned up for work.

A few minutes later, in came Davy.

"Sorry Sergeant, I slept in."

He too was spirited away to the sergeant's office for a telling off.

That left PC Penfold, the only member of our shift still to appear. The clock ticked away, and there was much discussion about why PC Penfold would not answer his phone and a question mark over whether he would turn up at all.

The hands on the clock kept turning, and just when we had all given up hope, PC Penfold appeared in the office at two forty-five (fifteen minutes before our shift was due to end). PC Penfold walked up to Sergeant

McHearty threw his arms wide and stated, "Sarge. I've nae excuse!"

He too was duly invited for a closed-door session with Sergeant McHearty, who was clearly struggling not to laugh - more out of relief that PC Penfold was in good health more than anything.

PC Penfold emerged from the sergeant's office none the worse for his reprimand. He then had his, now crispy, Christmas breakfast and went home. Not a bad day's work.

On boxing day Sergeant McHearty finished his briefing but stopped short of dismissing us.

"Guys, over the past week we have only had two days where everyone made it in time for the morning briefing. Yesterday took the biscuit. I can't have ninety-percent of my shift turning up late. That was ridiculous. I know it is the festive period and you all have parties to go to but we are a professional organisation. We are here to serve the public. We have to be ready to go to an emergency at the drop of a hat. I have to be able to send officers to calls and I can't do that if you are not here."

We sat with our heads down. I was a little bit miffed that I had to sit through this lecture despite the fact I hadn't been late but Sergeant McHearty was clearly not pleased and I wasn't about to interrupt him and protest my innocence.

He continued, "Since it is Christmas I am not going to do anything more, we have had a chat and that is it. Over and done. However, I am going to say one more thing, woe betide anyone who is late again. I'm not going to put up with it. I don't care how many alarm clocks you need to buy or if it takes you half an hour to wind them up - just make sure that you aren't late for my shift again."

He looked each of us in the eye. His way of ensuring we knew he was serious. I held his gaze for a moment then looked down at my crotch. He got up and left the room. Slowly we followed, silent and ashamed.

The very next morning, 7.15 am on the 27th of December, my colleagues and I crowded around the table in the muster room. In the centre of the table was a telephone, one that had a speaker so we could all hear. PC Penfold dialed a number and we waited a moment. It rang.

Ring ring, ring ring, ring ring.

It continued.

Ring ring, ring ring, ring ring.

Then we heard a click. The ringing stopped, the call had been answered.

"Hello," said a sleepy voice.

In unison, my entire shift shouted with one voice at the speaker, "SERGEANT MCHEARTY, IT'S QUARTER PAST SEVEN AND YOU'VE SLEPT IN."

CHAPTER 10

HARRY, BIG BOB, AND BUMJAR

One thing that remained constant throughout my career was that there have always been great characters in the job. I disagree with anyone who says the job doesn't have any characters anymore. I can assure you it does. The job of a police officer is such that it not only attracts great characters but it also breeds, develops and nurtures them. Modern day policing is no different.

First, some of the old characters:

Harry was a wise old cop. He had such pleasant manner with everyone and had the most reasonable approach to matters. Members of the public though highly of him, his peers held him in high esteem, and senior officers were thankful to have him working for them. Harry was a dedicated career cop. He had no ambitions to be promoted and no desire to work anywhere else other than the relatively small and quiet town where he was a community cop, a place he had worked for over a decade.

On the surface then, Harry was just the ideal officer. A trusted man of many years service. An officer who never put a foot wrong, he went about his business in a diligent and efficient manner requiring little or no supervision. That was maybe how it appeared on the face of it anyway. This incident made me raise an eyebrow.

One day I was in the front office, (control room) when a call came in about youths causing disorder in a park, on Harry's beat. The office clerk radioed Harry and passed him the call. Harry radioed back, "Roger, on my way."

As was commonplace with the old radios, his 'talk' button got stuck in the 'send' position. For the next five minutes, we could hear everything Harry would say. When radios stuck in the 'send' position, we got to overhear some juicy conversations. Not on this occasion, however, Harry was a gentleman and on his own. All we heard was his contented whistling. Harry headed on to the youth disturbance call cheerily whistling away and oblivious to the fact that his radio was still transmitting. We could hear every tune as he pursed his lips and forced air through the tiny gap. It was all agreeable. That was until he arrived at the park.

The brakes brought the car to a halt, the engine was silenced as Harry switched it off and the door clicked open and then clunked shut..

A moment later we heard him shout, "RIGHT YA WEE BUGGERS, AH KEN YER MOTHERS, GET YOUR-SELVES OUT THIS PARK NOW. I DON'T WANT ANY MORE CALLS ABOUT YOU LOT THIS WEEK, SO BUG-GER OFF!"

This caused everyone in the office to look at each other open-mouthed. There was a confused silence and a general air of surprise. Harry wasn't known for shouting. His outburst may have got his message across, but it was not how any of us believed Harry dealt with matters.

Following his rant, we expected that Harry, having identified the youths involved, would pass the names of the youths back over the radio and have them added to the call card. His final job would then be to ensure that we sent letters to their parents detailing why a police officer had spoken to them.

Harry was still oblivious to the fact that his rant at the youths had been transmitted across his radio for everyone to hear. A few seconds passed, and then Harry radioed in to control. "Harry to base, Harry to base, come in, over."

"Go ahead, Harry."

"Aye, that's the park searched – no trace of any youths, over."

Harry remained where he was until he retired, unlike the rest of us. Upon completion of my probation, I found myself transferred to a smaller station a few miles away. My new station covered a fairly large rural area and several towns all connected by the one main arterial road through them. The further east you went, the more opulent the houses and the nicer the clientele. I liked to work the towns in the west, rougher, more trouble and way more interesting.

My new partner was Big Bob, one of the nicest people you could ever meet. Big Bob was just a few years away from retirement but still as keen as the day he started. He would do anything for you and could fix just about anything, so he was always in great demand. Once he took the engine out of my car to change a seal when he put it all back he found there was still a tiny little leak. So he took the whole engine out again and changed the seal again. He fixed broken lintels, washing machines, cars, boilers - whatever it was. Big Bob could just about fix anything.

Big Bob was the handiest person to know. He was also one of the most pleasant people to be around, funny, companionable and full of mischief. I heard no one, including the people we arrested, say a bad word about Big Bob. He had a big heart and an innocent mischievousness that endeared him to everyone.

The predominant part of the job as a police officer is to protect the public, and you can't do that 9 a.m. to 5 p.m., Monday to Friday. When most people are out enjoying themselves or sat in their living room of an evening watching Rangers V Celtic, there are still police officers out patrolling the streets. They attend calls, fight with drunks, turn out to domestic incidents, direct traffic at road accidents or simply try to find a pal's house to watch the fitba.

One night when we were back shift Big Bob knew I was keen to see the football game so, as we had no calls to go to, he took me to his friend's house to scrounge a coffee, also hoping the game would be on the television.

Big Bob chapped the door. A minute later his pal answered wearing his dressing gown. He invited us in and said he would put the kettle on explaining that he had been running a bath, hence finding him in his dressing gown. Kindly, he put the television on and made us coffee. The game was a cracker. We had joined it twenty minutes in, but saw four goals scored by half time. It was only then I noticed Big Bob wasn't in the room. My cheery colleague had gone out to the toilet about ten minutes previous and hadn't returned.

Our curious host (Bob's friend) opened the living room door and on the stairs leading up to the bathroom was Bob's tunic. Halfway up was his white shirt, his trousers dumped in a heap on the top steps and on investigating further his pants socks and shoes lay just outside the bathroom door. Inside the bathroom, Bob had his pal's loofah and was luxuriating in a full soapy bubble bath, hard to be angry with him.

Being a rural station, we had some odd tasks. In those days, it was the duty of night shift personnel to check 'the magazines.' These were secure storage containers for explosives used by the coal mines nearby. We had four magazines to check on our beat, and they were, by their nature, kept away from the populace in inaccessible places. Any accidental explosions would, therefore, be less likely to do any serious damage because there was nothing surrounding them and no persons in the area to harm. The fact that they were in such out-of-the-way places meant it could take an hour or two to go round them all.

There was a set routine where we had to call in to control, via our radio, on approach to the magazine we were checking. Each magazine had a code name. Thus the process ensured our control knew we were approaching the danger area and could set alarm bells ringing if we did not call back in a reasonable time to say we had checked the magazine and all was in order.

Of course, police officers being police officers, we often short-circuited the process. Older cops, who were comfortable that nothing ever happened at a magazine, did their checks from the comfort of their canteen chair. As they sipped coffee, smoked fags and exchanged stories they would get on their radio and call in as follows:-

"PC Lazyboy to control."

"Go ahead."

Malky McEwan

"Off the air at Hotel Mike four."

"Roger."

A minute or two would pass by, and then he would call in.

"Hotel Mike four checked and in order."

"Roger."… and that was it done, all from the comfort of his canteen chair.

However, some of the more responsible officers did physically check the magazines now and again. Some were conscientious enough to check them every night. Some only checked them at the start of their week and then again at the end of their week. There were a couple who never checked them at all unless it was to show the new boy to the office where they were - just in case they were ever asked to go there.

While Big Bob was one of the conscientious ones sometimes, when we were busy, he deployed this 'check the magazine trick' from his seat in front of the typewriter as he drafted the custody report we had to complete before we left in the morning. It meant that instead of being held on past our finishing time we could spend the last half hour of our shift relaxing. The kettle would go on, and he would regale me with his stories of old. It was during one of those night shifts he told me about Billy and his invite to see the bull.

Late one evening Billy, a young cop, and Big Bob got a radio message to come and meet a couple of his colleagues at an out of way farm. Billy and Big Bob duly made their way to the farm. The track up to the farm was also the track to one of the magazines. Big Bob expressed his concern that there was something up. He wondered if there was a break-in at the magazine but suspected that their colleagues had driven into a ditch or something and just needed help to get out (a not unknown occurrence on the night shift).

When they arrived, they met their colleagues PC Smith and PC Jones.

"Come and look at this," they said, unable to contain their excitement, before escorting Billy and Big Bob up the farm track. The track bordered a field, and they took them to a part of the fence where a bull stood. The biggest, blackest meanest looking bull you were ever likely to see.

Normally these bulls stood in the middle of the field, and because they are further away, they look a lot smaller. But this bull stood right up at the fence. Its massive head stretched over the fence like the front end of a truck. It's neck resting on the wire, so big they were hard pushed to see the wires between the two wooden posts. The bull stood perfectly still, unfazed by the four uniformed officers standing in front of him.

PC Smith then encouraged PC Jones to 'do it again.'

"Do it again, do it again," he persisted.

Billy was not sure what PC Jones was to do again. He stood in awe of this incredible beast in front of him, curious as to what would happen. The sight of the bull at such close quarters was reason enough to call him up to see it. But there was more!

In front of them was a brute of a bull, a titan, a sight to behold. It calmy remained on its feet watching them, unruffled and immobile. PC Jones then did it again.

Without telegraphing his intention, he walked up to the bull and swung a haymaker of a punch at it. The punch connected with the bull's nose. Billy and Big

Bob were aghast. PC Jones had just punched the biggest beast they had ever seen, and it was propped against the smallest and weakest fence. To such a beast that fence would be no real problem. It had been punched squarely on the nose, and they were directly in the line of what would be an irate bull should it run amok. In unison, they turned and ran like skittery rabbits back towards their car at the bottom of the track. They only stopped when they heard PC Smith and PC Jones laughing.

The biggest bull in the world, standing behind the weakest fence in the country, didn't even flinch. It remained standing, eyeing up the four uniforms in front of it, apparently indifferent.

PC Jones demonstrated his pugilistic skills once more; the bull seemed not to notice his feeble effort. It continued to stand and take it.

Egged on to copy PC Jones, Billy agreed to have a go himself.

Hesitantly, he made his way up to the bull and positioned himself in front of it. Despite what he had seen he was still cautious enough to be ready to run. He edged closer and closer. He came within striking distance, his colleagues waited while he plucked up the courage to punch it. Then he went for it; he stretched out his index finger and lightly touched the bull on the nose. It was a tentative touch at best, no more pressure than a fly would exert landing on an elephant. The second he touched the beast all hell broke loose. The bull went berserk. Bellowing, snorting, and all sorts. Billy turned to run, but something blocked him from doing so. He screamed in fear for his life, dropped to the ground and rolled up into a ball. He put his hands over his head to protect himself from the pounding he felt sure he was about to receive from the angry bull that he had, stupidly, just touched on the nose.

It was a few moments before he realised that the bellowing and snorting had come from his colleagues and that self-same bellowing and snorting had now turned to belly aching laughter. His colleagues had stopped him getting away, and they were the reason he was now lying curled up on the muddy grass.

The bull stood completely static by the fence still unconcerned by it all. It nonchalantly eyed Billy while he lay on the ground. Later Billy swore it winked at him.

I continued to learn the job. You never stop learning. I learned how to detain and interview crooks, how to process them through the custody suite and then how to write a report to the Procurator Fiscal. I also learned that local knowledge was important, for example; It is good practice for police officers to know of the nicknames of their local clientele. Knowing a nom-de-plume when it is used to graffiti a wall or when some witness only knows the person by their nickname can save time.

Imagine getting told that 'Ginger Jimmy' did it. The persons telling you might not know Ginger Jimmy's real name. Knowing who 'Ginger Jimmy' is and where he stays will help progress your enquiry a lot quicker.

Now, in Ginger Jimmy's case, we could have a guess at how he came by that nickname. Similarly, 'Baldy Brian' or 'One Eyed Jack' would give us a clue to the origin of their nicknames. How some people got their nicknames is not so obvious.

One baddie went by the nickname 'Bumjar.' I hadn't a clue how he had come by this unusual nickname, even to fathom a guess was futile. One day we had him in the office caught red-handed for theft. During his interview, I built up a rapport with him. He admitted his wrongdoing, and I was preparing to charge him with the theft. Curious how he had gained his nickname I came right out and asked him.

"How did you get the nickname 'Bumjar?'"

He groaned and rolled his eyes, but explained, "I am forty," he said, "I have worked as a butcher, I have worked as a barman, I have been a darts champion in my local pub a dozen times. I got married and had four kids, I've been made redundant and I'm an alcoholic. But everyone still calls me 'Bumjar'... cause when I was in primary school I once farted into a jam jar, sealed the lid then opened it under the nose of some of my classmates."

What a bummer!

CHAPTER 11

THE NURBURGRING AND GANAVAN SANDS

Even more, than listening to the radio play Chrissie Hynde, Billy Idol and Kate Bush, I used to love listening to the stories from all the older cops. On one occasion I was sitting in the canteen with Big Bob. We were on our break when Tom and Fred arrived back also to partake of some tea and biscuits.

Tom would tell a story, and Fred would hit back with a more far-fetched story as they played a game of 'one-upmanship.' They had many stories, each one more absurd than the next. While I raised an eyebrow as to the reliability of their tales, listening to them was always preferable to getting on with the boring old paperwork.

Tom related a story about how the previous night he was five minutes away from finishing duty when he and Fred came across an abandoned car with its passenger window smashed. On checking his note-book, he saw he had noted, during his briefing at the start of his shift, that it was a stolen car. He recalled that the owner reported it stolen the previous night from a car park in an adjacent beat.

Neither he nor his colleague was happy about having to deal with it at that late stage of their shift. It would mean having to wait on a scene-of-crime officer attending, who would then carry out a lengthy forensic examination. Only then could they request a recovery vehicle uplift the car. As a result, they could be two or three hours late home. It wasn't even their crime; they reasoned, as it had been stolen from an area covered by a different station.

As the abandoned car was only fifty yards from the adjacent beat, they decided that the prudent thing to do would be to push it back into their neighbouring station's beat. Tom got into the driver's seat and steered while Fred pushed. Happy that no-one had seen them, they then radioed up to the control room, reported finding the car and requested officers from the adjacent station attend to deal with it, which they did.

Tom sat back on his chair in the canteen, proud of his story and the ingenuity of his quick thinking. Big Bob looked up and smiled, "That reminds me of the time I was on my probation."

"What happened?"

"My tutor and I got called to a dead body found at the side of a road. It was a poor tramp who appeared to have died of old age or the cold or something. It was near our border with our neighbouring force. A couple of their officers had found him and requested we attend to deal with it. When we arrived, we took one look, and I knew."

"You knew what?"

"I knew they had lifted this tramp from their area and carried him over the border into ours."

"How did you know?"

"Because we found him an hour earlier and had carried him into their area so they could deal with him!" Big Bob finished his story with his usual roguish smile.

As well as telling fantastic stories, Big Bob was also a bit of a boy racer.

Not long after I passed my police driving test, I was let loose on an unsuspecting public as a fully fledged general patrol vehicle driver. Big Bob still liked to drive most of the time, and it was during one of our patrols that he introduced me to the 'Nurburgring.'

The 'Nurburgring' was a series of bends about two miles long that weaved its way through some beautiful Scottish countryside. It was the most dangerous road in the county due to the number and frequency of crashes on it. Budding Ayrton Sennas used it a lot. The 'Nurburgring' connected two towns on our beat, and often we would have to travel the length of it to deal with emergency calls.

Big Bob was not only a first-class cop, a good mechanic, and all round handyman, he was also a fine driver. He drove his car everywhere fast. Many a time we would leave the office together, and before I even got my car started, he would disappear around the corner at the end of the street. Thankfully, he drove our police cars in a more sedate fashion. He was happy to toddle along unhurried, watchfully patrolling the streets. Unless there was an emergency.

Big Bob could handle a car at speed, but it was to my consistent consternation that whenever we got an emergency call, and just as soon as he floored the accelerator, Big Bob would remove one hand from the steering wheel to extricate his cigarettes from his tunic pocket. During the first minute or two of any emergency call we headed towards, Big Bob would fumble around with his cigarette and lighter. His lighting-up process always required the use of both his hands leaving the speeding police car momentarily unrestrained in its wild pursuit of the wrong side of the highway. The moment he got the end of his cigarette ablaze he would inhale deeply at the same time as he wrenched the steering wheel to direct the police car back onto the right side of the road.

Receiving an emergency call triggered my 'fight or flight' response. Kicking in and automatically releasing adrenaline to course through my veins, but when Big Bob was in the driving seat that flow of adrenaline became an absolute flood. I sat there unsure of what we were going to and in real fear that my puffing pilot would crash.

The first occasion we had to travel to an emergency through the 'Nurburgring' Big Bob told me to get my watch out and time him.

I set the stopwatch function to zero and as we approached the start point (national speed limit sign). Big Bob lit up his constitutional emergency cigarette and floored the one point six litre marked Vauxhall Astra through the 'Nurburgring' setting a blistering pace. The cigarette dangled from his mouth the whole way, dropping ash on his tunic as he drove. He dusted the ash off with whatever hand was free, depending on which corner he was skidding round. He passed the finish line in under two minutes. It was a masterful drive, a great feat of coordination, what with not only pointing the car in the right direction as it rounded bends at the edge of its possible grip on the roadway but with also having to contend with lighting up and subsequently smoking a cigarette in the process.

Timing the 'Nurburgring' became a regular feature of attendance to emergency calls in the next town. I would get my watch out whenever the journey required blue lights and a fast response. Big Bob's times were consistently good. Rain or shine he completed the 'Nurburgring' in under two minutes. The scariest time was during autumn. The road was wet and covered in sodden and slippery leaves. In those conditions, my butt cheeks gripped the seat tighter than a limpet on the hull of a ship. Big Bob always remained calm and on completing the 'Nurburgring' said, "Well sometimes you just have to go for it and trust to luck," which was never reassuring.

A few weeks later we were night shift. It was about four in the morning; sitting in the office doing our paperwork when a call came in to attend a house alarm on the other side of the 'Nurburgring.' We had been at this alarm twice already that night and five times in the past week. The alarm system was clearly faulty. However, police being police, we still attended and checked it every time - without fail. On this occasion, Big Bob thought it prudent that he get on with writing his custody report. He threw me the keys to the car and told to be careful.

Since this was a blue light situation (not really, maybe on the first occasion the alarm went off but not the sixth), I decided to have a go at Big Bob's 'Nurburgring' record. As I passed the start point, I glanced at my watch then gave the car the welly. The 'Nurburgring' was mine. I used every ounce of my ability and driving experience to race through the bends. Convinced that I was speeding through the bends faster than the best Stirling Moss could have done and certain I would smash Big Bob's record.

The engine screamed as I passed over the finishing line. I was positive I had beaten every time that Big Bob had ever recorded. Glancing at my watch and couldn't believe what I saw, I shook it twice and looked again to make sure. Yup - a full twelve seconds slower than Big Bob.

I continued to the alarm call and slowed right down as I entered the thirty miles per hour speed limit at the start of the town. There was a sharp right-hand bend, and I slowed further for this. I then dropped off speed as I rounded the sharp left-hand bend into the main street. I couldn't have been going over twenty-five miles per hour when a cat scampered across the road in front of me. Instinct took over, and I swerved to avoid it and in doing so clipped the nearside kerb. I wondered how I would explain that one.

The kerb caused the front nearside tyre to burst, and the blowout caused me to lose further control of the car. With the front nearside tyre ruptured, the car became uncontrollable. The steering wheel wrenched to the side, and the car mounted the pavement. The car's nearside connected with a wall and scraped along the full length of it. (A wall that belonged to the home of a Police Superintendent). I wondered how I would explain that one.

A sign post on the pavement prevented me going any further. The front of the car rammed it with such force that I catapulted through the windscreen onto the bonnet. I lay there, stretched out on the crumpled front end of the marked Vauxhall Astra.

I wondered how I would explain that one!

The irony was I had travelled as fast as I could through the 'Nurburgring,' but couldn't negotiate a left-hand bend at a sedate 'Sunday driver' pace.

Following my smashing time in a marked Vauxhall Astra right outside the home of one of our senior bosses, I got to go on a second driving course. Another two weeks of driving tuition.

At that time two Traffic Cops ran the driving course. There were six of us taking part, split between the two cars. We drove around our area and attained sufficient skill to impress our instructors we were all capable of passing. On the last day, our instructors took us a little further afield, and we shared the drive out into the countryside. Whether planned by our instructors or just the way it happened, we kept going out west, and we ended up passing through Oban, stopping in the car park of the beach at Ganavan Sands. It was the height of summer, glorious sunshine, and a gentle sea breeze washed over us as we stepped out of the cars.

The next bit seems surreal now but all eight of us, in our short sleeve uniform, got out of the cars and went paddling in the water. What better thing to do on a hot West Coast day? I found a perfectly rounded stone about four inches in diameter and kicked off a shot putt competition, which instigated a full on 'Olympics challenge.' We all took part in a thirty-yard sprint, the long jump, the hop skip, and jump and rounded it off with a javelin competition using a branch of a tree we found nearby. When it broke, I declared myself the quadrathlon winner, and we headed off back into Oban for lunch.

Somehow we persuaded our instructors to take us for a pub lunch. We sat in our short sleeve uniform around a large table in a pub at the sea front overlooking the bay. There we tucked into battered fish and chips, washed down with a single pint of beer, a frothy thirst quencher that topped a great day out. We were getting paid for doing something that felt like it was a family visit to the seaside.

The two instructors were sensible enough not to let any of us drive back. They took the controls and embarked on a demonstration of real driving skill, reducing the normal three-hour drive back to something just over the two hours. As you would expect, our instructors were the most accomplished and experienced drivers and could negotiate the tightest of bends safely, smoothly and as progressively as Stirling Moss in his heyday. We arrived back at the station right on time for our five o'clock finish.

It had been a blissful day in the police, a no stress training day that provided good memories and made up for much of the pressures we normally encountered in the job.

By that time I was nearing the end of my probation. Pleasurable days in the police, like the last day of my driving course were few and far between. I had had my eyes opened by all manner of things. People are capable of showing some awful behaviour to their fellow man. Police officers, unfortunately for me, are also capable of doing some awful things to unsuspecting probationers. I had learned a great deal about life, and I had experienced things that people in ordinary jobs don't see.

Two years into my career, the Chief Constable invited me to see him. He would confirm my appointment as a police constable, no longer a probationer. Sadly, it didn't work out like that for Doddit. I'm not entirely sure what happened or how Doddit got himself into bother, but there was a Professional Standards Investigation. Two weeks before we were due to complete our probation, he disappeared. Just got up and left. The gossip was that he departed the country in somewhat of a hurry. Packed a bag and got on the first flight out of the country. There were all sorts of rumours. Like every force across the country, police thrive on rumour and any newsworthy matters concerning other officers quickly spread. The rumours about Doddit were that he met several dodgy characters who knew him from his schooldays. Perhaps he turned a blind eye to some of their minor crimes. Maybe they got their hooks into him. I could only surmise that he must have done something illegal to drop everything and leave the country.

So it was just Hoddit, Bruce, and me that turned up at the end of our two years probation for our confirmation interview with the Chief Constable.

"Did you hear about Doddit?" I asked Bruce, who had worked in the nearest office to Doddit.

"Aye."

"Do you know what he did?"

"Aye."

"Was it something bad?"

"Aye."

I waited for Bruce to tell me but he kept quiet.

"Are you going to tell me what he did?" I blurted out in as impatient a manner as I could muster.

"Aye," he went quiet again.

I waited, but Bruce did not try to enlighten me.

"Well, tell me then!"

Bruce looked at me in the eye.

"He did the worst thing imaginable," he said.

"WHAT!" I screamed at him.

This time, Bruce held my gaze. A big smile

formed on his face, "Doddit didnae do what they said Doddit did, but Doddit did do what they said he didnae do. Doddit's just a diddy," and at that, he shut up.

I never found out what Doddit did.

At the end of our two-year probation Hoddit, Bruce and I walked into the Chief Constable's office for our confirmation interview without Doddit. I was now a fully functioning constable. My first important milestone in my career. The expectation was that I would now be self-sufficient as a cop. It was a daunting thought but I needn't have worried, there was always advice and assistance when I needed it. No matter how big a gang I came up against, being a police officer meant I always had a bigger gang to back me up.

Hoddit may have been destined for greater things, but it never happened. Probably he would have been a senior officer, had it not been for his soft spot for the female sex. Not that some senior police officers didn't also have a soft spot for the female sex, I heard many a rumour that was undoubtedly more than just gossip. But they didn't get caught. Hoddit got caught. He was caught in a compromising position with a policewoman, on duty, in flagrante, on the canteen sofa.

You can't do that. People are eating for goodness' sake!

I wasn't there, but I would imagine that such a thing might be somewhat disagreeable to the other diners. Imagine trying to eat your egg and cucumber sandwich only to be interrupted by the sight of Hoddit enjoying something entirely more palatable.

'I want one of those,' I might have said. Unless it was a rather splendid, bacon and tattie scone roll. Then I might think twice. Bacon and tattie scone rolls from the police canteen were somewhat excellent.

Perhaps Hoddit's ignominious departure from the police service was just what he needed. He moved on to a career befitting of his intelligence. He went back to University, studied law and became a lawyer. No more night shifts, or fighting with drunks or standing in the rain guarding a locus. He had enough to worry about as he worked his way through three wives and two maintenance payments. The extra money he made as a lawyer helped pay for his expensive divorces.

Bruce lasted a bit longer. He got to about fifteen years service and had made noises about getting promoted, but his face didn't fit. No matter what he did and how hard he tried he couldn't even get a temporary rank. I bumped into him at headquarters one day, and he explained it over a coffee.

"My face doesn't fit," he said.

"Fit what?"

"No matter what I do and how hard I try I can't even get a temporary rank," he bemoaned.

"Well stop moaning about it and do something different!" I replied in my usual sympathetic manner.

Bruce did exactly that. He resigned from the police and started his own business. The last I heard, Bruce was doing extremely well. His logistics company had taken off, and he was well on his way to living the life of a rich millionaire. I wonder if he will have some new stories to regale me with, and maybe a couple more fiancées, the next time we meet.

CHAPTER 12

ALWAYS TAKE THE RIGHT ROAD AND THE RIGHT ARM

Back at my station, we had different vehicles to those used by the Traffic Department. It is the belief of some members of the public that the police have extra powerful cars and that they get well cared for and looked after. Thus, when they come to the end of their useful service, we put them to auction. Some people are keen to buy them. They ignore the dull paint next to the removed livery; they take no heed of the extra high mileage and bid for them thinking they are getting a bargain. Nothing could be further from the truth.

Police cars are not top of the range, tuned-up supercars. Think about it, unless it is a Traffic Department car, we get the no-frills models purchased to save the organisation money. Why would they waste money on an electric window when a handle will do? General Patrol Vehicles are basic models and subjected to twenty-four hours round-the-clock abuse. Drivers of all shapes and sizes climb in and out ruining the fabric, breaking the adjustment mechanism and chipping paint with their handcuffs.

Not only that, these are cars that don't belong to the driver thus few take pride in them. Sticky sweets litter the carpet; sugary drinks get spilt on seats and goodness knows what gets excreted by prisoners in the back seats. They go unwashed from one week to the next and have all sorts of additional holes for blue lights, two tone horns, and radios. The car mechanics employed by the police have a service programme, but the mechanics have to deal with numerous accident damaged cars and breakdowns. All that unplanned work that can set back the service rotas for the rest of the fleet.

On top of all that, many police drivers routinely trash these motors. At least once or twice a day someone at the wheel is sent to an emergency. The car is put through a gruelling test, gunned to their top speed as they head to the crisis as fast as they can.

If it snows, drivers young and old find an empty car park to show off their 'handbrake turn' skills and if someone is serious about police work, they crawl along at a walking pace burning out the clutch or bumping into kerbs.

In the rural area where I worked, we had the use of a Land Rover. Needed because we had to get to some out of the way places across rough terrain. This Land Rover was a testament to British quality craftsmanship as it had endured all the above. It was battered and bruised but still just kept going. While it wasn't the most comfortable of vehicles to drive, it got us from A to B and back again.

One night-shift, at the start of the week, PC Prim and I were working together, in the days before vehicles or radios were fitted with Global Positioning Systems (GPS). We could drive anywhere without someone in the control room knowing where we were. It was a quiet start to the week. PC Prim drove to the far end of our beat and then kept going. He was looking for a reaction from me as he drove a few miles into another force area. I didn't say a word. He continued to drive further and further out of our beat.

We ended up about twelve miles from our boundary before he turned to look at me and brag, "I bet that's the furthest you have been off your beat!"

I agreed that it was.

The next night it was my turn to drive. I took out our Land Rover. Again it was another quiet night, and I drove the same route PC Prim had the night before. I got to the twelve-mile mark and just kept going. On and on. About one mile from the next major town PC Prim (a conscientious fellow) shouted, "Okay, okay, okay. You win, go back."

We were thirty miles from our beat boundary and a good forty miles from the office. It was only then I noticed the oil light was on.

I pulled up to the side of the road, opened the bonnet and checked the dipstick. There was not a lick of oil. The dipstick was completely dry (although the dipstick that was driving broke into a sweat). PC Prim and I weighed up our options and decided our best bet was to get back into our area. If the Land Rover seized up before we got there, then we would have to think of something else.

Land Rovers are built of sturdy stuff; it got us back to the office without so much as a hiccup. Thanking my lucky stars that Land Rovers can operate without the need of oil, I still thought it prudent to fill it up, anyway. We kept all the car stuff in the garage. I opened it up and found a four-litre plastic tub of oil. As I poured it into the Land Rover under torch light, I thought the oil seemed a little green. However, I was reassured by the viscous nature of it. I took the emptied tub of oil into the office and was just about to deposit it in the bin when I looked at the label, *'Washing up liquid - concentrate.'*

The Land Rover blew black smoke (I liked to think of it as bubbles) out of its exhaust for weeks after, but it survived none-the-less unharmed. It completed two hundred thousand miles of Sterling police service before being carted off to the market and being bought by some unsuspecting new owner.

If you think driving thirty miles off my beat was bad; what about the guys in the Traffic Department of the Metropolitan Police? It was about the same time that their story hit the newspapers. It might have been quite concerning for the public, but for those of us in the job, it caused nothing but amusement. I certainly admired their audacity.

Every night-shift about twenty cars left the Metropolitan Police Traffic Department to go on patrol around London. One day a crew came back into their office at their finishing time and intimated to their colleagues that they had been to Milton Keynes. The traffic crew explained that they had been following a boy racer in his Audi TT up the M1 but only caught it about Watford. After charging the driver for speeding they then followed him further up the M1 to ensure he kept to the speed limits, and they didn't turn back until they were fifty miles off their beat. It was a boast that couldn't be ignored.

The next night another crew returned to the office and whispered to their colleagues that they had made it as far as Northampton. There was a murmur of disbelief until the driver produced his notebook, which clearly had the Northampton Police Office desk stamp. Now the record for being off their beat stood at one hundred miles.

It soon became a habit for each crew to take it in turns. They would come back with their books stamped further and further afield. The distance off their beat increased week after week, month after month. Then one crew boasted of being the first into Scotland, a round journey of six hundred and nineteen miles with only a half hour stop for a pee and a stamp of their book; they had averaged eighty-two miles per hour for their entire journey.

With the latest challenge set, on a quiet Monday night, a particularly adventurous crew got a stamp at Motherwell Police Office (just short of Glasgow). By the time they returned to their office, they had completed a round trip of eight hundred miles and had averaged one hundred and two miles per hour but still managed to arrive back in time for their 7 a.m. finish.

Unfortunately for those Traffic Officers, they got rumbled. Their challenge fated not to remain a secret. When finally caught, every officer in the department ended up back on the beat. News of their exploits hit the papers. They had come unstuck as the result of a simple phone call back to the office.

"Hello, this is the captain of the P & O ferry to Le Havre, I was just enquiring... should one of your traffic cars be on my boat?"

Their antics put our little jaunt off our beat into the category of 'distinctly uninventive'.

PC Prim and I became good friends, despite me being the victim of his nasty prank. It was a well planned and well-executed practical joke of the first order; I had to give him that.

Every year I underwent officer safety refresher training. I became an expert. A honed practitioner of every technique. A disciplined and focused professional in using handcuffs and baton. A specialist in the art of controlled mental presence and formidably skilled in taking significant and decisive action. Yup, all this from a single morning of training once a year.

Following the officer safety training, I could go weeks, months or years even, with no real need to deploy my CS incapacitant spray (tear gas). I had no real use for my baton. Some officers go their entire service without even pulling it out of its holster, other than using it to smash a window and effect entry to premises. The truth is the baton and CS spray is rarely produced as a threat and even more rarely used in anger.

When I had to use 'force' to arrest someone it would be an amalgam of what I could remember from my officer safety training, which I adapted to the situation, and making it up as I went along. It was just a muddle of muscle and mayhem. I did, however, always remember the 'come-along-hold.'

The 'come-along-hold' is used for a compliant prisoner and comprises holding their upper arm with your strong hand and their wrist with your weak hand, although it doesn't much matter if you get it the wrong way round. The hold is a polite way to say 'come along' but affords the easy use of control techniques should they struggle. If they do struggle, then holding the wrist with the weak hand acts as a lever when pushing their elbow with your strong hand. The arrested person is bent forward and down making it tricky for them to kick, headbutt or punch you.

One night PC Prim and I were out and about when we got a call to deal with a habitually drunk female called Cathy McCrathie. I was new at the station and hadn't yet met her although I had seen her name on the log a few times.

PC Prim brought me up to speed. Cathy McCrathie was an alcoholic and a right royal pain in the backside, mostly for her family, friends, and neighbours. The regularity with which police dealt with her abusive and belligerent exploits was ridiculous. PC Prim warned me she was not averse to assaulting the police and we should be wary. At the first opportunity get her in the 'come-along-hold' he told me, "You take her left arm," he said.

That was his clear instruction, which he repeated several times. I thought this was PC Prim being overly cautious, but I agreed to follow his plan.

We arrived at the locus to find Cathy outside her neighbour's house shouting up at the window challenging her to come out and fight. Her neighbours were a middle-aged couple who had long since given up on trying to reason with Cathy and stood at their upstairs window firing as much abuse back as they received but declining, as impolitely as possible, to come out and fight with her.

PC Prim quickly made his way round to Cathy's right-hand side and, as per his plan, I took my position on her left side. I manoeuvred my way in readiness to grab her left arm in the 'come-along-hold' at the first opportunity.

As soon as Cathy realised we were there, she switched the focus of her vitriolic tirade from her neighbours and directed it towards us. Cathy's venom-ous and choice language was not for the ears of the innocent. I could not believe a woman, who was the same age as my mother, could be so vile and offensive.

PC Prim wasted no time in informing her she was under arrest and moved in to grab her right arm. At the same time, he nodded to me and without hesitation, I went for her left arm, just as instructed. It was only then I realised there was something about Cathy McCrathie that PC Prim had failed to tell me. An important omission if you ask me. If he had told me, it might have prevented me from almost having a heart attack. PC Prim had planned this a little too well methinks.

I took hold of Cathy's left arm just above her elbow with my right hand and grabbed her left wrist with my left hand. Cathy lashed out, resisting our attempts to arrest her. I applied a little more downward pressure on her upper arm, using my grip on her wrist as a lever. This lever action causes a person to bend over and thus reduce any likelihood of them being able to lash out as much. It was a textbook officer safety technique executed with speed, skill, and aplomb. It also revealed what PC Prim had omitted to tell me. As I applied the pressure, her arm came away in my hands, completely separated from her body just below the shoulder blade. Initially stunned, I stood holding her severed arm with feeling blind panic. My face drained of colour.

PC Prim had intentionally, and with malice aforethought, failed to tell me that Cathy McCrathie only had one arm. He had cruelly directed me to the prosthetic one.

Despite PC Prim's evil plan working so well and

him nearly causing me to have a heart attack, I forgave him, but I didn't forget. My carefully orchestrated and patient revenge was exacted on him twenty-five years later. However, that is a tale for the future.

PC Prim and I got to know how each other well. We were much alike in the way we dealt with incidents. Sometimes we just needed a look to know what the other was thinking. That was the case when we dealt with 'The Craw.'

The Craw lived in what was once a lovely cottage in a picturesque little village. Unfortunately, he didn't look after either himself or his property, and over the years the police had to get involved in many a dispute when his neighbours complained about him. The complaints were initially about him leaving litter everywhere. His rubbish was simply tossed into his garden for all to see. As his drinking increased, his mental health declined, and his odd behaviour became more concerning to the public.

The Craw was a hoarder; he never put the rubbish out for collection. Instead, anyone entering his house had to negotiate past all his empty tin cans and food packaging. He tossed his rubbish on the floor or out the window. The house inside was even worse. The hallway reduced to a narrow corridor you had to walk sideways down because of the rubbish piled up either side. Each and every room was full from floor to ceiling with years of rubbish. The only space to move was from his armchair to the telly (no remote controls in those days).

In reality, the Craw was an alcoholic with deteriorating mental health. Sadly, it manifested in him being found drunk in and around the village or saying inappropriate things to the villagers causing offence or even making people frightened, depending on their disposition.

One night I took a report of the Craw causing a nuisance at the other end of the town. PC Prim and I attended. We found the Craw lying in the front garden of a little old lady's cottage collapsed in a drunken heap having fallen over her hedge.

Before we even entered the gate PC Prim and I could smell him. The Craw had not looked after himself for many a year, but this was the worst I had ever seen him. He stank to high heaven. The clothes on his back not removed for several months, and despite it being a warm summer's evening he sported four layers of clothes all wrapped up in a filthy thick duffel coat.

The closer we got the more revulsion he caused our nostrils. A frail elderly lady, looked out her front window and was clearly frightened by the presence of this tramp in her garden. She didn't know the Craw, all she saw was this dirty frightening looking man, and she expected us to deal with him.

PC Prim and I looked at each other. Neither of us wanted an hour long trip to the custody suite with this smelly individual in our car. We both knew arresting him for being drunk and incapable would mean that once we got to custody, we would get instructed to take him to the hospital. We might have to sit there for up to three hours or more waiting on some busy doctor taking a brief look at him before telling us he was 'fit to be detained.' We also knew that when we returned to the custody suite, the custody sergeant would instruct us to clean him up. That meant stripping him and coaxing him into the shower until he got rid of the worst of

the muck. PC Prim and I looked at each other. Instinct-
ively we knew what we had to do. We didn't have to exchange a word. We lifted him off the ground and threw
him into the boot of our car, then we drove him home
and dumped him into the chair in front of his telly. We
couldn't get away quick enough.

Another of our strange characters was Bobby Bobrink.
Despite him being a bloody nuisance for most of his life
I think we all grew to have a little soft spot for him.

Bobby Bobrink was a farmhand, a great big lug of
a laddie. Six and a half feet tall, as broad as a bull and
with hands like spades, quite a sight. His blond hair sat
on his head like one big cowlick, and his ruddy face was
a beacon to the fact he spent all day, in all weathers,
outdoors.

Bobby woke at five in the morning and worked
on the farm until it got dark. He repeated this day in,
day out, except Sundays. Sunday was Bobby's drinking
day.

On Sunday Bobby Bobrink had a lie in. He might
wake up at the same time as normal, but on Sundays, he
stayed in bed until 10.15 a.m. He then rose, dressed and
left his little cottage on the farm and walked the two
miles to the nearest village. The first pub at his side of
the village was The Castle Inn, a rough-and-ready pub
with no entertainment other than a dart board and one
dart; even that one dart only had one bent flight left.
Not quite a sawdust on the floor, wipe your feet on the
way out type of pub, but close enough. The landlord
was a retired army officer who purported to have been
in the SAS, but nobody believed him. His habits were
too intemperate, his beer belly and cowardly personality more akin to someone who had perhaps been in the

catering corp.

The Castle Inn didn't open until eleven on a Sunday, but when it opened the landlord always found Bobby Bobrink standing there ready to come in and avail himself of the liquids on tap. Bobby sat at the bar and supped pint after pint, right through until closing time. Only ever moving off the barstool to relieve himself. He never even considered throwing the single available dart at the dart board. His sole purpose was to drink.

Bobby Bobrink's capacity to throw pints over his throat was remarkable. For the full twelve hours that the pub was open, he would down a pint in two or three gulps and then look forward to another serving. His right arm was like a metronome. Once he set the pace, he stuck to it and didn't waver. Bobby was happy, and the owner was happy that he was happy. Keeping Bobby happy guaranteed the pub's income on a Sunday.

Bobby was not one for conversation. Even when people got to know him, there would be little in the way of dialogue. He had been working on the farm all week, and that hardly provided the seeds for scintillating conversation.

"What have you been up to this week Bobby?"

"Working on the farm."

"Did anything exciting happen?"

"No."

Bobby knew nothing of the outside world, there was no newspaper delivered to his cottage, and he had no television, so he had nothing much to say to anyone. That was until he got drunk. When Bobby Bobrink got drunk, generally not until nearing closing time, he liked to engage in banter. He would bait whoever remained in the pub into having a go at him. His ribbing gave him much amusement and mostly went unchallenged, his sheer size was enough to put off anyone attempting to go tit for tat.

"Hey Jimmy," Bobby would say to his fellow drinkers.

"What?"

"You're fecking ugly!" which was a bit like Frankenstein having a go at Dracula.

"My name is not 'Jimmy,'" his fellow drinker would reply.

"It is now!" Bobby Bobrink would pronounce and forevermore he would refer to that person as 'Ugly Jimmy.'

"It's just Bobby being Bobby, ignore him," was the usual way of playing down him being a bloody nuisance to others.

For years Bobby Bobrink got away with his Sunday sessions. He supped pints from morning until night. Round about the late evening mark he got the urge for a little banter. That banter sometimes went a little too far, and some of the other patrons got upset. The excuse that it was 'just Bobby being Bobby' wore a little thin. The owner of The Castle Inn realised that for all that Bobby spent all his wages in his pub, he was losing customers and thus money. When Bobby got in the mood for banter, they upped and left. He was scaring the clientele away. The landlord had words with Bobby. Bobby ignored these words or at least didn't remember them because he was too drunk and turned up the next Sunday and did the same thing he did every Sunday.

Eventually, the landlord plucked up enough

courage and barred Bobby Bobrink. He didn't do it when Bobby was drunk; he was too much of a coward to do that, he waited until mid-week, popped up to see him at the farm when he was sober.

"Bobby, I'm going to have to bar you from the pub."

"What for?"

"Because you are a bloody nuisance to my other customers and they are not coming in when you are there," the landlord explained as hesitantly as you would expect.

"How long for?"

The subject of 'how long' hadn't crossed the landlord's mind. He was there to bar him for good, but it gave him a coward's way out of a full on confrontation. "Em, two weeks."

"Can you make it just a week?"

"Er, okay, you are barred for a week."

Bobby missed the next Sunday drinking session. However, the following Sunday Bobby went right back to being a pain in the backside. He couldn't help himself; it was what he did when he got drunk. The next time the landlord barred him for a month. No matter how long he was barred, just as soon as Bobby was allowed back in the problems started again. It took a long time, and even the police getting called in before Bobby Bobrink found himself barred from The Castle Inn for good.

The next Sunday Bobby Bobrink rose from his bed at 10.12 a.m., three minutes earlier than was normal for him on a Sunday morning. At 11 a.m. he was standing outside The Strathy Bar when it opened. The Strathy Bar was three hundred yards further along the road from The Castle Inn, and it became Bobby's hostelry of choice. The cycle was to repeat itself, and within a year Bobby Bobrink was barred forever from The Strathy Bar. Within two years he had been barred from all four of the pubs in the village.

Most of the local bobbies, at some time or another, had been called to assist the pub owners to help enforce their ban. Bobby would refuse to leave the pub; the landlord would refuse to serve him. With such a stalemate the polis were called to sort it out. Assistance rendered by his removal. I hadn't had that dubious pleasure, but Bobby Bobrink had been pointed out as 'one to watch' whenever we passed by him when we were out on patrol.

My first involvement with Bobby was about midnight, on a cold Sunday. It was a dark winter's evening I was on mobile patrol, travelling down a country road, with PC Prim. We saw a flashing yellow light ahead of us. The flashing beacon seemed to wave in mid air, and it wasn't until we got closer that we solved that little mystery. A tanked Bobby Bobrink was walking in the middle of the road trying to wave down traffic, using a method of hitchhiking that hasn't yet caught on. He held up a lamp, one of those, roadwork lanterns that had a big hook on top. Half a mile earlier we had passed road works and had commented to each other how poorly lit they were. We didn't have to be detectives to put two and two together.

As we neared Bobby, it dawned on him that he had just waved down a police car. So he put the lamp behind his back in an attempt to hide it. While he had fully concealed the lamp itself, the light was still flashing, and a burst of yellow light would explode from behind his back every second. First from his right-hand side and then from his left-hand side, each flash, alternately lighting up the shrubbery on either side of the roadway.

PC Prim pulled up beside Bobby and rolled down his window. Bobby adjusted his body so that the lamp remained concealed in his right hand behind his back. It still flashed every second.

"Right Bobby, give us the lamp, and we will put it back," PC Prim politely asked, showing his intention to do nothing more about it other than replacing the stolen lamp to its rightful position at the road works.

"What lamp?" Bobby asked.

PC Prim looked up at Bobby, either side of him blinked brightly as the lamp alternated its flash. He looked at Bobby and then looked at me, and we both shook our heads. There was no persuading Bobby to hand over the lamp. He simply kept denying he had it. The illogical alcohol fuddled brain at work. What a bloody nuisance. We had to get out of our car and wrestle the damn thing off him. No easy task, given the size and strength of him. We took about five minutes of huffing and puffing to recover it, but we managed. As soon as I had it in my hands, PC Prim and I took a step back towards our car and made efforts to get our breath back.

Bobby Bobrink stood on the pavement facing us and feigning innocence said, "Oh, *that* lamp!"

We couldn't help ourselves. All three of us burst out laughing. It was the most surreal evening on patrol I had had. Instead of arresting Bobby for theft we gave him a lift home.

We didn't want him getting run over in the dark

and, to be fair, he was due to start work early the next morning.

Having got himself barred from every pub in the village, Bobby moved on to the next town, a further four miles away. He now had to rise at nine on a Sunday morning to walk there, but he did it religiously for the next four years. The town had twelve licensed premises, and he took a full four years to end up barred from every single one. We all thought he might give up drinking. The next nearest town was a further three miles away, nine miles from Bobby's farm cottage. But no. Bobby rose an extra hour earlier and walked into his nearest village, out the other side, through the next town and onto the next one. This town had ten pubs he could frequent, and this time it took Bobby seven years to get barred for life from each of them, but barred he was.

It was a habit that Bobby just seemed incapable of breaking. He loved to spend his Sundays drinking, but after ten hours of it, he became a bloody nuisance, invariably police were called in to remove him, and he got expelled from one pub after another.

Years later I was driving through a town some twelve miles away from his farm cottage when I saw Bobby exit a dingy pub in a rather drunken state. It was closing time on a Sunday night, and I realised he was still at it. It was just a bit of a surprise to me he was still prepared to walk all that distance to spend all day in the pub. I had to admire his dogged determination and dedication to the ale. Here he was walking twelve miles from his cottage to spend a Sunday in the pub. Despite being barred from every other pub within an eleven-mile radius, he still wanted to spend his Sundays drinking from morning until closing time.

I decided it might be the decent thing to offer him a lift home. I pulled up beside him, rolled down my window and spoke to him, "Hello Bobby, quite some way from home, aren't you?"

"Hey, Jimmy! Do you ken that you are fecking ugly?"

"I'm well aware of that fact Bobby, now would you like a lift home?"

"Naw. I've got my bike here," Bobby informed me as he grabbed a large mountain bike from the side of the pub, "It's my pub transporter, Jimmy."

As he cycled off, I shouted to him that he should get lights for it, but I'm sure it fell on deaf ears.

A senior officer once suggested we should open Scotland's Secret Bunker, gather up the likes of Cathie McCrathie, The Craw, and Bobby Bobrink along with all our other ne'er-do-wells and lock them all in there. Then we could just throw away the key. They deserve each other.

I wasn't so sure that would be such a good idea. What if they ended up breeding? Imagine in a thousand years time when they opened the bunker up again and out popped all the flawed genes in one set of inbred offspring? The world would suffer. Anyway, they already tried and ended up with Cumbernauld.

CHAPTER 13

SERGEANT NAPOLEON

These were halcyon days, for me at least. In other parts of the British Isles, they had turbulent times. The IRA found themselves in jail for a bombing campaign across London, the Manchester air disaster killed fifty-five people, a riot in Brixton erupted after the accidental shooting of a woman by police, rioting at football matches by English supporters saw a blanket ban on their teams playing in Europe and the Sinclair C5 launched. Yes, a recumbent battery assisted tricycle stole the headlines. It was obvious from the start that the C5 would fail. The lack of steering wheel made it a difficult sell. It was an object of ridicule, as was Sergeant Napoleon.

Sergeant Napoleon was the source of many moans and groans. He was diminutive in stature and bereft of any sporting talent or physical prowess. People felt he tried to make up for it in his management style - hence his nickname. He micromanaged our tasks and demanded 'in your face' policing. Yet, he avoided confrontation with the public and would remain in his office from the start of his shift until it was time to go home (he wouldn't even answer the door to the public).

Sergeant Napoleon made life difficult for us. He was an over-officious bureaucrat who continually had to remind people of his status by pointing at his chevrons. He would command little or no respect without his uniform. His low standing in the human race and his power hungry hypocrisy was a noxious mixture.

It was with open amusement then when Big Bob stood looking out the canteen window and announced, "Watch out Sinclair C5 is coming."

"Sinclair C5?"

"Sergeant Napoleon!" Big Bob informed us and explained, "because he is wee, useless and has no control."

We made our way to the window, snorting.

"You can always tell when he has a good idea," Big Bob continued, "he has the habit of putting his hat on back to front."

I looked at Big Bob quizzically, "I've never seen him with his hat on back to front."

"Exactly!" he said and let out a great big guffaw.

Sergeant Napoleon chose that exact moment to look up at the canteen window and caught us looking at him and laughing. We dodged back into the canteen out of sight.

Sergeant Napoleon was not totally useless; he was quite a good communicator. Sergeant Napoleon loved to gossip, like a 'sweetie wife' he quizzed us endlessly, but only regarding other officers. The force experimented with newsletters, briefing documents and wall posters to find the best way to keep staff informed, the quickest and cheapest method, they found, was to have someone impart the news to Sergeant Napoleon with the words, 'can you keep a secret?'

Sergeant Napoleon was also ambitious and keen to advance his career. Thus he was eager to ensure that he knew all about everybody, especially those who also went for promotion. He spent a lot of his time trying to belittle his peers. He gave endless, disparaging commentary on others behind their backs.

When his mind turned to policing, his constant interference was like getting poked in the back every three minutes. The job didn't get completed any quicker or better, his meddling only alienated those who worked under him. I used to think his heart was in the right place, even when he was brusque with people for no reason, but I was wrong. I gave him too much credit. Micromanagement is the opposite of high-quality leadership. It slows the process, each little step of the task listed and detailed and run through and insured and okayed until every party involved is thoroughly demoralised. There is no trust in micromanaging. It is the enemy of loyalty, positivity and learning.

Those who worked under Sergeant Napoleon tried to avoid his beady eye and critical countenance. Some older cops, however, weren't averse to playing the occasional prank on him.

Sergeant Napoleon often came into work to find that the swivel chair in his office spun down as low as it could go, or conversely wound fully up so that his little legs dangled inches off the floor. His small stature made this amusing either way.

One day two cops set him up. Fred and Tommy were legendary; they made the job look easy and were universally adored for their ability to make the job fun for everyone. Well just about everyone, Sergeant Napoleon came to be mistrustful of these two.

One morning, before Sergeant Napoleon started

work, Fred concealed himself in a large cupboard in Sergeant Napoleon's office. When Sergeant Napoleon entered his office, he switched on his computer and then brewed himself a coffee. The coffee was always ready before the slow computer loaded itself up and became functional. He then sat at his desk and updated himself with all the goings on during the previous twenty-four hours, oblivious to the fact that Fred was hiding in his cupboard just a few feet away. A full hour passed. Fred remained quiet in the cupboard and went unnoticed for the full hour.

Tommy then came into Sergeant Napoleon's office and asked an innocuous question. Fred, still hiding in the cupboard, made a low whistle. Sergeant Napoleon stopped talking and looked around wondering where the whistle had come. Tommy ignored the whistle and continued talking. Fred whistled again. Sergeant Napoleon looked around confused, "What was that?" he asked Tommy.

"What was what?"

"That whistle?"

"I never heard anything!"

"You must have heard it that time."

"I don't know what you are talking about!" before continuing with his story, "...when the guy got to hospital they found he had a broken shoulder..."

Fred whistled again.

"There it is again," Sergeant Napoleon interrupted, and pointed at the cupboard next to his desk, "It's coming from there!"

"I didn't hear anything." Tommy informed him and continued his story, "... so because he had a broken shoulder we had to treat it as a serious assault..."

Sergeant Napoleon stopped listening to Tommy. He focused his entire attention on the cupboard. Nervously he approached it and slowly opened the cupboard door, at which point Fred jumped out waving his hands in the air and shouting, "AH HA!"

There was not one person in the office who did not think it was a perfectly justifiable use of Fred's time.

On another occasion, at the end of his shift, our wee Sergeant Napoleon bid his goodbyes and left the office. There was a general rush to peek out the window to watch him enter his car.

After a few minutes of revving his engine and nothing happening, Sergeant Napoleon got out and came back into the office. Everyone was back in place pretending to write reports or read statements.

"My car won't go," he announced.

"What's wrong?" we asked.

"Well, it starts up but when I put it in gear it revs up, and nothing happens."

We offered our sympathy, and he borrowed a radio to call an ex-mechanic cop working at a nearby station.

He then waited around for half an hour for the ex-mechanic to arrive. When he turned up, he had a quick look at the car and promptly announced that the problem was that a trolley jack was propping up the rear axle so that neither wheel touched the ground. Fred and Tommy had been watching from a bush at the other side of the car park, giggling away like schoolboys in a brothel. All the funnier that Sergeant Napoleon hadn't even noticed that his car sat on a jack.

Sergeant Napoleon suffered many an ignominious prank at the hands of Fred and Tommy. For having nonsense, they were a partnership made in heaven. Fred was the senior cop nearing retirement but still keen as mustard to get the job done and have as much fun as he could while doing it. Tommy had nearly twenty years service but was still hardworking and conscientious. He liked to do the job properly but couldn't help getting dragged along into scrapes with Fred. I worked with both these guys at different times and thoroughly enjoyed their company. They were as equally engaging and entertaining on their own, but together their nonsense and shenanigans were a joy to behold.

One day an apprehension warrant arrived at the office for a bad guy. Fred and Tommy were night shift and had started at eleven. Fred knew the bad guy was a nasty piece of work and decided that it was worth getting him out of his bed and locking him up. So off they went to the bad guy's house about arrived at midnight.

The lights were all out, and they presumed the bad guy had retired for the evening. Fred walked up to the door and tried the handle to find it locked. He opened the letter-box, but before he could say the bad guy's name, a big dog behind the door barked furiously. Fred and Tommy took fright and a couple of steps back before looking at each other not sure what to do. Neither of them happy about the prospect of tackling a ferocious big dog. Just then the upstairs curtain opened, and the bad guy looked down from his bedroom window curious as to why his dog was barking.

He saw Fred and Tommy standing in full uniform at his door; both anxious about getting savaged by the dog. With a smirk he concluded that his dog had frightened them off, he sneered at them, gave them the V sign and headed off back to bed. Fred was livid.

"He is not getting away with that," he told Tommy, "we've got a warrant, and it is getting executed right now."

The arrest warrant gave them powers of forced entry but only if they had reasonable cause to believe the subject (i.e., the bad guy) was there. Well, they had just confirmed it. They knew he was in and they knew he wasn't opening the door for them.

Fred formulated a plan. Tommy would hold the handle down on the front door while Fred shoulder charged it. They would both charge in and kick the dog out the door. Once the dog was outside, they could then close the door and arrest the bad guy at their leisure.

The first bit of the plan went well. Two shoulder charges and Fred burst the lock and gained entry. Fred and Tommy both rushed into the dark hallway despite the dog barking even more furiously than before. Fred got past the dog and started booting it towards the open front door. He couldn't see much in the dark hallway but was surprised his efforts to remove the dog from the house didn't work. The dog snarled and growled at them determined to stay where it was.

The dog continued to bark, despite receiving several hard kicks in various parts of the body. Fred put more effort into it striking the dog with his boot. He kicked it hard enough to launch it outside whether or not it wanted to go but this was one determined dog. It stayed in the hallway barking and yelping like a Tasmanian Devil.

Fred decided there was nothing else for it the

dog was so frenzied he would have to kill it. He removed his baton from his holster; it would be him or the dog.

Just as he was about to swing the baton at the dog; the bad guy clicked a switch, and the hallway flooded with light. The frenzied dog, they saw, was trying to exit the front door and escape their violent attack on it. It could not escape because his owner, the bad guy, had tied him to the hallway radiator with his lead.

Fred had his baton raised in readiness to strike the dog but realised there was no need. He turned to the bad guy, baton still raised. "You're under arrest... and if you have any nonsense you're getting the same."

It was years after the event before I heard that story. Fred and Tommy kept some things close to their chest. They couldn't keep the next one quiet though.

Masquerading as reliable, hard-working pillars of the community Fred and Tommy were, on the face of it, fine upstanding members of society. They came to work, put on a uniform and got on with whatever they had to do. They attended road accidents, dealt with shoplifters, stopped cars and warned drivers for speeding or for having dangerously bald tyres. They dealt with sudden deaths, assaults, served citations, locked up bad guys, patrolled the streets and wrote up their paperwork. They did this in a cheerful and efficient manner. That was until Sergeant Napoleon came on the radio, "Aye, Fred and Tommy, return."

"But sergeant we are dealing with..."

"Aye, return now!"

And at that, Fred and Tommy dropped what they were doing and headed back to the office to speak with

Sergeant Napoleon.

"How did you get on with that call?" Sergeant Napoleon asked them.

"Which one?"

"The housebreaking in the village?"

"We haven't been to that yet."

"Why not, what have you been doing?"

"Well, we were locking up a prisoner when we got sent to it. As soon as we lodged our prisoner, we drove to the housebreaking call and just as we were about to arrive you called us up on the radio and asked us to return to speak to you. I tried to explain to you that we were going to be dealing with the housebreaking, but you instructed us to return immediately. That's why we haven't been to it yet," said Fred.

"We don't get many housebreakings in the village, and I need to know about it. So get yourselves there and give me an update as soon as you can," Sergeant Napoleon instructed.

Fred and Tommy, mumbling under their breath and shaking their heads, got back into their car and drove the five miles back to the housebreaking. No sooner had they parked their car outside the house, Sergeant Napoleon called them on the radio again.

"Aye Fred and Tommy, return to the office."

"But Sarge, we have just arrived at the village for that call..."

"Aye, return now!"

"But we haven't been to deal with the housebreaking yet."

"Return NOW!" Sergeant Napoleon demanded.

Fred and Tommy turned their car around and headed back to the office.

Sergeant Napoleon was standing at the back door waiting for them and looking decidedly distraught.

"I need you to deal with the dog in the front foyer."

"Dog?"

"Someone found it roaming the streets and handed it in."

"Could you not have put it in the kennel out the back?" Fred asked.

"No, I couldn't. It's too big."

"How can it be too big for the kennel?"

"It's too big for one person to handle. Just go and do it."

Fred and Tommy went out to the front foyer and found the dog, a Great Dane.

Sergeant Napoleon recoiled at the sight of any dog. He wasn't a doggie person. Man's best friends have had close relationships with humans for millennia. They follow us without question, they won't ever let you have dinner alone and once you finish eating they act as mini-dishwashers.

No matter how long you leave them alone they are always over-the-moon to see you again - they forget it was you who left them alone. They also have good long-term memories, if you mistreat a dog they remember it. A dog stands by you in prosperity and in poverty, in health and in sickness. He will sleep on the cold ground, to be near his master's side. He will guard the sleep of his master whether he is rich or poor. When all other friends desert he remains to lick your wounds. The faithful dog asks no higher privilege than to be by your side. So when I meet someone who isn't a doggie person I ask myself 'why?'

Perhaps they once did something bad to a dog? Teased it, threw stones at or something like that and it retaliated. People who don't like dogs recoil from them for a reason. They have evil in their character, they are capable of despicable things.

They do not see the boundless good in dogs. And they show the same animosity towards people - people not like them. I have witnessed them, dog haters have no time for other cultures, branding them all as biters. Such intolerance breeds bigotry and racism.

People who don't like dogs aren't nice people, we should distance ourselves from them. We can't change their minds so we should isolate them so their poison can't infect others. So pat a dog and feel their love or forever bear my suspicion.

Sergeant Napoleon asked the finder to leave the dog in the foyer while he remained behind the counter. He couldn't even be in the same room as it. Fred and Tommy took the friendly Great Dane to the back of the office and lodged it in the kennel, no problem at all.

With the friendly Great Dane safely caged they got back in their car and headed on back to deal with the housebreaking. This time they alighted from their car and were walking up to the door of the house when Sergeant Napoleon called them on their radio again.

"Aye, Sergeant Napoleon to Fred and Tommy - return."

"Sarge, we are at the housebreaking, just about to get the details."

"Aye, return now."

"But Sarge, we haven't..."

"Aye, return NOW!"

Once again Fred and Tommy made their way back to the office. Sergeant Napoleon was sitting in his office typing on his computer.

"What did you want us for now Sarge?" Fred asked.

"I need you to take that dog back to its owner; she's been on the phone. Will you manage to get it in your car?"

"Well we can try, but it seems friendly enough so it should go in no problem. Where does the owner stay?"

"It is a Mrs Wilcox, 7 Denniston Way."

"Denniston Way?"

"Yes."

"How long have you been stationed here, Sarge?"

"Nearly seven years, why?"

"Because Denniston Way is the street at the back of the office. The one you drive through and into the car park every day when you come to work. It will take longer to drive the dug home than it would walk it from the kennel across the street."

Sergeant Napoleon reddened a little and became a little flustered; he changed the subject, "Have you got details of that housebreaking yet?"

"Not yet Sarge, because every time we get up to the door you call us back to deal with a bloody dog."

Fred walked out, dealt with the Great Dane and decided that it was time for some karma. Tommy was joyfully roped in.

Sergeant Napoleon was a creature of habit. A man with over two decades of police experience, the last five years of which he had entrenched himself at our local office. Monday to Friday working nine-to-five hours he always arrived into work at ten minutes to nine. His first port of call was his computer to switch it on, then to the kettle. The kettle was older than the computer, but it still came to the boil before the computer had loaded up and was ready to go.

Armed with his coffee, Sergeant Napoleon sat at his desk and caught up on what had been happening in his area. At ten he boiled the kettle again and his second coffee sustained him until lunchtime. Regular as clockwork.

Lunchtime for Sergeant Napoleon was at 12.30 p.m. on the dot. He would vacate his seat and take up the same plastic chair in the canteen he sat in every lunchtime for the last five years. Sergeant Napoleon's lunch box contained the same things every day. His lunch box comprised a cheddar cheese sandwich, a packet of salt and vinegar crisps and an apple.

Sergeant Napoleon religiously opened his cheese sandwich and spread half the packet of salt and vinegar crisps on top. Closing the sandwich, he pressed it firmly together with the palm of his hand. As he munched away at his sandwich, the remaining crisps in the packet became a side dish.

At lunch time his preferred beverage was tea, the making of which was somewhat obsessive. The kettle boiled, and the contents poured into Sergeant Napoleon's special mug, a green and white striped juggernaut of a mug with an embellishment on the front that said 'Simply the Pest,' the bottom curl of the 'B' in Best having been scrubbed off by a disgruntled cop years earlier. Once the mug had had two minutes to heat up, he poured the contents out and filled it again from a freshly boiled kettle on top of one standard tea bag. He commenced a stir of exactly sixty seconds before removing the tea bag. The milk was always last to enter the cup and never over the tea bag - that would have been sacrilege. The fanatically prepared cup of tea helped washed down his cheese and crisp sandwich.

Then Sergeant Napoleon ate his apple, tossing the bare core in the bin. The process took half an hour which left Sergeant Napoleon a full quarter of an hour of his lunch break to complete the last of his customary routine. As regular as the sun came up, as soon as Sergeant Napoleon finished his sandwich, crisps, apple and tea he would declare his next intention, "I'm off for a shite!" and he would toddle off to the toilet with his Daily Record firmly tucked under his arm.

On this occasion, Fred and Tommy were up off their seats as soon as Sergeant Napoleon made his way to the toilet. They donned their tunics and stood at the back door ready to leave. They didn't want to be around when the shit hit the pan. Their idea, planned over several weeks, and with much debate whether they should execute it or not. Fred had the deciding vote, and Sergeant Napoleon's fate was sealed when he Fred declared, "To hell with it, he deserves it!"

Moments later there was a barrage of loud expletives from the toilet as Sergeant Napoleon discovered the mess you can get into when you don't notice cling film carefully stretched across the bowl.

"RIGHT YOU TWO. MY OFFICE NOW!" Sergeant Napoleon shouted from his cubicle as he immediately realised who would have been responsible.

Fred and Tommy, however, made a run for it and didn't return to the office until Sergeant Napoleon had finished for the day, despite him calling them on their radio every half hour with the instruction, "Aye, Fred and Tommy. Return NOW!"

Sergeant Napoleon may have stretched the patience of many a cop, and I don't think many would regret the pranks they played on him but there is more to people than the job they do and the way they do it. When he retired, he devoted much of his spare time to charitable work and raised an awful lot of money for good causes. On balance, the world is probably a better place because of him.

CHAPTER 14

HOW TO GET INTO THE CID

Our station wasn't the most up-to-date, we didn't have the best cars or equipment, but the people who worked there were great. It was a good place to work, and I would have happily remained there for many years. However, just as I was getting comfortable with the station and the people I dealt with, my boss called me into his office. Sergeant McDonnell, one of the best gaffers I ever had, a quick-witted, knowledgeable officer respected by all who knew him. I jumped up from my chair and headed through to his office.

"The Criminal Investigation Department are looking for aides," he said.

My ears perked up. I liked the thought of joining the CID, I felt there was kudos accompanied with the title of a detective. I liked the thought of wearing a suit to work. I hoped Sergeant McDonnell would recommend me.

"I'm going to recommend you," he said.

What a great opportunity for me, the beaming grin on face couldn't hide my delight. With only four years under my belt I was young in service to be going to the CID, so I took pride from the fact that I was even getting recommended.

"I think you have the right attributes, and I'll tell

you why," Sergeant McDonnell continued.

I respected Sergeant McDonnell. He was one of the good guys. A hard working, down-to-earth man who had a great way with people. He would now tell me why he thought I was worthy of going to the CID. Perhaps he recognised my intelligence. He knew I worked hard and had a great detection rate. He saw that I was good with people. I could talk to anyone and easily built rapport. He had no issues with my work ethic or my report writing or anything, for that matter. Yup, I doubtless deserved the opportunity to join the CID, for all those reasons.

"Yes," Sergeant McDonnell continued, "I think you should fit right in... because you can drink!"

As it turned out, my penchant for a pint stood me in good stead when I swapped my uniform for a *Ralph Slaters* suit.

There was certainly a drinking culture in the police at that time. That drinking culture seemed magnified in the CID. Senior officers didn't condone drinking on duty, but they didn't seem to mind us having the occasional libation after work. While sometimes officers finished duty and retired to a back room for a drinking session, this was a practice that was becoming much less common even then. Nowadays that practice is neither tolerated or ignored. Anyone caught drinking within the confines of a police building could find themselves out on their ear.

So with my bum fluff moustache I joined the CID. I discovered, were a hardworking, hard-drinking bunch. By Friday night everyone was ready for a drink, and as the aide, they sent me out at five or six in the evening to purchase a carry-out for the office. It never ceased to amaze me how quickly this was consumed. Then we'd make our way to the pub to continue to wind down.

One Friday evening our boss, Detective Inspector Jagielka, was in fine form regaling us all with his stories and castigating anyone who wasn't part of his hardworking crime fighting team. Before long the carry-out lay empty in the buckets for the cleaners to dispose of in the morning. DI Jagielka still hadn't quite given vent to all his feelings about the week's events. He declared he needed something more to drink. I was despatched again to the local off-licence to buy further sustenance.

Within an hour the further sustenance had been guzzled. A heated discussion commenced. The importance of this heated discussion would be lost on me forever. However, it was deemed important enough to warrant more drink.

At this, our good Detective Inspector Jagielka recalled that a bottle of vodka had been lodged in the production room earlier in the week, following the recovery of stolen goods from a break-in at a pub.

"Go and get that vodka out the production room," he decreed, "we can replace it with another bottle tomorrow."

There were no protestations about keeping best evidence or even any qualms about the ethics of such action. We would replace the bottle the next day, so no harm done. We unanimously approved the decision as a great idea. DI Jagielka removed the bottle of vodka from the cupboard, stripped of its production label and unscrewed the bottle cap, which he tossed into the bucket. No point in keeping the redundant screw cap, it would never be reunited with the bottle.

Detective Inspector Jagielka took on the job of taster and poured a generous helping into his little white plastic cup. He took a gulp and almost instantaneously he spat it out spraying everyone with the contents, "FOR FECKS SAKE!" he shouted, "THAT'S WATER."

A quick look around the room identified two guilty looking detectives who had been on duty the previous two nights.

Nowadays, police officers don't get together for a drink so much. When I first started it was almost a duty; everyone joined in. There was a local 'police' pub for every area. Often it is the nearest pub to the nick, handiness being more important than ambience. Those working Monday to Friday, nine to five often made it a daily routine. Those working shifts made it a weekly visit, after their last shift. Even after the night shift.

Not everyone in the police was a drinker, but there was a definite drinking culture. I remember being open-mouthed in surprise at Herbert's admission he couldn't remember the last day he didn't have a drink. That was alien to my upbringing - my parents being teetotal. Herbert took my astonished surprise as an invitation to relate another outrageous drinking story. He had woken up in the middle of the night and made his way to the toilet in desperate need of relief from his bulging bladder. Upon finishing, he went into the kitchen and, by sheer force of habit, opened the fridge, took out a can of beer and popped it open. It was only five o'clock in the morning.

"What did you do when you realised you had to start work in less than two hours?" I asked innocently.

Herbert's puzzled stare indicated that I had asked a rather stupid question. "I drank it of course."

In those days most all the cops worked and lived in the same town, or close to it. They could easily go for a drink and then stagger home. Today, cops rarely live and work in the same town. Cops have to travel from all over to get to work. For the early part of my service I was a twenty-minute walk from the office, a ten-minute cycle or five minutes in the car - so I took the car. It wasn't unusual to have to leave it and walk home though.

When I joined the CID, as an aide, it was a different matter. One pub near our headquarters was known as the 'CID' pub. Every night of the week, and especially on Fridays, the CID would finish up their working day and head to this pub. Sometimes the drink would take over and a couple of hours would extend right through to closing time. Fridays were always a heavy session, commencing with a carry-out in the office, then a night in the pub. The drinking finishing when the barman threw us out at closing time. Occasionally, the session continued when DI Jagielka invited us back to his house, there we were fed drink by our host and food by his long-suffering wife.

The local 'CID' pub was quite an education. It was rough and ready. Ironically, classed as a 'working man's pub,' other than the CID, most of the patrons were unemployed. They sat there all day nursing a 'half and a hauf' (half a pint of lager and a nip of whisky).

Dotted around were the police:

The entire Special Branch Department (all two of them) stood feeding the bandit all night, only ever dragging themselves away to replenish their glasses and empty their bladders. The Drugs Unit secreted themselves at a table at the back of the pub sharing their secrets and pitchers of beer in relative privacy. The rest of the CID propped up the bar where the recently promoted Detective Chief Inspector held court. He had moved to the Complaints and Discipline Department. The more he drank, the more we heard about the stupid things that cops had got themselves into bother for, who had done what and how to avoid getting into trouble ourselves.

As his tongue loosened, I glanced down and saw he was standing on a briefcase. I assumed it might have been a height thing so he could hold court more easily by standing on the heavy black briefcase.

"Why is he standing on his briefcase?" I asked my detective sergeant.

"Oh, that's just his way of ensuring he doesn't forget it again. He had a habit of leaving it behind after a few drinks."

"What does he keep in it?"

"All his complaints and discipline cases!"

As much as I loved their banter and stories of old, I often left early to avoid getting into the habit. More often than not, a good idea.

CHAPTER 15

JUST TO SET THE RECORD STRAIGHT

I settled into my new role and learned a great deal. I seemed to get on well with my colleagues and was in awe of my experienced and exceptionally competent boss, Detective Sergeant Billy Black. DS Black and I worked closely together; he was great fun and no matter how challenging our work he breezed through it, making it look easy. His knowledge rubbed off on me, and I was soon taking on more serious cases. After a few months, I had solved a robbery, made headway in a five-year-old fraud case and learned how to drink five pints of lager on an empty stomach. Yes, it was all going well, right up until the mishap!

Before the police hiring 'Scene of Crime Officers,' the job of dusting for fingerprints was the remit of the CID. Most mornings our first jobs were to do Scene of Crime examinations. The duty detective sergeant would divide these out to the junior detectives.

To dust for fingerprints, we used a fine powder made from aluminium. The powder sticks to the greasy residue left on the object where touched. Every finger has tiny ridges, and the greasy residue forms a pattern in the shape of these ridges. Each pattern is unique to an individual human. Thus if we find a fingerprint at the scene of a crime, it can be matched to the owner. The powder is sparingly applied using a fine-haired purpose made brush. We lightly dust the places that the house-breaker has most likely touched. The best chances of getting a print are smooth objects, such as glass and plastic. We start at the point of entry, where they broke in, and dust everything that may have been touched by the crook.

The fingerprint powder got everywhere, no matter how careful I was. The powder would find its way onto my suit, my shoes, my fingernails, my hair even and it was a devil to get off. Often I felt sorry for householders who would find that their biggest inconvenience was cleaning the aluminium powder off everything after we had completed our scene of crime examination (no easy task).

I recall turning up at one house and seeing the telltale signs of silver coloured fingerprint powder all around the entire window frame at the point of entry. I presumed that someone had already been to do the scene of crime. The householder informed me it was still there from the last time he had had a break-in, over a year previous.

One cold Sunday morning I got the job of doing a scene of crime in a rather posh house near to our headquarters. The culprit had pulled open an insecure front window, climbed in and rummaged through the sitting room. Clearly, the owners were not short of a bob or two going by the expensive plush carpet and ornate art treasures that adorned the room. The crook had gathered up all he could carry and left via the same window he had entered. I set to work, took the cap off the fingerprint powder and dipped my brush. Almost immediately the plastic container of powder started to slip through my hand. The excess of fingerprint powder covering the container made it slippery. I couldn't do anything about it. I lost purchase, and it headed towards the floor. As the plastic container fell towards the Axminster carpet, I froze, unable to do anything to prevent it.

Then I couldn't believe my luck. The tub of fingerprint powder landed the right way up. The luxurious carpet cushioned the tub, and it stayed standing. Saved - but only for a split second.

The sudden impact caused the aluminium powder to explode from its container in one big mushroom cloud. It floated up to the ceiling, puffing ever further out then spread out covering every possible item in the room, settling into the smallest crevice. It left the room looking like a 'Cyberman' and the room looked like an accident in a 1970's disco. My apologies to the householder were not enough to prevent my force having to dip into its pockets for a new carpet and a rather hefty cleaning bill. To add insult to injury, we never caught that housebreaker.

Back at the office, late on a Friday afternoon, Detective Sergeant Billy Black, introduced me to two suave detectives from Liverpool. They had made the journey north to interview one of our locals who they suspected had been naughty in their area. I was asked to accompany them, assist in the arrest and facilitate the detectives in their interview of our naughty local.

Happy to help, I shook their hands and offered them a cup of coffee before getting on with the job. It was during this short break I formed the opinion that the two Liverpudlian detectives were full of themselves. They were not impressed with our headquarters and they treated me like I was a country bumpkin. Their designer suits and patent leather shoes looked out of place, in the heart of working-class Scotland. While they were not quite in the same fashion league as Don Johnson and Philip Michael Thomas from 'Miami Vice' their shiny suits and greased back hair made them stand out just as much. Their accents were the killer for them though. They might just have got away with their contemporary dress if their accents hadn't made them stand out so much. The strong Liverpudlian accent made us all wince. They were as conspicuous as two turds floating in a swimming pool.

I raised an eyebrow as to their ability to garner any information from any self-respecting Scottish ned, not with accents like theirs. Over coffee, I gathered that all they wanted to do was get their business out of the road as quickly as possible. Their underlying purpose, as they were staying overnight, was to go out on the town for an evening, have a few cocktails and meet some lovely Scottish lassies.

I took them to the address of their ned, helped arrest him and brought him back to the station. As soon as the custody sergeant processed him, I showed them all to an interview room. Their interview of our naughty local took all of five minutes. In that short time, their haughty manner and cringing accents alienated our ned so much that he sat arms folded refusing to speak. They released him without charge.

Unperturbed by their failure and happy to be done with their case, the two suave detectives formulated a plan for their evening's entertainment and overnight stay. Their plan involved drinking and chatting up our local lassies. Their confidence in their own prowess and their eagerness to get going was downright nauseating.

My boss, DS Billy Black, was a tough and capable detective, one of the 'old school'. Years of service in the CID had hardened him to regular and copious consumption of alcohol. He took the Liverpudlians out on the town and show them round a few of our bars. It was a matter of hospitality; we normally take such visitors for a good night out in the hope that we would get the same treatment should we venture into their area. I was working until midnight and was a little miffed. I wasn't impressed with their attitude and said so to my boss. DS Black just winked at me and said he might call me later for a lift home.

Some two hours later DS Billy Black rang me at the office and asked me to meet him on a side street down the town. I jumped in a car and headed down to pick him up, thinking he had had his fill of our Liverpudlian colleagues.

When I drove into the side street, my jaw dropped. The two, now not so suave, Liverpudlian detectives were sprawled on a bench, looking dishevelled and drunk as a Russian miner. My boss sat in the middle of the two with his arms around them making sure neither fell over. He grinned and winked, "You better drop these two at their digs," he said and headed back to the pub.

There is a lesson here for everyone. It is fun to come to Scotland and drink with the locals. The only proviso I would put on that is; if that local is a detective sergeant then you should not try to keep up with them drink for drink.

There were other real characters in the CID; my boss

wasn't the only detective sergeant with immense capabilities and an abundance of wit.

During some foundation work on a building, a digger was working away when it uncovered a shallow grave. The grave revealed several bones and a skull that was clearly human. The likelihood was that this was an old grave from an ancient burial site but, like everything the police do, we like to make sure. After all, it could be a murder.

They called for the CID, and I headed down to the scene. After some discussion, we decided that we should call out a pathologist for some expert opinion. In due course, the pathologist arrived with Frank Johnstone, an old school, rough-and-ready detective sergeant. The pathologist examined what had been dug up and confirmed the bones and skull were most definitely of human origin. He stated that he would need to remove it all to the lab where he would, "sex it and age it."

Before decomposition, there are clear differences between the male and female form. Here, the body had decomposed, and the bones were the only clues to determine which sex. The accuracy of such a determination will depend on the age of the person; there is little to differentiate the skeleton of a male or female child. It is not until adolescence that the real divergence takes place. You can make a guess by looking at the bone size, for the most part, male bones are larger than female bones, but this is not always exact. The pelvis area is where the most indicative signs are. The area around the pelvic inlet is larger in females than it is in males and a female will have a larger sub-pubic angle to that of a man, indicative of childbearing requirements.

Thus a pathologist would make careful measurement, to avoid any mistake.

"You don't need to take it to the lab to sex it," declared Frank, "it's a woman."

"How do you know?" enquired the pathologist with genuine interest. Here he was, an expert in his field, and he felt he needed to take the remains to his lab and carry out tests to be sure of the gender that bones had been in life. Yet, this gruff detective sergeant seemed confident in his diagnosis.

Frank pointed at the skull and declared, "It is obviously a woman.

The pathologist bent down and carefully inspected the skull again. Puzzled he stood up and looked at Frank. In all his years as a pathologist, he still couldn't come to such a verdict without further stringent tests.

"But how do you know?" he asked.

Frank just shrugged and said, "... because her mouth is open."

(In no way do I condone this sexist stereotyping from anyone or excuse old detective sergeants from it. I just thought it was funny in the circumstances.)

One of my favourite times in the police was at the end of the day, work all done, when we would sit about and discuss our cases. Often old war stories would come out, and I always listened with intense interest at the experiences of my colleagues, particularly of the times, long before I joined the job when they seemed to get away with all sorts of misbehaviour.

Things were different in the police in the old days before I joined. This story about the kind of things they got away with in those days. The characters are known to me, and it made it all the more real and a little less unbelievable.

Detective Sergeant Dowie arrived back at the office with information that The Red Lion pub would get broken into that night. The information was hot, and his informant was allegedly trustworthy. Detective Inspector Jagielka, who was keen to catch the bandits in the act, convened a meeting and together they came up with a plan of action.

DS Dowie, having been the recipient of the information, alerted the publican that his premises might be a target. He got his agreement to conceal himself and three other detectives within the pub so they catch the thieves in the act.

DI Jagielka didn't want to leave anything to chance, so he arranged to borrow two unmarked cars from the drug squad and use them for covert surveillance outside the pub. They would park up at either end of the street and alert DS Dowie inside if they saw anyone coming.

At midnight DS Dowie secreted himself and his three detectives inside. The publican locked up and made his way home. The detectives familiarised themselves with the layout inside. As they heard the doors bolted from the outside DS Dowie waited inside the door for a few seconds to ensure the footsteps of the publican had disappeared down the street... then he declared the bar open!

He made his way behind the bar poured four pints and served up several chasers, from the gantry. After two stiff ones he then switched on the jukebox and set the party into full swing. His thought process appeared to be that as two unmarked cars plotted up at either end of the street, they would alert them to any movements via radio. When the alert came, they would switch everything off and wait. If the break-in didn't happen, well they would have missed an opportunity to have a good time.

In the meantime DI Jagielka sat in his car at the end of the street, with his driver, watching and waiting. He was excited to be out on the job again for the first time in several years. Often perceived as a tough man, DI Jagielka stood no nonsense. The harsh facade he put on could be quite intimidating. In fact, there was no-one more supportive of his staff. He had worked hard to get to where he was and was an immensely capable detective. Underneath the tough exterior was a man with a keen sense of justice. He hated it when criminals acted despicably and detested when they got away with their crimes. He drove his team to do as professional a job as possible. His promotion to detective inspector took him away from the front line more than he liked. So he was more than happy to get out of the office, away from all the paperwork, even if it was just waiting in a car for something to happen. Scanning the streets around, he waited some more.

About two in the morning, just as he was getting a little bored, everything changed. The monotony instantly disappeared, adrenaline pulsed through his veins and his heart raced. The reason for this change in his physiology - he had spotted something. Two likely lads were coming down the street, dressed in black, carrying a sack and looking decidedly shifty. They would walk right past his car. DI Jagielka leant forward to turn off the car radio and ensure that they didn't notice him. In his haste, instead of switching off the radio he switched on the vehicle siren. Panicking he tried to switch it off. However, being unfamiliar with the layout of the car and the emergency response buttons he then activated the vehicle's blue lights. In the unmarked car the blue lights are hidden in the front grille, they flashed brightly on alternate sides. The hidden red lights in the rear also activated. So much for their covert operation!

By the time DI Jagielka's driver switched the lights and siren off, the two males dressed in black had disappeared. They radioed to DS Dowie and informed him they had blown their cover. DS Dowie suggested they go home and that he would wait with his colleagues until the publican returned in the morning to let them out.

The fellow relating the story to me suggested that they drank so much it might have been cheaper for the publican if he had been robbed.

There may be some old cynics who will tell you that 'it isn't the same as the old days.' They make disparaging remarks like 'the recruits these days can't speak to folk,' or 'they don't know how to do the job anymore.' However, there is a lot of things that happened in the good old days that simply would not happen now. There will be many a serving officer today who carries out their role in a professional and dedicated manner who would shake their head at us old retired cops.

The CID was a fantastic place to learn the job. It was also a place rich with characters. Intelligent men and women who worked hard and had boundless energy and determination. There were occasions when serious situations arose, murders or robberies or rapes. On those occasions all other work went by the wayside, plans were cancelled and nonsense instantly replaced with serious intent. A well oiled, hard working evidence gathering machine emerged in its place that doggedly persisted until the crime was solved.

One such serious incident was a 'tie up' robbery in one of our remote villages. Two attackers, armed with sawn-off shotguns, barged their way into an elderly couple's large house, tied them to chairs and blindfolded them. Threatened, robbed of all their valuables and then left frightened and sore. The elderly couple suffered through that ordeal, and there would be little to comfort them from the memory of it for the rest of their lives. It was a despicable crime and one that warranted our best efforts to detect.

The crime, understandably, garnered a great deal of media interest. With such an appalling crime, the press wanted to know as much as they could. The press were desperate for a police spokesperson to give them information that was true. What is not true was that the TV cameras did not come to Police Headquarters. It was also not true that they waited outside headquarters on the detective superintendent. Detective Superintendent McGonagle was not preparing a briefing and was not putting together a press release and appeal for witnesses. What is also not true was that a young aide to the CID (me) emerged from the office and stood in front of the cameras before Detective Superintendent McGonagle could get there. The entire CID did not look out the top floor window aghast as the young aide gave the TV cameras an interview.

That was just how the mischievous Detective

Malky McEwan

Sergeant Billy Black ended up embellishing the story.

Yes. Okay. I appeared on TV that night, and I said it was a wicked crime and I appealed for witnesses. That bit is true. But I was out at the locus in a remote village at the time; there were no senior officers there. The TV journalist said they were heading back to their studio so if I didn't give the interview we would not have the opportunity to make an appeal. I was just acting in good faith if I hadn't given the interview then and there, no-one would. There would have been no police representative (superintendent or otherwise) making an appeal for witnesses and information.

My boss, Detective Sergeant Black, often told his version (the former) of that story and always gave me a big wink after telling it.

CHAPTER 16

TRAIN FARE

So here is my way of getting him back. The following is the story of DS Black's trip to pick up a prisoner wanted on a warrant.

Occasionally, a wanted person would turn up drunk in Blackpool or Manchester or London, get themselves into bother, and the police there would put his name into the Police National Computer and find out he was wanted on warrant back in our area. In the days before private security firms got the contracts to transport prisoners from custody to court that job was the remit of the police.

Depending on where they were and what the risk assessment was, we'd send either one or two officers to collect them.

There were occasions I travelled by car to pick up prisoners at other stations. If our journey lasted only an hour or two, they would offer a coffee before we got back on the road. If it was any longer, we might get a bacon roll or even a full lunch. However, I had never had to travel so far that required an overnight stay.

On one occasion, I was in the middle of writing a complicated fraud report when Detective Sergeant Billy Black interrupted. I had been working on writing my fraud case all day as it was due first thing the next morning. It was a complex case and required going into great detail, which makes it hard to keep it simple to read. It had to be easy to read otherwise a procurator fiscal might just throw out the case from the start. I would be there until midnight, at least. Not only that, I had several other cases and full statements to write up. Even if left undisturbed it would take me two weeks to complete them all. I had to get my head down and get them done.

DS Black broke my train of thought, "Malky, how do you fancy a trip to London?"

"What for?"

"There is a prisoner escort duty. We need a plain clothes detective to travel down and pick him up."

I didn't have the time. What with the fraud case and all the other urgent paperwork. I needed to sit at my desk and get on with it and hope that nothing else serious happened. I couldn't afford the time away on an escort. Paperwork is important, you need to get it right, but most of all you need to get it done. Nobody will do it for you. Deadlines must be met, or questions are asked. We are accountable for any delays, and it was impossible for me to fit anything else in.

So I said, "Yes, okay, "... well it is tough saying no.

I had never been to London before. Here was my chance to see the sights of the big city. I had been nowhere so far afield. I imagined myself wandering through Piccadilly Circus and Pall Mall. Dipping my fingers in the fountains at Trafalgar Square, eating in China Town, taking in a show and spending a pleasant few hours in a London pub drinking Samuel Smith's Organic Lager before getting a little rest in some hotel, all paid for from the police budget.

As it turned out, I got on an aeroplane flew to London, found myself ushered off the plane into a police office at the City of London Airport, then handed my prisoner. Minutes later they showed me back onto the same plane I got off. No night on the town for me.

Detective Sergeant Billy Black had a little more adventure on his escort:

Kent Police traced a man we wanted on warrant. Because of the serious nature of the charge, two cops had to go. As the journey would take so long the trip required an 'overnighter.' The wily old Detective Sergeant Black didn't like to miss out on such an opportunity, so he decided to go himself and picked Tam to go with him. Tam was a detective constable, a good friend, and drinking buddy. Billy and Tam sorted out a travel warrant, booked bed-and-breakfast, arranged their expenses and before anyone realised what they were up to, they were on the train heading south, accompanied only by their small overnight bags and large carry-out of various alcoholic beverages.

The arrangements were that they would travel down to Kent, stay overnight in their bed-and-breakfast accommodation and pick up their prisoner first thing in the morning. By the time that Billy and Tam had arrived in Kent, they had consumed the large carry-out.

Kent Police met Billy and Tam at the train station and turned out to be obliging hosts. Despite our two detectives already being well oiled, their Kent colleagues took them out on the town, where they showed them the sights and fed them more drink. The Kent CID seemed intent on ensuring their Scottish colleagues enjoyed themselves, and the tour included some of the best pubs and clubs in the town.

It was about 5 a.m. before the obliging Kent hosts poured Billy and Tam out of the blue-light taxi onto the pavement outside their bed-and-breakfast accommodation.

By arrangement, at 6 a.m., two sober uniformed Kent police officers chapped the door of the B&B and took our now worse for wear detectives to the police station. With their bellies empty of any breakfast, furry tongues and fuzzy heads Kent Police handed them wanted man and deposited them back at the train station. Billy and Tam boarded the early train back to Scotland, with their prisoner.

Billy and Tam sat on the train with their untouched overnight bags, a handcuffed prisoner and two serious hangovers to nurse. Recognising the need for sustenance, having missed any opportunity for breakfast at their digs, Billy suggested to the prisoner that he use some of his ill-gotten gains to purchase breakfast in the buffet car. He reasoned that he would not need his money where he was going. The prisoner readily agreed and trotted off up the carriage to the buffet car. A few minutes later he returned to the table carrying three cans of beer. Not quite the breakfast Billy had in mind. While they required thick black coffee, as opposed to any more alcohol, Billy and Tam were not inclined to turn down any form of freebie. Thus they proceeded to down more beer, courtesy of their prisoner.

The prisoner saw it as his opportunity to get drunk one last time before going to prison, so he continued to buy more beer and share it with his escorts for the rest of the morning. All three got well-oiled and reminisced about the old days, albeit the prisoner's memories were perhaps not recalled as fondly as his drinking buddies.

Come two o'clock in the afternoon; the buffet car had taken a buffeting. The copious amounts of alcohol and lack of sleep had also taken their toll. Billy lay spread across two seats, head pressed against the window sound asleep. Tam slumped in his chair, arms folded and snoring loudly. The train was at a standstill.

The comforting and soporific rhythmic clickety-clack helped induce their sleep. Stopped at some unknown station in the North of England, the reassuring clickety-clack had ceased. Tam's snoring roused Billy from his slumber, slowly Billy rubbed his eyes and came back to the land of the living. Tam also woke, with a start, and took a few seconds to realise where he was. Billy and Tam put their hands on their overnight bags, relieved that they remained untouched. Then with a sudden panic, they both realised their prisoner was no longer attached to the handcuffs which lay discarded on their table.

Billy and Tam looked at each other and groaned in unison. The thought of returning to Scotland without their prisoner was about as appealing as colorectal surgery.

Before they could gather themselves and raise any form of alert, their agonised expressions turned to puzzlement as they looked out of the train window. There, on the platform, was their prisoner. He was walking back towards the train smiling at them. His hands were full of bags displaying the McDonald's logo. Their obliging prisoner had left the train, purchased food and returned to the train of his own accord. He spread his purchased fare over the table. I can, even now, picture the relief on their faces.

The only reason I know this story is that one night I was working with Billy and in a quiet moment, looking to make conversation I asked him, "what was the best meal you ever had?" You might guess it was a 'MacDonald's, quarter pounder and chips.'

Billy was one person I most admired. He was an incredibly experienced detective and a thoroughly great bloke. He never told me to do anything, instead he always asked 'would you mind...'. His polite style of management was such that I jumped to assist. He had an air of confidence, was highly respected and was proficient at his job.

There are many books on management and leadership. You can walk into a large bookstore and see shelves upon shelves of books on the subject. Much of those that have their merits. There will be those that might apply to some people, but not all. I might disagree with some theories and those writers might disagree with me. However, my experience told me that Billy had a perfect balance. He had a lot of great qualities, and he applied them depending on the situation.

So what were these qualities? Well foremost, DS Billy Black could talk to anyone. He gained respect because he treated people like people. He listened, understood and appreciated. At the back of that was his competence. He didn't know everything of course, but it felt like he did and he had an instinct about the way to deal with things.

On one occasion I was working on a Saturday afternoon when the front office phoned up to the CID looking for a bit of advice. I answered the phone. They had a man in at the counter who wanted to confess to stealing a television.

"Who is he?" I asked.

"He won't say."

"What?"

"He is refusing to tell us his name."

"Where has he stolen the telly from?" I probed further.

"He won't say," said the office clerk, "he just told me he felt guilty about stealing a television but is afraid to give us any details."

I smelled a detection, dropped what I was doing and went to get him. I escorted him up to our interview room. He was a middle-aged man. A perfectly ordinary individual with no distinguishing features: average height, weight and just showing the first signs of greying.

I interviewed him for the next hour and a half. He was clearly remorseful. He felt guilty about depriving the owner of the television he had stolen. But that was as much as he would tell me. He said he had not been involved in criminality before, and he sat there shaking, frightened about what would happen to him if he came clean. Feeling sorry for himself, and penitent but too worried about the consequences to tell me who he was or from where he had stolen the television.

In an hour and a half, I didn't even get him to tell me his name, or where he stayed. I tried building rapport; I tried forgiveness, I threw in the threat that he was attempting to pervert the course of justice and wasting police time. All I got was an anguished reply but no answers. I researched recent crimes, but there was no stolen telly. Left with nothing to go on I sought advice.

I left him in the interview room and went to speak to my boss. DS Billy Black listened carefully to my story of the man with the guilt complex and nodded. "I'll speak to him," he informed me.

Billy entered the interview room and didn't even bother to sit down. He looked my man up and down and asked, "What's your name?"

"I don't want to say," he replied worriedly.

"Where did you steal the telly from?" my boss asked him, getting straight to the point.

"I don't want to say," he repeated.

At that, my boss grabbed him by the collar pulled him to his feet and marched him out of the room. He is a big man and easily manhandled my ordinary looking interviewee along the corridor, down the stairs and out to the front door where he physically threw him out of the office. "Come back when you want to say!" he shouted after him.

I must have looked downtrodden. "Don't worry," Bill said "he'll be back. In the meantime, we are too busy to be dealing with that time-waster."

Sure enough, about two weeks later I came into the office to find that my anguished man with the guilt complex had returned and been interviewed by another detective constable. This time, he had admitted to the theft of a telly from a local hotel. The hotel had been unaware it had been stolen so hadn't reported it. The Detective Constable had got the easiest confession of his career. He became a Detective Superintendent (I sometimes wonder if that could have been me).

CHAPTER 17

THE MICROWAVE COOKBOOK

The senior detectives had concerns. There had been a round of promotions across the force and no-one from the CID was on the list. There were a lot of hardworking dedicated and capable officers within the CID. Why were none of them being considered? What could they do about it?

From my perspective, the CID was keen to draft in the best cops to their ranks. The CID dealt with the more serious crimes; detectives had to be diligent, thorough, patient, and dedicated. So they recruited those from uniform who stood out by demonstrating those qualities.

(I should point out that there are plenty of just as intelligent, hardworking and dedicated officers in all others roles within the police and not everyone wants to join the CID. There are many other members of the police in front line roles and other departments with equally valuable skills, abilities, and qualities - although some would say that doesn't include the Traffic Department).

When an officer is plucked from his front-line duties, where he or she is doing well, and take their place in the CID, they go from being one of the more senior and experienced officers in their group to one of the most junior. Sent from the top of the pecking order to the bottom. Where they might have had a chance at promotion in uniform in a year or two, they join the CID and are expected to remain a detective constable for much longer.

The senior officers in the CID wanted to redress this balance. While they didn't want to lose their best people they wanted to see more opportunities available for their detectives.

They came to a decision. The CID bosses decided they would solve this problem by moving all those detectives who didn't have promotion exams back to uniform. My understanding was: they thought if they only had detectives who were pre-qualified by having their promotion exams under their belt, then they would likely have more promotions from within their department. Thus the senior officers in the CID came downstairs from their meeting and announced that I was one of four detectives, who didn't have their promotion exams, and we would be sent back to uniform.

At the time I was gutted to leave the CID. I was enjoying the work, and it was great working with my colleagues and supervisors. I went back to uniform, but it didn't take me long to realise that there was more to life than being in the CID, that it could be more fun and it worked out well for me in the end.

My bosses were accommodating and allowed me to choose whatever station I wanted. I opted for a small office in a small town. The office comprised a room and a toilet. There were only five cops stationed there, no sergeants. The cops seemed to get moved there and just stay forever. I was to remain at the station for seven years, but others stayed for much longer.

The guys at the station were absolutely the best people you could hope to meet. Each different in their way but I think we complemented each other which made the station work. We were proud of our wee station, and we consistently delivered a higher than 70% detection rate. That was a pretty incredible figure when you consider that the average in Scotland was 40% and in England, it was less than 20% in most places.

Ironically, the four of us who were moved out of the CID later passed our promotion exams, and all of us ended up promoted to at least the rank of an inspector (one made it to superintendent). We found ourselves promoted quicker than if we had remained in the CID.

Back in uniform, at my newest station, I settled into the team. I knew them all from before and, as I say, they were a great bunch of guys. We had a crossover on weekend nights with one working 6 p.m. to 2 a.m. and the other 8 p.m. to 4 a.m. If one of us were on holiday, the officer on weekend off would come back out and work 10 p.m. to 2 a.m. Although they paid us overtime for these four hours, this could be our only weekend off in the month, and thus we could often work the full summer months without getting a single Saturday or Sunday as a rest day.

The office itself comprised two rooms, a report room and a locker room come kitchen (although a plug-in kettle and microwave were all that would point towards it to being called a kitchen). It was a busy wee station, and we often worked on our own during the weeknights. We had an official log to complete at the end of every shift but, as we had nobody taking over from us, we also used to leave an unofficial log as to what happened during our shift. It meant our colleagues could start in the morning and quickly read about all that had happened the night before.

Our unofficial log was an A4 lined book, and we would detail in it what we had dealt with and any issues that required their attention. In the back of the book, we kept a running log of minor undetected crimes (small value vandalisms and the like) reported 'for information only.' Because it was quite an insular place most of our crimes were committed by a small minority of those that lived in the town. We built up a good local knowledge and interaction with the town residents. We kept the book hidden away in the micro-wave – hence 'The Microwave Cookbook.'

You can't cook the books these days (well not unless you are the Chief Constable).

Occasionally, I would come in and read a note in 'The Microwave Cookbook' that was particularly revealing. The following is just a selection:

19th July

1) See nightshift log - HELP!! - I FORESEE A MURDER!

2) Another puncture on our car. (Barbeque Bill)

21st July

Strip light fixed and cleaned (Do I get money?) - (Alec)

22nd July

Excellent job on the strip light. YOU'LL GET A CAN OUT OF THE CASE LIKE AWBODY ELSE!! (Barbeque Bill)

PS. I wish whoever uses the toilet would dispose of 'SKID MARKS' left by Exocet missiles being fired.

23rd July

Morning Malk

1st slag of the day - fatty!!

re the attempted suicide - Adam Hunter had taken a (blunt) razor blade to his body suffering from multiple lacerations, all superficial...(Deek)

25th July

Busy yet again. I want to transfer to East Beirut!!... (Barbeque Bill)

29th July

Last night a young lad came into the office asking about a football tournament that I am running? He told me the fat-cheeked polisman said I was organising it - any idea?... (Duggie)

30th July

Re football tournament - I haven't a clue what you are on about...(Malky)

30th July

Re football tournament. I have had 3 different laddies ask about it. I keep telling them to see PC Duggie about it. I haven't a firkin clue what it's about either!

PS Any knowledge of the correspondence book No. 152/573 - BLANK ENTRY? (Barbeque Bill)

31st July

Who keeps telling the kids I am running a football tourna-

ment? (Duggie)

1st August

Watchman reports finding ladies undergarments, skirt, and blouse on the 2nd hole at the golf course. Area searched and door to door negative. It would appear that someone has been playing a round. (Malky)

2nd August

Does anyone read my notes??? Any knowledge of the correspondence book No. 152/573 - BLANK ENTRY? (Barbeque Bill)

3rd August

Duggie - are you organising a football tournament? I've left details in your drawer of two laddies who are interested... (Deek)

4th August

I am not running a football tournament. Stop telling the kids I am. They have been at the office all day pestering me about it. (Duggie)

5th August

Seriously! Does no-one read my notes??? Any knowledge of the correspondence book No. 152/573 - BLANK ENTRY? (Barbeque Bill)

6th August

Duggie - I've left details of another two kids interested in the football tournament you are running. (Malky)

7th August

I have had a constant trail of kids at the door all day asking about this football tournament. Can I make it any clearer that I am not running a football tournament? Stop telling the kids I am running one. It is not funny anymore! (Duggie)

8th August

Cancel the correspondence book blank entry - it was me by mistake. (Barbeque Bill)

PS Duggie are you running this football tournament or not?. (Barbeque Bill)

11th August

I am just back from two days off and I have another 18 names interested in a football tournament. I am not running it. That's it! (Duggie)

15th August

Mrs. Harvey had her bamboo plant stolen from her front porch last night - did you see anyone cutting about? (Duggie)

16th August

There was a rotund guy with a white patch on his eye wandering about last night (Deek)

17th August

About 4.30am I was just about to finish, daylight drew nearer and the sun came up. It flashed its rays across the sky igniting every cloud with the most beautiful display of reds, scarlet, then orange. I decided to prolong my knocking off time and drove to a quiet part of the county which afforded uninterrupted views of the dawn breaking and flooding across the rapeseed field in front of me.

Normally a splurge of yellow, the field now glittered with gold and greens and ever-changing hues as the sun rose. The minutes ticked away and as I gazed across the field, I picked up a movement out of the corner of my eye. I wasn't sure if it was just the wind rippling across the rapeseed or even just tiredness playing tricks on my eyes. I settled my gaze on this movement. Sure enough, something was making its way through the field of rape.

As the light brightened all around, I was able to identify what it was. A hat. A little top hat. At first, I thought it was black, and then, as the light improved, I saw it was most definitely green.

Curious as a cat, I alighted from the panda car and stealthily made my way to intercept this little green top hat. I sat in wait as it edged towards me at the end of the field of rape. An astounding sight rewarded my curiosity and patience. Out plopped a leprechaun. He was no bigger than a Labrador and resplendent in Irish green garb.

"Oh bugger!" said the leprechaun, at once surprised and annoyed at being seen.

"What on earth!" I exclaimed even more surprised.

"Damn" said the leprechaun; "now that you have seen me, I must grant you a wish."

"What?"

"I need to grant you a wish"... said the leprechaun... "every time a human sees me I need to grant their wish".

"What?"

"Oh begorrah! Don't you know? Us leprechauns sleep for fifty years, then we get up for one night and walk as far as we can until dawn, then we go back to sleep for another fifty years. If I'm seen, then I have to grant that person a wish."

"You mean I can wish for anything."

"Anything at all."

I grabbed the moment with the first thing that came into my head - I pulled out my map of the UK and said, "See that whole area? I think I could do a better job than the people that are running it just now, so... I want to rule all of that."

"My goodness me" said the leprechaun; "I don't know about that, that's a rather tall order. I don't know if I could pull that off."

I thought about. I might have been a little hasty in making my wish. "Okay, okay, maybe that is not what I want. I couldn't be bothered with ruling it all. It might be more hassle than it's worth. I am actually quite happy with my lot. Perhaps you could do just one small thing for me?"

"Yes, whatever it is."

"Could you get Duggie to run a football tournament for the kids in the town?"

"Begorrah - you better give me that map back!" (Malky)

18th August

Duggie - The Chief Inspector heard you were running a football tournament this summer. He thinks it is a good idea and wants you to speak to him. (Alec)

19th August

Anyone with any names of kids that want to get involved in a football tournament, can you pass them to me. It is organised for a week on Saturday. (Duggie)

CHAPTER 18

PHONE US BACK THE 'MORRA'

Today we have one Police Service to cover the whole of Scotland, the eight forces having amalgamated in April 2013.

Before the amalgamation, if we required an enquiry completed in another part of the country, which was not in our force area, we had to make a request to the Police Service that covered that area to do it for us. We often had enquiries in other areas. I would phone the service centre of the force I required and ask to get put through to the office that would handle my enquiry. Whether I got my enquiry completed depended on the person on the other end of the phone.

Invariably, in my experience, when I phoned one particular force, the person on the other end of the phone would come up with some excuse why they couldn't help. "Aye we are dealing with three assassinations, five robberies, and an abduction, phone us back the 'morra.'"

I would end up having to send a fax (this was the time before we had emails), which would go missing and there would be countless phone calls to establish who was dealing with the request. It would take so long I would often end up travelling through to do the enquiry myself.

One day, I arrested a Glaswegian who had been drunk driving. The custody sergeant correctly insisted that I verify my prisoner's address before releasing him from jail. If I didn't confirm his address, I would need to write a custody report. I was already late for an evening out with Mrs McEwan, and she wouldn't be best pleased if we ended up missing the show we booked.

I chanced a phone call and was put through to the office that covered the area where my Glaswegian drunk driver lived. A few rings later a broad Glasgow accent answered, "Aye, whit ur ye wantin?"

I explained my situation, and he replied, "I canny take a note of that just now."

Trying not to show my impatience, and fully expecting him to tell me how busy he was with all the assassinations and other major incidents he was dealing with, I enquired why not?

"I huvnae got a pen," he said.

I was speechless for a few seconds, dumbfounded by his answer. "For goodness sake, you are in a police office; surely you must have a pen!"

"Wait a minute," he said.

I looked at my watch and the second hand ticked off exactly sixty seconds. The cop came back on the phone. "Okay, I found a pen," the Glaswegian on the other end paused before hitting me with his next line, "but I canny find a piece of paper," and before I could say another word, he hung up.

I cursed and swore, ranted and raved, worried about Mrs McEwan's reaction to the news that, once again, she would miss an evening out due to my work. Then I had an idea.

I phoned Strathclyde Police back and asked for

their CID. My call was put through to the relevant CID office, and a young detective constable answered.

"Hello," I said and introduced myself, "this is Detective Chief Inspector McEwan," giving myself three consecutive promotions in the space of two minutes.

"I need you to drop what you are doing, get into your car and check if this guy stays at this address in your area and I need it now."

The young detective may have been a little intimidated by my new found rank but had the backbone to ask, 'why?'

"I can only tell you it is a matter of life and death."

This wasn't entirely untrue because Mrs McEwan would have killed me if I was late again. Within ten minutes he came back to me, address confirmed. I had my answer and was on my way home.

Sometimes you have to use a little cunning to get the job done.

CHAPTER 19

THE NUDE PHOTO

One of my favourite people to work with was Barbeque Bill. Ironically, Barbeque Bill was so nicknamed because he didn't, in fact, have a barbecue. He kept threatening to have a barbecue and get all the boys round for a beer, but it never happened. Every time I see him I always ask, "When will you have that BBQ " He never fails to respond with, "When I get a barbecue," but he never does.

One day Barbeque Bill and I attended the sudden death of an elderly lady, found dead in her bed by the home help. She was eighty years old and by all accounts had had a good life. We attended at the single bedroom bungalow where we met her doctor, who pronounced life extinct. There were no apparent suspicious circumstances, however, due to her keeping good health, her doctor could not certify the cause of death.

In such circumstances, the police take over. We take possession of the body, investigate the circumstances and submit a report to the Procurator Fiscal detailing the facts surrounding the death. The Fiscal invariably instructs that a post-mortem examination is carried out to establish the cause of death. A process designed to ensure the old dear hadn't been murdered.

The procedures require us to strip the body at

the house and examine her for any signs of violence. We do this prior calling an undertaker who will then convey her to the mortuary.

On this occasion stripping the body was like trying to strip the bark off a tree. Our little old dead lady was a slight woman and wearing a camisole top that just wouldn't budge over her skinny bones. I decided that the easiest thing to do would be to cut it off. I asked Barbeque Bill to have a look in the kitchen for a pair of scissors. Bill disappeared from the bedroom and raked around the kitchen while I remained in the bedroom. From the bedroom, I espied a sewing box sitting on the windowsill in the living room.

Barbeque Bill returned and told me he couldn't find any scissors. "Hold on," I said, "I'll ask her where she keeps them."

At this, I turned to our poor wee deceased woman and asked her where she kept her scissors. I then bent down and pretended to listen to her as if she were whispering in my ear.

"She says she keeps them in her sewing box," I told my colleague, wide-eyed and innocent. I then turned back to the old dear and asked her where she kept her sewing box and again bent down so she could whisper the answer in my ear.

"She tells me her sewing box is on the windowsill in the living room."

Barbeque Bill's face showed a wry smile, but as he turned from the bedroom door to look into the living room, his eyes rested on the sewing box sitting proudly right in the middle of the windowsill. He looked back at me, narrow-eyed and slowly made his way to the window. Cautiously he opened the sewing box and sitting right on top of everything was a gleaming pair of scissors. "YA BASTARD! YA BASTARD YOU KILLED HER JUST SO YOU COULD SET THIS UP YA BASTARD!"

I'm still not sure Barbeque Bill has forgiven me for that one. He certainly hasn't invited me for a barbeque yet.

Another of my favourite people to work with was Tom. Tom was a worrier who didn't like to draw attention to himself. So he worked hard and made sure he completed all his responsibilities efficiently so that no-one could criticise him. Tom had a dry sense of humour, and on the occasions he wasn't worrying about something or other, he was very, very funny. Unassuming and self-deprecating, which was a shame because he had all the skills to go far if he put his mind to it. Happy to do anything for you, he would unselfishly give up his time and effort to help out whenever needed.

One evening, before the days of computers, I was sitting in our wee office waiting on Tom finishing typing his report. I was rather impatient and kept cajoling Tom to 'hurry up' so we could get back out on patrol. Tom was conscientiously trying to complete his report as fast as he could on the office typewriter. He tried to concentrate all the harder and type even quicker.

I paced up and down our small office, which wasn't helping him concentrate. Impatience is my big weakness. Distractedly I opened and shut drawers as I went. In the last drawer, I found a large ball of string. Tom continued to type, doing his level best to ignore me. I tied the end of the string over the aerial on his radio, which sat sticking out of the top pocket of his tunic on the right side of his chest. I then unwound the string wrapping it round and round Tom and round the back of his chair. Tom continued to type and ignored me.

I kept wrapping the string round and around. The more I wrapped it around, the tighter Tom's arms wrapped into his body. However, he remained free from the elbows down, and although I was making it difficult for him, he continued to type his report.

Eventually, the ball of string came to the end. I tied the end of it to the aerial on his radio completing the loop. Tom was now firmly secured to the chair but continued to type as best he could with the restriction of his upper arms secured to his body and the chair back.

No sooner had I tied the knot (and I couldn't have timed this any better) we heard a female scream from outside the office, then the sound of someone running away. It sounded exactly like a girl was in real distress. Without a second thought, I jumped up and ran outside.

The office door overlooks a wide pavement and parking bay, which we used for our police car. Instead of a murderous assault, I was confronted with a male and female smiling at each other as he chased her down the street. They were both university students in the early stages of a romantic relationship. They had been at the pub and were now on their way home. The scream turned out to be a playful one in response to their 'chase me, chase me' game.

Satisfied that all was in order, I made my way back into the office remembering, only then, that Tom was a little tied up.

Tom had also heard the scream and was as concerned as I had been. He jumped up to run out and assist. Regrettably, he was still attached to the chair. What I saw, when I returned to the office, was like a beached walrus flapping about in panic. Tom and the chair had toppled over and he lay on the floor still attached to it as he writhed to get free. I couldn't help but see the funny side; I burst out laughing. Tom looked up at me and with a beetroot red face told me to, "Get knotted."

There were occasions when I got all tied up as well, although, not quite as literally as Tom.

We used to get regular calls from Irene. She was a single female in her fifties and an alcoholic. She attracted many ne'er-do-wells to her home who ended up getting drunk with her. It wasn't quite a party; it was just a place for drunkards to drink. If they weren't there, they would drink somewhere else, on their own. I suppose it made their lives a little less sad. The problem was, after copious amounts of alcohol, they would all end up arguing, and Irene would call the police and ask to have them removed. She would call us for the most trivial of matters:

"Can you send someone round? Senga just drank my cider."

"I need the police; Bobby just called me a slag."

"There is a mouse in my wardrobe."

"Jimmy has been in the toilet for forty-five minutes and won't come out. I need a pee."

"A monkey ate my chocolate."

Our attendance was a waste of our time.

Getting called to her house became an exercise in diplomacy. A case of how quickly could we get in and out without offending her. We would assure her we were doing everything we could to resolve her imaginary problem and then get out and on with some real work. It was a minor annoyance as, other than being a neurotic drunkard, Irene was harmless.

Irene was not harmless to herself. She showed the signs of ageing and the effects of prolonged alcohol abuse. It was a surprise to me then, when my colleague, PC Annabel Zapatski, told me that Irene had once been a nude model. He (yes Annabel is a man) had been dealing with Irene's imaginary complaints for a few more years than me. He told me that, in fact, she had been a stunner in her younger days.

She had been a nude model and attracted the attention of many men. In a stroke of good fortune, she met a businessman. He'd started a building company in the sixties. It was just the right time. The Conservatives had returned to power, and there was an emphasis that shifted Government policy towards slum clearance as millions uprooted from overcrowded, rundown inner-city terraces and re-housed in purpose built new towns. He was to piggy-back the money-train ride all the way. Land was cheap, labour was plentiful, and business was abundant. He became seriously rich. Irene was attracted to his money, and he was attracted to the easy removal of her knickers.

The relationship appeared to suit both well and, following a brief and bare courtship, they tied the knot. The downfall for Irene was the long hours her husband worked. He was away to the office before she woke and didn't return until late, sometimes seven days a week. Irene's nude model gigs dried up, not that they were all that plentiful. She amused herself by visiting her local pub of an evening. Her visits became so frequent you could see the outline of her bum on her favourite seat. Her visits started earlier in the day and soon she was having a liquid lunch, a liquid afternoon tea and a liquid dinner. The drink took its hold, and she ended up in a self-destructive downward spiral.

Irene's relationship with her millionaire husband did not last long once she became dependent on alcohol. The drinking problem affected her mental health (and took a toll on her looks). It was rare for her husband to get a sensible conversation from her and even rarer for him to want to remove her knickers. So her millionaire husband decided he had had enough and sought a divorce.

Once separated, Irene received enough maintenance money to continue to slate her daily thirst for vodka, white wine and soda no longer did the job. Her continued drinking caused further deterioration in her mental health. Thus she ended up in a small semi-detached council house in our police area, associating with many ne'er-do-wells and would call the police for the least imagined problem.

After one of my first visits to Irene's small council house, PC Zapatski asked me if I had spotted the nude photo.

My ears perked up, "What nude photo?"

He revealed that there was a nude picture of Irene, in her prime, tucked away at the back of the sideboard in her living room. "Have a look next time you are in," Annabel urged.

So I did. The next time I was there, as I was walking out of the room, I had a squint at the sideboard. Sitting at the back behind some drinks glasses was a small Polaroid picture of what appeared to be a naked young woman posing for the camera. All I had was a glimpse. It was such a small photo that I couldn't be sure it was Irene.

A plan hatched.

The first opportunity to look at the photo close up didn't come for a few weeks. I was with Barbeque Bill, and we had discussed the photo and the possibilities of getting a peek.

The regular call came in, Irene complained that her neighbours were spying on her. We visited Irene, and she persuaded Barbeque Bill to go to her bedroom with her so they could look out the window and see where the male was allegedly spying on her. I remained in the living room. I waited until I heard footsteps in the bedroom above me, I then sneaked across to the sideboard and carefully opened the glass front. I moved the glasses as quietly as I could and extricated the photo. I took it over to the light of the window, and I examined the picture.

The photo was indeed of a young woman, but I had been stitched up. The woman in the picture was neither naked nor that of Irene in her prime. It was just a photo of some woman in a pale coloured dress. I replaced it and returned to my seat. Irene and Barbeque Bill returned downstairs, and we gave her further assurances we would do everything in our power to prevent her imaginary peeping Tom from carrying on his unsavoury ways. And then we left.

Once outside Barbeque Bill couldn't wait to ask. We hadn't even got to the car before badgering me, "Well. Is it Irene? Is she nude?"

I whispered to him, "Aye. It's Irene, and she's gorgeous."

As soon as he could, Barbeque Bill went through the same process with a younger colleague. The younger colleague distracted Irene and Barbeque Bill entered the display cabinet to get a proper look at the photo, only to realise that I'd stitched him up.

Once they left the house, the younger cop was eager to know if the naked photo was Irene. "Yes, it is," he lied. He stitched up his younger colleague. Thus the myth that is 'the nude photo of Irene in her prime' perpetuates and still catches out young cops to this day.

CHAPTER 20

MORE MICROWAVE COOKBOOK

I could get used to most things. I got used to getting up in the middle of the night for early shifts, and I got used to staying awake during night shifts when every fibre of my body was telling me to shut my eyes and go to sleep. I got used to stripping dead bodies and examining them for signs of violence. I got used to being verbally abused, being spat on and even wearing heavy woollen sweat-inducing police issue trousers in the height of summer. Yes, I could get used to most things, but the one thing never got used to was giving evidence in court.

Getting to court is a long slow drawn out process. You need to gather the evidence, take statements, lodge productions and after all that you have to write a report. Your report is read over by your sergeant to ensure that the basics are there and if it passes muster he forwards it to the report checker. The report checker has a more in-depth look. His viewpoint is a little more detached than the sergeant. He has no vested interest in whether it is a good case or bad. He only wants to know if there is a sufficiency of evidence to present it to the Procurator Fiscal. If there is insufficient evidence, he sends it back. When it arrives with the Procurator Fiscal, she makes the final decision whether or not there will be a prosecution.

The Procurator Fiscal has the final say. She reviews the evidence with an even more critical eye. Not only will she assess whether the evidence is sufficient and competent, but she will also consider whether or not it is in the public interest to pursue the case. I'm sure there was formula she used that went something like this:

$$E = mc^2$$

E = energy expended on a case
m = mood
c = cantankerousness

So let's say you investigate a crime. You gather evidence, and at the end of your enquiry, you see that all the evidence points towards a particular person as responsible. You then charge that person with the crime and submit a report. Your sergeant signs the report, happy that there is enough evidence, it satisfies the report checker, and the Procurator Fiscal considers it a good enough case to take the accused to court. The Procurator Fiscal kicks off the process by issuing the accused a 'copy complaint.' The copy complaint details what the charge and seeks a response from the accused. Do you plead 'guilty' or 'not guilty?'

If the accused pleads not guilty, then the Procurator Fiscal will arrange to 'try' the evidence in front of a judge. In most cases, the accused will appoint a lawyer to represent him. The Procurator Fiscal sets a date, all the witnesses and the accused will appear in court on that day. Each witness gives their evidence one at a time. The Procurator Fiscal will lead the witnesses through their evidence as they described in their ori-

ginal statement to the police. Then you, the police officer, are called to the stand. The Procurator Fiscal will
lead you through your proof. What statements you
took, what evidence you gathered and what actions
you took.

Easy enough you might think. Unfortunately,
after the Procurator Fiscal has had his go, it becomes
the turn of the defence lawyer. He gets to cross-exam-
ine you.

I was always nervous about appearing in court.
As soon as I received a citation, I would read over the
case, check my notebook was in order and ensure that
I had all the productions labelled properly. The day beforehand I would refresh my memory again, go through
all the evidence and run through potential questions
I might get asked. Even so, I was still nervous turning
up at the court. I never liked entering that forbidding
building and always had to stop at the gents first before
to making my way to the witness room. I would get
increasingly worried as I waited for hours (sometimes
days) to get called. Despite all my preparation, I was
a jittery wreck by the time I had stood in the witness
box and presented my evidence to the Procurator Fiscal. For I knew the defence lawyer stood waiting to rip
me apart. He'd shred me of all dignity like a revolving
hunk of processed meat hanging in a kebab shop. These
lawyers were smart; they trained to trip me up. Some of
them did it with such aplomb. I mean, how do you answer the question:-

"Tell me, Constable McEwan, is this the first time
you have lied in court?"

"Er um, yes. Er, um I mean, no. Um yes, noooo!"

There is no correct answer to that.

When I escaped the court invariably needed light relief, so I headed back to the office to read the Microwave Cookbook.

8th September

Life being as it is, I have a very important League rugby match on Saturday afternoon, but I am 10 a.m. - 6 p.m., so a wee problem, I don't know what to do about it. I suppose I will have to call off, <u>but</u>, maybe there may be a friend somewhere who might be in a position to come in and work for me (2.30 p.m.). I think I have friends but then again maybe not. Anyway if there is a friend who could do this for me I would be very grateful. (Annabel)

9th September

Annabel - Life being as it is - you are right - you have no friends!!!

- Ok - this will cost you a pint. See you 2.30 p.m.. (Barbeque Bill)

11th September

Well, what a night! First two hours spent watching Brian S. McNutt in a house in Hill Road (we were at the back). He had presented a gun at his girlfriend then shot a hole in his telly. We saw him through his rear window injecting something. Then he came out with the gun and wandered about his garden brandishing it. He tried to escape by climbing over his back fence but then saw us and about turned - which was a bit of a surprise as we were running away as soon as he approached. Kamikaze MacKenzie arrived and just breenged right in and talked him into handing over the gun. (Barbeque Bill)

18th October

Superintendent McHatchett had his sundial stolen from his garden. The sergeant was a bit concerned that we weren't doing anything about it and has marked up the crime report with some tasks. Task No.3 reads 'If found take a note of the time in case it has stopped' - clearly, he is in the dark about how a sundial works. (Tom)

16th November

*As I sit here in the silence of your office, I'm left to think - What a F****N toon this is. Tonight was like the wild west - fighting at the pub - what a fight!!...*

...two hooses broken into on Main Street and their boilers stolen...

...Surprise surprise - 2 shites missing from the children's home, what a novelty...

...Ice cream war kicked off again, brick through van window, full statements required by tonight...

...Davy Lumsden conveyed to hospital for stitching after being glassed by his wife, no complaints made...

...fire at the nursery, malicious by the looks of it...

...car stolen from Orchard Road found crashed and abandoned in Galloway Terrace...

... and a bad day at Black Rock, 5 windows smashed at the office...

...how can you work in this place? (Written by a cop covering the station for one night only)

17th November

For a change - nothing to report, except we need bog roll. (Barbeque Bill)

25th January

Break in at the Windyhill Restaurant, Dominic Dobson, across the road, reported it saying he heard the window smash and saw a drunk Ali Broon running off. Something sounded fishy about his story. Got Ali Broon in and he was sober and alibied. Dobson is so ugly that he has got to be up to something - worth watching... (Malky)

26th January

We saw Dobson wandering about at 3.30am in the morning last week with big gloves on. He is one ugly laddie... (Alec)

27th January

Bale of hay set on fire down by the distillery. Can someone view security video at the distillery to see if anyone passed after 2 a.m.... (Annabel)

28th January

Viewed video, not clear but it looks like one ugly guy. Security says he is down there regularly during the night, don't know his name but he looks like 'Plug' from the beano.. (Tom)

29th January

Interviewed Dominic Dobson, (he is really ugly!) Not admitting to setting the bale of hay on fire. Get the impression he might not be telling us the right story about the break- into the restaurant, but he stuck to his story... (Malky)

30th January

Got information that Dominic Dobson is prowling about during the night. Maybe worth a wee surveillance operation... (Duggie)

2nd March

Kept watch on Dobson's house. No movement between midnight and 3 am... (Malky)

3rd March

Windyhill Restaurant broken into again. Looks like it happened about 3.30 a.m.. A lot of foodstuffs stolen including two whole salmons... (Duggie)

4th March

Security at distillery reported seeing the same ugly guy as before wandering past last night. He had a sack with him. We went down and found a fire in the same place as last time and it looks like he has been trying to barbecue two salmon... (Annabel)

5th March

Bill - are you having a barbecue on the cheap? (Malky)

7th March

Got a search warrant and turned Dominic Dobson's house. Recovered stuff from stolen from Windyhill Restaurant. Dobson interviewed and admitted 18 other break ins over the last 6 months. He is in custody for court tomorrow - he is so ugly at least he won't have to worry when he goes to prison. (Annabel)

8th March

Sorry to phone you so early Annabel, but some DIPSTICK left the car keys in your tunic!!! (Barbeque Bill)

9th March

Locked up Scott Montgomery and Jason McKee for breach of the peace. I was on my own and they gave me dogs abuse but got a couple of locals to provide statements. No more favours for those two. They even called me 'BIG EARS' - I mean how imaginative!!!... (Barbeque Bill)

15th March

Returned the productions in Malky's case to Jemima Sinclair!!! What a <u>honey</u>. What a bod. Spent as long as I could next to her (I'm in love) before asking her ~~out~~ to sign the production labels. Her family eventually threw me out the house but they couldn't get rid of me that easily HAH! Mind you I got soaked standing in the back garden watching her bedroom window.
Anyway, back to work, smashed window at the rear of 1 Derwent Road and he had two tyres punctured on his Range Rover. When I returned to the police car, guess what - both front tyres punctured.
Lots of French students hanging around. They are worse than our lot. They pretend they don't understand English and I am sure they are taking the pish. Maybe I am getting PARANOID. Anyway - what have you been saying about me?
I think I am cracking up. I could fill this book with crap. (Deek)

16th March

C'est la vie! (Malky)

Deek - at the meeting the other night, I met a chap who I think you should have a word with. His name is Mike O'Connor, Senior Psychologist, Health Board. I am sure he would have an interesting time with you. (Duggie)

Saturday Night

AAAAAHHH!!!!

CHAPTER 21

A CLEAN SWEEP

One of my colleagues, Shuggie, ended up getting divorced (not an irregular occurrence in the police). He made it clear he was hunting for the next Mrs Shuggie and there were the occasional embarrassing moments when I had to turn about and leave his side as his patter and chat up lines became more and more desperate if not downright inappropriate.

One night we were called to a country farmhouse by the farmer's wife (a stunning woman, drooled over by every red-blooded male who had ever seen her). She requested our help as she had been to a dance and her husband had got so drunk that, on the drive home, he had collapsed into a drunken stupor in the passenger seat of their Range Rover. She had tried everything but she couldn't wake him.

Shuggie rubbed his hands with glee, he knew her from his schooldays. Not only was he going to see his old school pal (who he was still burning a candle for) but her husband was drunk and incapable of interfering with any advances he might make. "I'll deal with this," Shuggie informed me.

"Yes, okay," I answered as I drove leisurely towards the farm.

"You stay in the car," Shuggie instructed as he

mulled over the situation, planning his tactics for our imminent arrival.

"Yes, okay."

"You're married, I am divorced," he explained.

"Yes, okay."

"If I get invited in, you stay in the car."

"Yes, okay."

"If I am over ten minutes, then you disappear, and I will give you a shout on the radio when you can come back."

"Yes, okay."

"I get on really well with her. I think she is just making an excuse to get me there."

"Yes, okay."

"I'll deal with it. You stay in the car," he reiterated.

"Yes, okay," I said as I drove the car into the farm entrance.

I saw the Range Rover parked outside the farmhouse, and our gorgeous farmer's wife stood at the passenger door. Her husband slumped in the passenger seat comatose. I drove the police car right up to a dry-stone dyke and parked the nearside about an inch away so that Shuggie could not open his door; not even slightly. There was no way he could extricate himself from his side of the vehicle. If he tried to climb out through the driver's side, it would have just been too embarrassing for him. He looked at me and fumed. I smiled, got out and assisted our damsel in distress. I helped manhandle her husband to a couch in their living room before making a dignified exit.

Shuggie didn't speak to me for the rest of the night.

Back at work!

'Annabel, the thief-catcher,' had a remarkable ability. Annabel had a nose for sniffing out when something was wrong. It sometimes bordered on the psychic. I'm not sure how his insights came to him, whether he used reasoned and logical thought processes - like Sherlock Holmes - or just gut instinct.

One night Annabel and I were sitting outside a disco waiting on it spilling. It was about two in the morning. We were there as we had had a lot of complaints from nearby residents regarding the noise from the patrons as the disco emptied. Annabel was in the driving seat; I was in the passenger seat talking to another colleague who standing next to our car on the pavement.

Annabel interrupted our conversation with, "That's our stolen moped!"

I looked up and fifty yards away a moped had emerged from a side street. It turned onto the main road heading away from us out of town. It was a dark night, and from that distance, I could not make out what kind of moped it was, far less a number plate or even any other clue why Annabel thought it was our stolen bike. Annabel started the car and went after it.

The moped had a maximum speed of 50mph, and thus we caught up with it easily. I clocked the number plate and radioed into the Control Room asking them to check it on the Police National Computer (PNC). A minute later, sure enough, the result came back – it was our stolen moped.

Stolen five miles away and five days previous, so it wasn't a crime that was fresh in my mind. How Annabel knew it was our stolen moped, I will never know. I looked at him open-mouthed at his spooky ability.

Annabel put the blue lights on and flashed the moped to stop. It didn't stop, and that was when the fun started. The rider was wearing a helmet, and neither of us could identify him. He looked round, saw the blue lights and hurtled off as fast as the moped would take him. He clearly had no intention of stopping.

Annabel remained a safe distance behind, mindful that it was a hell of a lot more dangerous for the rider if he crashed. I got back on the radio and requested assistance. As it was a 'police pursuit' I had to provide a running commentary to the Control Room.

We followed the moped for about three miles before it entered a town, signposts showed the built-up area had a speed limit of 30mph. The rider paid no attention to the legal limit and continued at his top speed of 50mph, straight through. Fortunately, there wasn't a lot of traffic or pedestrians at that time of the morning.

The moped carried on out of the town heading towards the countryside. We entered the 'Nurburgring' and its series of bends. The rider maintained his speed increasing the danger to himself tenfold. He misjudged one bend, went too fast and edged further out, crossing the double white lines. Annabel and I breathed in deeply as we believed the rider would lose control. At that precise moment, a car came round the corner towards us. The moped strayed to the wrong side of the road and was heading straight for it. The oncoming driver swerved, but the moped struck the offside of the car. The swerve saved the rider and bike from careering off the road into a wall.

Annabel and I sucked in our breath again as the

moped wobbled then recovered and on it continued. I kept up my running commentary over the radio and requested another crew attend to speak to the driver of the car it had struck.

The moped made it through the series of bends, and we continued to follow. We passed through another two towns in close pursuit and headed out into the countryside. Annabel and I had plenty time to discuss our tactics. We considered going for a little clip of his back wheel but dismissed that as being much too dangerous. There was an opportunity to get alongside the moped and nudging him to the side of the road. Annabel dismissed that idea as too uncontrolled. Considerations for the rider's safety prevented any reckless intervention.

"What about overtaking it on a long straight and then slowing down in front of it?" I suggested. He dismissed that too, "He might turn around and we could lose him."

In these situations, adrenaline flows and the rush can often result in rash action. Annabel was old enough and wise enough to let the rider and moped carry on without interference. If the rider was going to crash and injure or even kill himself, it would not be because of anything we did.

The moped continued at full pelt for another five miles. We ended up in the middle of no-where. Then, without warning, it slowed down. Then it sputtered to a stop; the rider pulled over to the side of the road. We thought he was just giving up, but we later discovered he had simply run out of petrol. On our right was a field and on our left, there was a small wire fence which bordered a large wood. Despite us thinking our rider had given up we were still on edge. Sure enough, the rider dismounted and climbed over the fence, he was heading for the woods to continue his escape on foot. With the night so dark if he made it into the woods we might never find him.

I got out the car as fast as I could and ran towards him. He had just cleared the fence, so I dived head first over it and rugby-tackled him to the ground. Once I had a grip on him, I wasn't about to let go. I bundled him back towards the fence until Annabel could grab hold of him and haul him back over. Annabel cuffed him, then removed his helmet. We both recognised our most prolific local thief, Jed the Ned. Caught red-handed, Jed was now going back to jail.

As I climbed back over the fence, I realised it was one of those fences with barbed wire. The barbs were about three inches apart on the top. When I leapt over it, my right trouser leg had caught the barbs and ripped the skin down my thigh. The trousers themselves were ripped in two tramlines from just below the groin all the way down to the bottom where it flapped around revealing my entire bare and bloodied leg.

We got back to the office, lodged our prisoner and went off to see the sergeant. My ripped trousers were flapping about, but thankfully my leg had stopped bleeding. Sergeant Pocock took one look at me and the state of my uniform, he rubbed his chin in contemplation and mustered up the comment, "Well you can't go out on patrol like that, you can take the office."

"But Sarge, my trousers are ripped right up the middle."

"The world doesn't want to hear about your ripped trousers, McEwan. It wants to tell you about its ripped trousers. You can man the phones."

I sat for the next four hours taking calls and feeling a draught about my leg. At our finishing time, I got up to go home and was walking through the corridor towards the locker room when the early shift inspector walked in the back door, ready to start his work. He looked me up and down, saw my trousers in a state of disrepair so he lambasted me for my untidiness.
"B b b but." I stammered, intimidated by his severity and wanting to explain, "but Inspector... "

He cut me off, "Don't 'but-but' me son, get yourself sorted out and don't come into the office looking like that again," and off he marched. That inspector must have read all about the incident in the night log, but I never got an apology from him. I kept a spare uniform in my locker ever since.

While working at our tiny office Harold, our community cop, had the job of keeping the office clean and tidy, for which he received a small cleaning allowance. Harold was a gentleman, a mild-mannered considerate human being. Although, he was a worrier. He worried about anything and everything, the stock market, the price of petrol, giving a talk to primary school kids, whether he would get transferred, whether he wouldn't get transferred - he even worried about the shape of his orange (to be fair this one was quite worrying, it looked like the Hunchback of Notre Dame). He worried about getting a cold, if he had a cold he worried that it was the flu, if he had the flu he worried he would die. He worried about what people thought of him; he worried about his job, his family and life in general. He worried about things he couldn't control, like death and taxis. (He paid his taxes willingly but always felt ripped off paying for a taxi). Yes, he was perpetually anxious and apprehensive about everything. The following prank I played on him was all the more cruel for that.

Harold had it in his head that there was something in his cleaning contract that said he was not allowed to clean above waist height (health and safety reasons). Thus the cobwebs on the ceiling were only ever hoovered up when they fell to the floor. The windows were never clean enough to see through unless just replaced after being smashed by vandals (which happened frequently).

Once every three months, the local inspector (Johnny Elvis) would take a trip to our office and carry out a quarterly audit of the station. Inspector Elvis checked all our books, found property, lost property, accident books, housing repairs, etc. and then run his beady eye round the rest of the office. Harold took the responsibility on himself to keep things ship shape and sort out any court productions that weren't properly labelled, and any other issues. Thus Inspector Elvis would write a favourable report. A copy of which he always sent to Harold as a wee pat on the back.

One back shift, a few days after Inspector Elvis's audit, I was picking up the mail for our office and saw a letter addressed to Harold. I recognised Inspector Elvis's handwriting on the envelope. I carefully opened the envelope so that it could be put back without anyone knowing I'd tampered with it and read his typed report. It was all mundane. No real issues to speak of, things were running in a efficiently according to the audit. The final paragraph read:-

"An excellent audit. Once again I congratulate Harold on maintaining a well-run office regarding compliance with all

matters. The office itself is clean, tidy and maintained to a high standard."

Now this made me laugh because our 'in joke' was that Harold did not clean above waist height and this was a bugbear for those of us who had to work and live in the office. *'Maintained to a high standard'* was debatable and more akin to the Inspector's benevolent outlook than reality. A plan formed in my head.

I photocopied the report and then tipp-exed out the last paragraph. Then I photocopied the tipp-exed document leaving a nice blank space for me to type in the following amended last paragraph:-

"The audit revealed no compliance issues, and clearly, all officers are working hard to ensure that matters are attended to without the need for any supervisory intervention. I'm sorry to say the office itself is a disgrace in terms of its cleanliness, cobwebs cover the ceiling, and you can hardly see through the windows for the dirt. Presentation for callers at the counter is an important aspect of our first contact with the public and the office requires immediate remedial attention for this basic hygiene issue."

I then photocopied the doctored letter and carefully resealed it in its original envelope before depositing it in Harold's tray.

Two days later I was working day-shift on a Sunday. I had been out dealing with a few matters and returned to the office about midday. Harold was there. He was cleaning the office. Not only that, he had enlisted the help of his three young children. One had a mop in hand and was washing the floor, another kneeling on the desk cleaning the windows, and the third had a duster on the end of a broom and systematically removed the cobwebs from the ceiling.

Harold showed me the audit report from In-spector Elvis by way of explanation.

"Oh! That's a bit severe," I sympathised.

"I know. You think he (Inspector Elvis) would have said to my face, I used to get on well with In-spector Elvis," Harold bemoaned.

I kept quiet.

I had to go out again and didn't return until a few hours later. Harold and his children had completed their tasks. The office was sparkling clean. I had never seen it so free of dirt. The windows gleamed, the ceil-ing was visible again, and you could eat your supper off the floor. The toilet was in pristine condition and gave off a lovely lemony smell. The furniture had a polished sheen, and even the threadbare carpet in the back room looked as if it had been steam cleaned. 'Job well done,' I thought.

The next day Harold and I were working to-gether. I praised him for such a splendid job. I even bought sweeties to take to his kids as a thank you. Something still rankled with him though.

"I will ask Inspector Elvis to come out today and see the office again," he stated, "I want him to know I have cleaned the place up as he asked before you lot make a mess of it again."

I had a wee smile to myself as I produced the original letter from Inspector Elvis and handed it to Harold. "I think you might want to read this first," I said, then grabbed my coat and ran out of the office. I jumped into my car to escape. As I was driving off, Harold ex-ploded out of the office, shouting angrily at me. Some-thing about never cleaning the office again, I think.

No change there then!

I knew Harold would forget about it after a while, so I carried on working away and smiling to myself every time I remembered the scene with Harold and his three kids in the office. Much of the week, at our wee station, I spent working on my own. Occasionally, I was paired with a spare officer from headquarters. Handy for the corroboration. I was pleased, therefore when one night my old friend PC Penfold came out to join me.

It was a nice night, and we had no calls to attend, so we went out on foot patrol. We sauntered around the town then out towards the local golf course where we had had several complaints about youths hanging around and causing damage to the greens.

We walked down a narrow path on the far side of the course and crossed the 5th fairway. We'd both played that course before and reminisced about our bad luck, missed putts and an occasional stonking drive. The course opens out and offers splendid views across the valley. That night the moon was out and the glow it provided was almost enough to play a round of golf in it. With nothing much going on we sauntered back up the hill along the side of the sixth fairway. That was when PC Penfold spotted a hare. It was a big fecker of a thing just sitting on top of a grassy mound minding its own business.

I took out my newly purchased 'Maglite 3 D-cell PRO LED torch'. The torch was an expensive bit of kit and ideal for police officers patrolling the beat on night shifts as it has a high-intensity 500-lumen linear, focused beam. I switched on my new powerhouse of a torch and pointed at the hare.

The hare froze.

It was incredible; instantly the hare went into a trance. The light acted like some magical hypnotic beam. The hare remained completely motionless, fixated by the beam of light trained on it by my magical hypnotic 'Maglite 3 D-cell PRO LED torch'.

PC Penfold was equally mesmerised by the power of the torch. Fascinated by the effect of the light beam on the hare. Without thinking it through, he circled round to the back of the hare. Slowly but surely he inched his way towards it.

"I think I can grab it," he informed me. I kept my 'Maglite 3 D-cell PRO LED torch' trained on the hare.

PC Penfold moved in closer and closer until the hare was only an arm's length away. He then lunged forward and grabbed it by its big ears and lifted it clean off the grassy mound so it hung from his arm. He had caught this oversized hare with his bare hands.

Now, this is where it became farcical because if there is one thing that is going to awaken a big fecker of a hare from a trance-like state, it is grabbing it by its ears and pulling it clean from the ground.

On being roused from its trance, the hare bucked, kicked and struggled in PC Penfold's grip. Its thumping big feet kicked out in rapid fashion striking PC Penfold on his lower stomach, groin and upper legs with such force that PC Penfold felt it necessary to point it out.

"It's kicking me in the nuts!" he screamed.

"So I see. I don't think the hare is best pleased with you."

"Ooh ouch, ah, ooh ouch," he said.

Despite the big hare's instantaneous and furious response PC Penfold continued to hold on to its ears and complain that it was causing him no little discomfort. As you would expect from anything that was kicking the living daylights out of your groin area.

"What am I going to do?" PC Penfold enquired of me as I continued to focus the torch on the hare.

"Well, you could let it go," I suggested.

So he did. He dropped it to the ground, and the hare bolted. Battered and bruised, PC Penfold crashed to the ground holding his groin area and moaned. I ended up on the ground beside him, holding my stomach, unable to stop laughing.

About two weeks later I was lying in my bed, getting my necessary eight hours beauty sleep before my early shift in the morning. The telephone rang. I let it ring off. It rang again. It rang and rang and kept ringing. I checked my clock to see if I had slept in. The clock said it was one o'clock in the morning. I decided that I better answer it, assuming that it must be important. I picked up the receiver and listened. It was PC Penfold.

"Malky, Thish is important."

I detected a slight slur in his voice. PC Penfold was not averse to having a few libations of an evening and ending up in a scrape. I wondered what it was. I was already preparing myself to get out of bed, get dressed and pick him up somewhere.

"What is it?" I enquired.

"I'm in the pub."

"Yes?"

"Well the guys don't believe me that I caught a big hare with my bare hands – could you tell them!"

I was on early shift in the morning. I needed my sleep. Being a police officer is a demanding enough of a job without having to do it when you are tired and irritable. PC Penfold, couldn't care less, he was drunk, not working the next day and totally insensitive in phoning me at one o'clock in the morning, whether or not I was working the next day. You would think I would have just hung up - but I'm an obliging fellow, I find it hard to say 'no,' so I spent five minutes relating the story to his mates before going back to sleep. Despite being woken up, I still had a smile on my face from recalling the circumstances of the tortoise and the hare.

CHAPTER 22

ACCELERATED PROMOTION

It was round about seven years service my inspector suggested I have a go at the 'accelerated promotion scheme. 'My first response was, 'what's that?'

The accelerated promotion scheme, he told me, identifies potential senior officers early in their service and then helps to train, prepare and develop them for senior level posts. So, in my naivety, I filled out the self-nomination form and applied. I was one of several hundred who applied and had little expectation I would get over the first hurdle. It was a surprise when I received a letter inviting me to go to an initial assessment and interview.

The initial interview took place at The Scottish Government Offices in Edinburgh. I travelled through with another officer from our force, PC Phil Smirnoff.

I only knew Phil because he drank in one of my local pubs. He was dating the barmaid there, and every time I saw him, he was as drunk as a skunk. I don't think I had ever spoken to him while he was in a sober state. When I popped into the pub for a quiet drink, no matter what time of the evening, there was Phil propped up at the bar guzzling vodka martinis. I would nod in his direction, and he would bob his head up and down. I wasn't sure if he was acknowledging me or just struggling to keep his head up straight. Occasionally I would end up standing next to him at the bar when I ordered my drink, and we would have a brief conversation. I say conversation, I asked how he was doing, and he would look at me with his bloodshot and bleary eyes, half recognise that I was someone who worked in the same occupation and then burp in my face - a reply of sorts.

On one such occasion, I nodded to him as I stood at the bar awaiting service from his barmaid girlfriend. Phil was nodding away trying to fend off the alcohol in his belly that was now affecting his ability to keep his head in an upright position.

"How are you doing?" I asked, concerned that he would fall over backwards off the stool.

Phil looked up and kind of recognised me. I could almost see his brain cells working away as he fought with them to formulate a reply. His chin went down and pressed into his chest for a second before he flung his head up and said, "I'm fine," then belched at full volume for ten seconds.

(I later looked it up; ten seconds wasn't quite a world record that was an honour held by an American called Tim Janus who burped for a full 18.1 seconds at the World Burping Championships in New York - yes there is such a thing.)

Rather taken aback at such a forceful and unexpected belching, I asked Phil, "What on earth are you drinking?"

Phil's lack of ability to string two words together was suddenly forgotten, and he managed three words, "Vodka Martini, thanks!"

At that precise moment, his girlfriend magically appeared at the opposite side of the bar and overheard our brief exchange thus sealing my charitable donation to Phil's liver cirrhosis by saying, "Vodka Martini coming up, what about you?"

With little thought, I said I would have the same. Then I watched in amazement as Phil's girlfriend poured our Vodka Martinis, a cocktail I had never tried before. I was neither a fan of Vodka nor Martini and, other than in a James Bond film, had never heard or seen anyone ask for or drink one.

I admit I was inexperienced in the actual preparation of a Vodka Martini. I presumed there might be a little of Vodka and a dash of Martini topped up with lemonade or other such sweet mixture to make the whole thing palatable. Nope. The glasses received four measures of vodka and one measure of dry vermouth, which she stirred with an olive on a cocktail stick. That was it.

Phil grabbed his glass and guzzled it half down before making further conversation. I supped at my Vodka Martini; it was vile. After a few sips and some unintelligible chat with Phil, I decided that the best way to consume this cocktail of poison would be to down it in one go. I steadied myself and forced it down my throat. The fire worked its way down my gullet and into my belly. The after effects were not only warming to my stomach but also my mood. I laid my glass down on the bar where another two newly prepared Vodka Martinis sat, Phil's girlfriend expected the first two wouldn't last long.

The second Vodka Martini was a lot less vile, so I bought another round, and soon I had consumed my third Vodka Martini, all in the space of ten minutes. God knows how many Phil had consumed before I got there but the more he drank the quicker he seemed to pour them down his throat. Before I had even taken a sip of my drink, Phil had ordered another two for us.

My third Vodka Martini was my last. My head spun, and I could feel my legs wobble. I recognised the effect of the alcohol was having on me, and without another word, I about turned and unsteadily made my way out of the bar. Time to go home. Phil, no doubt, consumed the two Vodka Martinis and a few more on top.

So that was my entire knowledge of Phil Smirnoff as we headed through to the initial assessment and interview for the 'accelerated promotion scheme' together. It was the first time I had seen him sober. We had a comprehensible conversation en route. It turned out that Phil's father had been a senior officer in the force. Phil had applied for the 'accelerated promotion scheme' the year before and had made it through to the weekend assessment but had been unsuccessful.

"So why are you going for it again?" I enquired

"I was told to!"

I wasn't sure who told him to or why, but I found out a little more about the process from him as we made the drive through to our capital city.

"If you get through the assessments and interview, you have to go to the Scottish Police College for the full weekend assessment. That is tough. There are only a few places, and out of the sixty odd who get there, only about half a dozen get picked to go forward. The tests and interviews give the cerebral muscle a vigorous workout and make it the most exhausting weekend."

"You must be keen to get on it then if you are

going through it again?"

"I'm not bothered."

The tests turned out to be IQ type tests, puzzles, and conundrums. These are right up my street. I love puzzles, crosswords, number games and the like. We spent two hours at a desk doing these with about thirty others before being interviewed by a panel of senior officers.

My interview must have gone well enough because about a week later I received another letter - this time an invitation to attend the full weekend assessment at The Scottish Police College. That was despite lying during the interview.

"What is your biggest weakness?" a rather forbidding superintendent asked me.

"Em, chocolate!" I said (when it was really beer). It raised a smile, though, and I bet it was the first time that particular superintendent smiled in years.

A few weeks later I turned up at The Scottish Police College on a Friday afternoon, along with a load of other bright hopefuls, for the gruelling assessment process. There were only four officers from my force chosen to go, and I ended up going the same weekend as Sam Gordonson. Phil Smirnoff was also one of the four, but he got to go on a different weekend from me.

We were straight into it. Ushered into a lecture theatre, we all sat in a row in front of a team of assessors. The superintendent in charge mentioned a burning topic in the news and said, "Discuss!"

I'm not a political animal. I have views on lots of topics, I am interested in a lot of things and can voice my opinion eloquently enough on them, but not politics. If the conversation was about the best sitcom on television, I have an informed opinion. I can talk about business, books, and biscuits. If there is a discussion about football I can dismiss, Pele, Maradona, and Ronaldo as candidates for best footballer in the world and explain, enthusiastically, why that title goes to Davie Cooper of Glasgow Rangers fame.

(Davie Cooper was a left winger with an abundance of skill. He could dance his way past the opposition even if he did it in slow motion. He could kick a ball too. On one occasion, during the warm up at an Old Firm game, he went up to the Celtic end placed the football on the penalty spot. He lined up a shot and kicked it toward the empty goal. The ball flew into the air and struck the bar, bouncing straight back to him. The Celtic supporters were beside themselves with glee; laughter rang out from their end. Unperturbed, Davie Cooper replaced the ball back onto the penalty spot and took another kick at it sending towards the empty goal. Once again it flew a little too high and struck the bar, rebounding directly into his hands. The laughter from the Celtic fans diminished somewhat as Davie laid the ball back to the penalty spot and smiled at the Celtic supporters. He kicked the ball straight at the bar again. For the third time, it bounced back off it straight into his hands. He waved at the now silent Celtic supporters and skipped his way back up the pitch.)

However, politics I could do without. With enough research, I might have been able to formulate a viewpoint on the recent relinquishment of sole power in the Soviet Government by the Communist party. I might even have postulated on how it would affect policing in Scotland - or at least decide that it would be of little concern. My approach would have been careful and measured. However, sitting in a large group of intelligent and highly ambitious, prospective senior officers I was aghast at how quickly those people shouted their opinions across the room. No sooner had the superintendent uttered the word 'discuss' the young lady next to me screamed her beliefs towards the rest of the group, at the same time as several others shouted even louder. My definition of 'discuss' appeared to be skewed from the rest of the protagonists in the room. We were at war. Fighting for the limited positions on the accelerated promotion scheme, and the best way to to fight, it appeared, was to yell as loudly and convincingly as you could. Getting heard became a battle. As soon as one person stopped talking, three or four others barged in. They went feral - this lot belonged in the House of Commons.

I sat back. *Was this what senior officers were supposed to do? Was this practice for the 'bunfights' they had at senior level?*

Some weren't even saying anything that made any sense. It was just babble. Big words strung together and exhaled as a tumultuous clamour. 'Whoever boomed their opinion longest wins,' came across as the object of the debate. I suppose the whole point of the exercise was to see who commanded the situation. Which of us would they listen to when we spoke? Sam Gordonson managed it. He talked, and people listened. And he talked sense, people nodded. As soon as he stopped talking, the rabble started up again.

After some minutes the superintendent interjected and then asked each of us our opinion in turn. His interjection calmed the herd as they had their say without having to shout over someone else. I was last in line, and until then, I hadn't spoken a single word. I felt it unnecessary and rude to interrupt anyone.

By the time the superintendent asked for my opinion, the entire group had had their say. The group had touched upon every sort of belief and judgement. I panicked.

How on earth could I come up with something original? Every possible thing I could think of had already been said. Some suggested planning to deal with the potential fallout from the news and outlined how they would go about it, what people should be involved, what meetings would need to happen, what records were needed and what they would have to do in every circumstance.

What could I possibly say that would add to that?

"I don't think we should be concerned about it," I said with a decidedly dodgy frog in my throat.

The superintendent furrowed his brow and stared at me, waiting for further explanation. I froze.

What else was I supposed to say? Who cares what the bloody Russian Government does? It is not as if they are starting a war is it?

There was a pregnant pause. A hush as I desperately tried to think of something else to say. Everyone was looking at me and waiting. It was an awkward moment. It was then that Sam Gordonson took the pressure off. I am eternally grateful. He recognised my predicament and perhaps because of the affinity he felt because we were from the same force he chirped up saying, "I think what Malky is trying to say is that the adjustments in the Russian Government should provide a stabilising effect for the inherent threat that has been hanging over the east-west political landscape since the inception of the cold war. The communists relinquishing full power could do much to reduce the tensions."

"Yes. That's it. That's what I meant to say," I said and nodded at the superintendent and Sam Gordonson one after the other.

I knew that my little episode effectively put paid to my chances of getting anywhere further in the process and that it ensured Sam a place on the scheme. I didn't much care. I was grateful to Sam, who went on to be one of our most respected senior officers.

The following day I spent sitting various IQ tests and taking part in group activities, each one more gruelling than the next. It was an intensive selection process. By the Saturday evening we were exhausted, and although free for the evening there was still the next morning's round of tests with which to contend.

Someone suggested that we retire to the local golf club for a libation or two as a way to unwind. Everyone accepted that this was a good idea and off we went.

At the golf club we sat supping our pints. A pack of cards appeared from behind the bar, and Gillian handed them to me with the request to 'show a trick' (she remembered that I could do card tricks from our 'get to know each other' session earlier in the day).

My willing assistant was Gavin McBarrhead a young cop from Strathclyde. Both his father and mother were senior officers in Strathclyde, and there was an expectancy for him to follow in their footsteps.

"Okay Gavin," I said as I shuffled the cards, "I will show you a trick, but it might cost you a pound. But don't worry after I take your pound I will show you how to do it and you can make your pound back as many times as you like."

(This might sound like a pyramid scheme or con, it isn't, it is perfectly legal. My willing assistant only loses a pound, but I do show how simple the trick is so they too can make their pound back. It is a money-making, magical entertainment course.)

"Pick a card. Look at it and put it back on the top of the deck."

Gavin did as instructed.

"I will now shuffle the cards behind my back so that no-one, including me, can know where your card ends up."

Now, this is the trick, observe; Instead of shuffling the cards I pretend to do that, but I turn the card he has chosen upside down, so it is now facing the other way. I bring the pack of cards around to the front and show the bottom card to Gavin, "Is this your card?"

Of course, it isn't, but I can now see what his card is sitting facing me on top of the deck. The only thing you have to be careful of is that no-one else sees that I can see it.

"I'll shuffle them again."

I put the cards behind my back again and turn the chosen card back over so it is facing the same way as all the rest of the cards. This time, I do shuffle the deck. I even bring them back round and shuffle them in front of everyone.

"You see Gavin; there is no way I can know where in the deck your card is, I will go through the deck one by one and stop when I think I am coming to your card. Don't tell me if you see it."

I then turn each card over one by one until I see

Gavin's card. The secret here is not to stop but to keep going for five or six cards more. I then tap the top of the deck and say, "Okay Gavin. I bet the next card I turn over is your card."

Gavin has already seen me deal his card onto the table five or six cards previous and he knows that the next card on top of the deck can't possibly be his.

"I'll take that bet, " he said, smiling.

Carefully, I spread out the cards on the table find his card and turn it over. Et viola the next card I turned over was his. That wiped the grin from his face.

It is a nice neat and simple trick that uses a little deception. Once used, however, you cannot show the same trick to the same person twice. They wouldn't fall for it again. At least you might think that. I pocketed Gavin's pound and explained how I did the trick and how he could do the same thing to make his pound back. At the end of my explanation, Gavin looked at me and said, "Can you show me it again from the start?"

"How to do it?"

"No. Just the trick."

I was a little puzzled."You want me to show you the trick again?"

"Yes!"

So I picked up the deck of cards asked him to pick a card and went through the whole process again. At the point where I said, "I bet you a pound the next card I turn over is your card," Gavin produced another pound from his pocket and laid it on the table.

"Okay," he said.

Gavin lost another pound coin to the same simple trick I had just shown him how to do. I couldn't believe I was sitting in the company of one of the most intelligent officers in the country and a potential senior officer in the making. If you ever come across him, I would wager the trick might still work on him.

With Sunday morning came further exercises and tests. The last ordeal was a sneaky one where we all had to grade each other and assess whether the others were suitable for senior ranks within the police. I was as honest as I could be. Head and shoulders more impressive than anyone else was Sam Gordonson. Gavin, not so much.

In the end, Sam, Phil Smirnoff and incredibly Gavin, were both welcomed onto the programme. I wasn't successful. I got feedback from the process and did well enough on the IQ tests, with some of the highest scores they had seen. The superintendent giving me the feedback suggested that I read a little more highbrow newspapers. I'm not sure what he meant by that - did he think I read *The Beano* or something?

Despite being unsuccessful, I did take a lot from it. I identified my need to project myself more, to have more firm opinions and formulated ideas - it helps to think about these things beforehand. A little preparation can go a long way. Also, I cancelled my subscription to *The Dandy*.

CHAPTER 23

EVEN MORE MICROWAVE COOKBOOK

7th June

Newsagents broken into, £30 taken from the till and a box of paperclips! (Barbeque Bill)

8th June

I now have sufficient evidence to charge Windy Miller for the break-in to the Masonic Hall. ..(Tom)

9th June

Windy Miller detained for the break-in to the Masonic Hall. Interviewed and admitted it. He also took the shed at the back of Main Street, the break-in at the butchers, the shed on the golf course and the bike stolen from Findlay's Farm... (Deek)

10th June

If I was keen and ambitious, I might get upset at somebody 'stealing' my cases without a 'by your leave'. Did he not admit to the break-in at the newsagents?... (Tom)

11th June

Re Windy Miller, it wasn't a matter of stealing cases. I was told to do a custody report. In any case, you had written it off! Next time I will phone you out your bed and see what you want to do... (Deek)

12th June

What about the newsagents?... (Tom)

13th June

No, he didn't admit to the newsagents... (Deek)

14th June

Did you ask him about the newsagents?... (Tom)

15th June

Um, don't think I did ask him about the newsagents. He is back up in court tomorrow, maybe you could see him then... (Deek)

16th June

Busy day... (Tom)

18th June

Did you speak to Windy Miller about the newsagents?... (Deek)

19th June

Windy Miller didn't admit to the newsagents... (Tom)

19th June

I just happened to be in at the custody suite when Windy Miller was getting taken out to go back to HMP Barlinnie. In his property was a box of paperclips!!! I have charged him with the break-in to the newsagents and left details for Deek to add to his report. (Annabel)

3rd February

Where is radio No. 34?... (Barbeque Bill)

4th February

I left radio No. 34 in the tray, don't know where it is now... (Malky)

5th February

Radio 34 still missing...

Who ate my doughnuts?... (Barbeque Bill)

6th February

I ate your doughnuts, I'll buy you more doughnuts, don't know where the radio is though... (Malky)

7th February

WHY ME!! AGAIN!!

Another body in the pond, 80-year-old, it's a sideyways - I'm reporting... (Barbeque Bill)

8th February

Found the radio. Someone had stolen it and then craftily hid it in Annabel's locker. (Duggie)

9th February

More doughnuts for the boys. I'm not looking for any favours - HONEST - YET!! (Barbeque Bill)

10th February

Who ate all the doughnuts - not one left for the backshift!!! - ie ME!... (Barbeque Bill)

11th February

Tom off sick, puking and shitting. Guess it was Tom who ate all the doughnuts... (Duggie)

12th February

Bill - DO NOT buy any more doughnuts!... (Annabel)

2nd March

Per Sergeant Napoleon, we have to go to The Scottish Police College on Monday and pick up a video production from DC Cardwell. I know I am in on Monday and it will be up to me to go and get it. This note is so I don't forget - please remind me... (Malky)

3rd March

Malky , don't forget to pick up the video production at The Scottish Police college... (Deek)

Malky - remember the video... (Annabel)

4th March

Malky, mind you have to pick up the video... (Duggie)

Malky, remember you have to get that video from DC Cardwell... (Tom)

5th March

Attended at SPC, spoke to DC Cardwell, she forgot to bring the video... (Malky)

29th March

Break-in at Main Street again, a welder stolen. Obviously not a real live welder with a mask and gloves. The gas thingy that lights up and burns stuff... (Barbeque Bill)

30th March

I think Barbeque Bill has lost it... (Malky)

31st March

Bit of criminal intelligence gained - apparently, there is a strong rumour in the village that Malky is a wwww-waannkkah!!! (Barbeque Bill)

All to note:

SIGNED BY: (Deek)(Annabel)(Duggie)(Billy)

1st April

Having conferred with senior management, middle management, and lower management, it was decided that the Personnel Department initiate a workshop. This they did over the weekend, and the conclusions reached were as follows:-

1. Barbeque Bill has lost it.
2. Barbeque Bill is a PLONKA.
3. Barbeque Bill is one step away from sticking his underpants over his head and pencils up his nose. (Malky)

CHAPTER 24

THE WORST PRANK IN THE WORLD

Nobody liked to work on their own. It can be dangerous out there. But the police are paid to go out there and patrol, so if there are bad guys wandering around, the likelihood is that the police will happen upon them. If those bad guys are up to no good, then we got sent to sort them out. So it was always good to have a partner to back you up.

It was a small station, so I had to work on my own a lot. Whole shifts would pass going from one call to the next and the only other cops I would see would be when they passed by in their car on their way to a different call. A brief wave and they were gone. The people I ended up talking to were the ones who didn't want to speak to me. However, sometimes working on your own was an advantage. When there were embarrassing moments, I might admit them to my colleagues if it was likely to get a laugh. This one, however, I kept to myself - until now.

On my beat, there was a long stretch of road that followed a flat flood plain along the foot of the hills. For many miles, it was level and straight. The towns developed on either side of the main road. One of them had grown so much it extended the 30 mph speed limit for almost a mile.

Malky McEwan

About 2 a.m. I was driving slowly through the town; the street lights threw down their orange glow on either pavement. In the distance a car drove towards me. I could see it had its full beam on, but it was far enough away it was not an inconvenience, yet. I dipped my lights and expected the oncoming car to do the same.

It didn't.

It kept coming towards me, full beam blazing. I'm quite a patient fellow, so I waited. It kept coming. The lights got brighter the closer it got. I put had to put my visor down and my hand up to my eyes to stop getting dazzled. It was time for me to do something about it.

I flashed my lights. A quick two jerks of my hand and my full beam lit up twice. A simple gesture that said, 'Hello, I'm here, dip your lights please.'

The car trundled on towards me. Its lights stayed on full beam, resolute in their mission to blind me.

Annoyed I flashed again, three times. Instead of just quick ones I held each flash on slightly longer as if to say, 'Now you are getting on my goat. Dip your lights dipstick.'

It didn't.

It kept coming. If the driver didn't dip his lights, I was going to have pin holes for pupils. My mood went from happy to miffed to irritated.

The nice thing about being a police officer is that when irritated you can do something about it.   I came to a stop, wound down my window and put on my blue lights. The oncoming driver would now realise that he was blinding a police officer and do something

276

about it.

He didn't.

He kept coming and his full beam blazed brighter. I stuck my arm out waved it up and down. The universal sign to slow down or stop.

Remarkably, the oncoming car still failed to dip its lights. Now it was real close, I couldn't see anything beyond the glare of his headlights. The car slowed down, and I kept waving my arm. It drew up beside me and came to a stop, driver's window adjacent to mine. There was a concerned look on the driver's face, a middle-aged man with a moustache.

"What's the matter officer?" he asked.

"Do you not realise you have been blinding me with your lights?"

"What? Er... Um...I'm sorry."

He looked at the controls of his Ford Escort and checked the light switches. He pulled the lever that switched the lights from dipped beam to full beam. The front of his car lit up even more. The full beam hadn't been on at all.

"My full beam isn't on, officer."

"Well, there must be something wrong with them then. Your lights must be set too high. I was being blinded all the way as you came towards me. Where are you going at this time of the morning, anyway?"

"I was just picking up my daughters from the disco. I'm just taking them home," he nodded towards the back seat of the car.

It was only then I noticed his passengers. Two girls sat in the back of the car. These weren't just any girls though. These were two portly girls. Enormous in fact. There was no room for anyone to sit between them. Squashed into the back seat, both compressed against their respective doors and each other. The combined weight of the two heifers sitting over the back axle had strained the rear suspension so much that it had torpedoed the front of the car into the air.

The heifers in the back hung their heads. The driver looked at me embarrassed. My face flushed red. All four of us comprehending my error.

"Well, see and get those lights fixed," I said and drove off.

We played a lot of pranks on each other.

Some were funny, some were cruel, but the worst prank in the world was despicably evil. I cringe in shame when I think about what we did to Special Constable Hughie Hefner.

The worst prank in the world just happened. I didn't wake up feeling malicious or evil. I didn't sit and plan it out over weeks or months. I felt no animosity towards Special Constable Hefner. In fact, I liked him; it was just one of those things. No reasoning behind it, it just happened.

I was still working out of our small five-man station. We had to work much of the week on our own. As a result, we used to welcome having 'Special Constables' come out and work with us.

Special Constables are volunteers. They go through a limited amount of training, but put on a uniform and accompany us on our duties. They see it as a hobby or a way to give back to the community. It can be interesting being a special constable, they get to accompany cops on the job and assist in arrests, travel in police cars at 90mph on their way to emergencies, chase people and hear all the gossip. It can be exciting.

They make friends with the police officers they work with and many prefer it to getting drunk on a Friday or Saturday night. The best part is they have no paperwork to do; that is the remit of the cops. The worst part of the job for them sitting around waiting while the cop does his or her necessary paperwork.

I was lucky as we had some cracking good guys who gave up their spare time to put on a uniform and work with us. I had many a great laugh with lots of special constables, and many ended up as good friends.

Special Constable Hughie Hefner worked twice a week, regular as clockwork. He enjoyed the camaraderie and relished getting involved in the calls. I enjoyed his company too and counted him as a good friend. Hughie got a buzz from going to emergency calls, intrigued by what went on in the big bad world. He was a good lad and had considered joining the regulars but the paperwork was a deciding factor in putting him off.

Hughie and I built up a good relationship and enjoyed each other's banter, which often degenerated to downright mockery.

Being single, Hughie felt it necessary to regale me with his dating exploits, of which there were many. He seemed to find it funny that he could go out and 'play the field' while I remained 'under the thumb.'

One Saturday night he came out and we paired up. We were driving around on patrol and to make conversation, I asked what he had been up to. He told me about his latest date.

The night before he had been in a bowling club and chatted up the delightful 'Senga Bucket,' a buxom blonde barmaid. Senga was rather taken with him, and at the end of the night, he accompanied her home. Special Constable Hughie Hefner wasn't shy about giving all the meaty details. He was proud of his night's work and went into just a little too much detail. Gentlemen should be a little more decorous, I think. Hughie related his energetic evening with his buxom young barmaid in a no holds barred fashion.

I asked, "When are you seeing the young lady again?" and he laughed. He considered it a one night stand.

The next afternoon Hughie came out to work with me again. We patrolled the streets for several hours, dealt with some calls and stopped a few cars. When we got hungry, we headed to the station for a break. The rear entrance opens into the custody suite, and we had to pass through to get to the canteen. In the custody suite, there is a large whiteboard which displays details of those in custody. It contains information such as the name of the prisoner, the crime, the cell they are in and any special requirements (medication, etc.).

As we walked past, Hughie looked up and noticed the name 'Senga Bucket' on the board. The same name as the young buxom barmaid that had been his Friday night conquest. Her name written in capitals. The board showed that she had been arrested for drug offences. Right next to her name, in red, was a warning marker that read 'HIV+.' The colour completely drained from Hughie's face.

Hughie looked at me and pointed out her name. His voice trembled a little and his eyes darted back to the board to read the name over and over again as if he could somehow magic it away. I tried to reassure him, as best I could, that it might be a coincidence. It could be someone else with the same name; it couldn't possibly be his buxom barmaid buddy. After much babbling from Hughie, I told him I would check the cell and just confirm that it wasn't the same girl.

On my return, Hughie was pacing up and down. He could tell from my serious look it was bad news. Sure enough, it was his barmaid buddy. His Friday night one-night stand was now having a two-day date with a cell wall.

Hughie gibbered that he had been wearing a condom and looked for reassurance that he would be all right. I hit him with the further news that Senga had repeatedly been asking for him. I then came right out and asked him if he had partaken of drugs in her company and he looked at me aghast. He hadn't even thought about the implications of that. All he had been running through his head until then was 'HIV positive.' Now he might become a suspect in some drugs case. Vehemently he professed his ignorance and innocence.

I suggested that he would be better having a little word with her to ensure that she would not make things up about him. While he wasn't sure, I persuaded him it would be the sensible thing to do. It would give him a chance to work out a strategy if, on the off chance, she would cause him any problems.

I handed Hughie the keys and made his way down to the cells. There are only two females cells, and the first one was empty. He had a quick look through the spy hole and saw the outline of a body curled up underneath a blanket on the mattress. He plucked up his courage, opened the door and went across to speak to her.

At this point, Big Billy, my gregarious colleague,

and partner in the prank jumped up from underneath the blanket, held his arms wide and gave Hughie a great big bear hug. All the time screaming with laughter. I entered the cell behind Hughie and joined in.

Hughie was dumbstruck with relief. He put his hands on top of his head, went down on his haunches and bounced up and down like 'Basil Fawlty' shouting, "Ya Bastards! Ya Bastards!"

We had doctored the whole event, Hughie may have called us for everything, but he was more relieved than anything.

It is a testament to Hughie's forgiving character that he still counts me as a friend.

CHAPTER 25

LOYALTY POINTS

There was always work to do. In the early days of my service, it was the cops job to deliver correspondence (citations, copy complaints, etc.). We used to have to go from call to call and, in between this, deliver any correspondence allocated to us. It was a bugbear because there was never enough time to do it all. We knew it needed to be done; the alternative was a court case not go ahead or even for the case to fold.

The police now employ ex-cops or similarly suitably qualified civilians as process servers to carry out this function. They quietly go about their business, making sure the wheels of criminal justice remain lubricated and keep turning. They never cause any issue for cops or supervisors. They get paid a third of the wages a cop does so it makes good sense to use them. Due to tight budgets and cost savings, it was suggested that their jobs might go. Anyone with a modicum of commonsense would know that it can't possibly save money to dispense with the services of someone and then pay another person three times as much to do the same job. It would be an incompetent idiot who ever got rid of them and gave that job back to police officers. (It did happen).

Delivering correspondence, before we had process servers, was irritatingly tedious. Often there was no reply and we had to call back repeatedly. We left calling cards asking them to call into the office and collect their court citations, but people routinely ignored these. I always felt like I had more important things to do. Squeezing in the delivery of citations was always difficult - in between playing Scrabble and drinking coffee.

Still, the job needed to be done.

So whenever we had a quiet moment, we would take the opportunity to whizz round our beat getting as much of it delivered as we could.

One Saturday morning Barbeque Bill and I were doing just that. A load of correspondence arrived on Friday, and we got on with delivering as much of it as we could over the weekend.

I was driving, and Barbeque Bill was running in and out of the addresses with the correspondence dropping it through the letterboxes or getting signatures of receipt, whichever was required.

While I sat in the car waiting for Barbeque Bill, my boredom turned to mischievousness, so I wound the back of his seat forward. He found it difficult to get in the car. The next stop reclined his seat so that when he sat back, he ended up in a recumbent position. Just a tad annoying for him but slightly amusing for me.

Being 'just slightly amused,' was all that was required to keep doing it.

In the afternoon we swapped roles, and I had to get in and out of the car and trudge up flights of stairs to deliver the correspondence. Barbeque Bill reciprocated my earlier nonsense and I found my seat altered to some degree or other.

While on the last delivery of the day, Barbeque Bill slid my seat as far forward as it would go. He also put the incline of the seat forward so that it was leaning towards the windscreen.

Awkwardly, I climb in.

I sat so far forward that I had to turn my hat around back to front, as the skip was pressed right up against the front windscreen. Barbeque Bill drove off, and we both had a wee giggle as he drove through the streets towards the main road. I remained in that position, with my seat as far forward as it would go, my hat on back to front and my face pressed up against the windscreen.

As we drove through Main Street, we saw a group of our local troublemakers hanging around at the bus stop. The bus stop was their usual hang out, where they passed the time of day, smoking, occasionally drinking and annoying the rest of the townsfolk. I burst out laughing at the thought of us driving past this group. I pictured them having a double take as they spied me with my hat on back to front and my head pressed against the window. Barbeque Bill also started laughing. It would be a hoot seeing their faces as we disappeared off up the street.

At this point, I should describe my colleague; Barbeque Bill was one of the best guys I ever worked with. Hard working, dedicated, kind and considerate. But he also had a wicked sense of humour. His liking for nonsense and shenanigans, in fact, knew no bounds.

Barbeque Bill didn't drive past the group of youths as I thought he would. Instead, he pulled into the bus stop and came to a stop.

Despite my undignified and embarrassing position squashed up against the windscreen, I couldn't stop laughing. I had to turn away from the youths as tears of laughter rolled down my face. I looked at Barbeque Bill, and he was laughing so hard it took him a minute or two before he was able to compose himself enough to drive off.

I remained, hat on back to front, with my nose pressed up against the windscreen in front of that bus stop for what seemed like an eternity.

Here were the respectable uniformed local bobbies acting like idiots. Would anyone ever take us seriously again?

How could we ever remonstrate with these troublemakers when our nonsense was worse than theirs?

The next day Barbeque Bill was once again the designated driver and he took to hiding from me when I made a delivery of correspondence. I came out of a block of flats and had to wander around until I found him hiding around to the back of the flats or behind a lorry or up a side street.

The last occasion I came out to find him gone I noticed a taxi parked just up from me. I recognised the driver as an ex-cop, so I had a wee chat with him. It turned out he was heading back in the direction of my office, five miles away, so I cadged a lift. I hopped in, and he drove me out of the village and dropped me back at my office.

About an hour later Barbeque Bill called me up on the radio, "Alright," he sighed, "Where are you?"

"I'm back at the office writing a report," I informed him.

I'm not sure I ever told him how I managed to get

the five miles back to the office.

Sooner or later, all good things come to an end. The force recognised that the toilet I had worked out of for the past seven years was no longer fit for purpose (some would say it was never fit for purpose). They built a new office on the outskirts of the town. It was a sports centre compared to the two tiny rooms we had occupied until then. A brand spanking new office. But I didn't get to move there. Instead, I transferred to another station a dozen miles away.

Scotty Boy got a move to the new station.

Scotty Boy was young in service and full of nonsense. One of the funniest guys I came across in my career, sadly he is no longer with us.

Scotty Boy was a hard working, loyal cop who ended up in the role of 'Detective Constable.' He was also an incorrigible prankster. In his early service he brought in a WWII pilot's helmet to work, not a real one, this was made from latex. During the quieter hours, he would drive around at night, in the marked police car, wearing his latex helmet. Members of the public had to look twice. We could see them in our mirror walk away not believing their eyes.

"Did you see that? It looked like the driver of that police car was wearing a pilot's helmet."
"... Nah, surely not?"

Scotty Boy made me laugh. He made me laugh when he greeted me in the morning with some joke he had made up about the previous night's football. He made me laugh throughout the day with his funnies, and he made me laugh when he extolled the virtues of his beloved Glasgow Rangers Football Club. He made me laugh at myself, and he made me laugh at the most inappropriate times.

You see, Scotty Boy had a habit of trying to make you laugh all the time the worst of which, was when a member of the public came to the counter. In our small office, there was a partition up to separate our room from the callers who came into the foyer. As we walked round to attend to callers, I could see them and the rest of the office, but the rest of the office remained hidden to the caller behind the partition.

No matter who came in, Scotty Boy would stand behind the partition with a smile on his face, put on his WWII pilot's helmet and salute you with his tongue hanging out. It was difficult to remain professional, keep a straight face and deal with the member of the public on the other side of the partition.

The week before our wee office was due to shut, the night before I transferred to my new station, we had a clear out of all the cupboards and drawers. We unearthed about twenty footballs, balls we had found or confiscated but remained unclaimed. We decided to reunite the footballs with the community. We made our way to various locations around the town and kicked them down the street for the kids to find in the morning.

The next day the locals found balls everywhere. An abundance of free footballs for the kids. This resulted in several more telephone calls that night, instigated by complaints of youths playing football in the street. Those on duty ended up having to confiscate half the footballs back again!

One of Scotty Boy's favourite tricks was to pull a 'Marigold' glove (one of those rubber cleaning gloves) over his head until it stretched over his nose. He would then draw in a breath through his mouth and expel it through his nose so that the Marigold glove blew up and up and up and up.

The first time I saw him do this I watched in amazement. He blew it up to the size of a football. The red glove made him look just like a cockerel as the fingers extended up into the air. My amazement turned to complete hilarity as he pranced around the room clucking like a chicken.

The second time I saw Scotty Boy pulling a Marigold glove over his head and prancing around like a chicken brought similar hilarity.

The sixth time I saw Scotty Boy pulling a Marigold glove over his head and prancing around like a chicken still brought a smile to my face. You might think the more I saw it the less appealing it would be. However, it was around the hundredth time I saw Scotty Boy pulling a Marigold glove over his head and prancing around like a chicken that I thought I would die with laughter. My sides were so sore I thought I might have seriously injured myself.

I suppose if you pull a Marigold glove over your head, blow it up and prance around like a chicken often enough, then the Chief Constable and his deputy will to walk into the office on an unannounced visit and stare in disbelief.

On that occasion, Scotty Boy had been prancing around the front office with two or three of us as an audience. Altogether unexpected, the Chief Constable and his deputy walked in. We all had a sudden panic - what on earth would they make of Scotty Boy? Would we all be in trouble?

Scotty Boy was totally oblivious to their presence. He continued to prance around like a chicken, clucking, and 'puck pucking.' He continued to blow into the Marigold glove until it could take no more. The elasticity of the glove is such that it can only take so much and with the size increasing as the air expanded it from within there was only one outcome - it exploded. With his hair dishevelled from the blast and bits of Marigold glove stuck to his tunic, Scotty Boy opened his eyes and stared into the face of the Chief Constable. It was the first time I ever saw Scotty Boy speechless.

None of the rest of us, however, could contain our delight. In trouble or not, the situation and Scotty Boys' angst ridden face was just too funny. Grunts of laughter turned into bellows of hilarity. The Chief Constable couldn't help himself, he cracked a smile, tried to hold it in but couldn't - he too burst out laughing. Scotty Boy's face went as bright red as the Marigold glove he had been wearing.

Scotty Boy, despite all his nonsense, was a good worker and intelligent with it. He ended up posted to the CID as a temporary detective. A stint that would identify whether he had the skills to become a fully fledged detective or not. It was a small department, so there was only Detective Sergeant Frank Johnstone and him. Scotty Boy did all he could to impress and ended up with a good working relationship with his boss. Instead of doing the bare minimum or even just what was asked of him he went the extra mile. Scotty Boy turned up at 7.30 a.m. every day. He printed off the daily log and crime return so it was ready for Detective Sergeant Frank Johnstone when he came in at eight.

Frank Johnstone arrived at work, sat down at his desk and had all he needed to update himself right there in front of him. Scotty Boy made coffee, engaged him in football banter and then got on with his work.

There are two kinds of cops. There are cops who wander around oblivious to all that goes on around them. They couldn't detect a cold if it slapped them in the face. And there are cops who have an inborn instinct, a sixth sense almost. They tune themselves to listen to their gut. If something is out of place their unconscious mind alerts them to it long before anyone else suspects a thing. So when Sergeant Cathy Sharp felt that tingle in her belly that told her something wasn't quite right, she decided to investigate for herself. It was in the middle of the night and two of her cops had attended a call to a block of flats were a resident reported hearing a scream. They attended, chapped a few doors but couldn't find anything untoward.

"Area searched, no trace," was passed back as the write-off.

Cathy put on her jacket, drove down to the block of flats and wandered around to the back. There on the concrete drying green was a body. A man, about thirty years of age and as dead as a dinosaur. His body traumatically injured. Blood pooled underneath him and spread outwards until it congealed into a sticky dark gel. A gruesome find. The question was, 'did he jump or was he pushed?'

Detective Sergeant Frank Johnstone was the senior on call detective and thirty minutes after being woken; he was at the scene directing a possible murder investigation. By 8 a.m. he had got a handle on things, so he phoned Detective Inspector Jagielka at headquarters and gave him an update. At the end of his call, he asked DI Jagielka to phone Scotty Boy and tell him he was tied up and wouldn't be back to his office that day. Scotty Boy could hold the fort and deal with anything else that came in.

About 8.30 a.m. Scotty Boy had prepared the briefing and made the coffee. Detective Sergeant Johnstone's brew was now almost cold. He remembered that Frank had planned to go to a Burns Supper the night before and, putting two and two together, reckoned he must have had too much to drink and slept in. Then the phone rang. Scotty picked it up.

"It's Detective Inspector Jagielka here," who was just about to explain to Scotty Boy where DS Frank Johnstone was and what he was dealing with, he continued with, "Your detective sergeant..."

Before he could go any further Scotty Boy interrupted, "He's out at the moment."

Scotty Boy assessed the situation. He presumed the DI Jagielka was looking to speak to Frank and decided to cover for him. Now you don't get to be a detective inspector without having a few smarts. DI Jagielka played along.

"Oh, where is he?"

"He went across to the Procurator Fiscal's office, he should only be five minutes," was Scotty Boy's spur-of-the-moment reply.

"When did he go across there?"

"About ten minutes ago, sir."

"Well he should be back any moment then," DI Jagielka surmised. "I will just hang on for him then."

"... er well he might be a little longer, I think he was going to discuss a case as well."

"Oh, I see, what case was he going to discuss?" Scotty Boy got deeper and deeper into his lie and was now desperately hoping his boss would walk into the office, hung-over or not.

"I think it was the fraud he has been working on, it's complicated, and he said it would be easier to explain some aspects to the procurator fiscal face to face, sir."

"Oh yes," DI Jagielka played along, "well you have no doubt discussed the crime return with him this morning haven't you?"

"Yes, sir."

"What did Detective Sergeant Johnstone identify as today's priority?"

Scotty Boy made a stab at what his boss might have considered a priority.

"He said we would look at the housebreaking up the High Street, sir."

"I see," said DI Jagielka, "not the murder he got called out to in the middle of the night then?"

Scotty Boy realised he'd been busted and true to his likeable rogue character stated loud and proud, "Well that's me caught then, sir!"

The next week Scotty Boy's temporary detective role came to an end. They took away the temporary bit and made him a fully fledged detective constable (you can't buy loyalty like that).

CHAPTER 26

SHIT HAPPENS

My new station was a nice building, modern, well equipped and a million miles away from the toilet where I used to work. The office was ideally situated to cater for the needs of the area. Just like any workplace anywhere in the world, it isn't the building that makes it a good or bad place to work; it is the people. I knew a few of the cops and sergeants working there before I moved, so I settled in pretty quickly. The people were great. There was a good deal of friendly rivalry amongst the cops, and that made it a fun place to work. We boasted whenever we had any successful detections, and those who were unsuccessful took a fair amount of ribbing.

The station covered a sprawling residential town and three rough and tough mining villages. It was a place that ticked over during the week with various minor calls keeping us going. At weekends, however, it was frantic. The calls came in thick and fast, and we would rush from one village to the next to break up fights and stem the tide of blood and guts.

Not long after I arrived my sergeant took me aside and asked me to work with PC Goodwillie, a young cop with five year's service.

"You need to keep an eye on him," Sergeant Mac-

Mufty warned me.

"Why?"

"He is a liability, at some stage he is going to embarrass himself and that will reflect badly on us all."

"What makes you say that?"

"Trust me on this, he is a bomb scare. You will need to be on your guard all the time. Sorry to land you with him but I don't think there is anyone else who could keep him out of bother."

I didn't think my new partner could be as bad as all that. Most people embellish things to make their point. Surely Sergeant MacMufty was exaggerating. As I got to know PC Goodwillie, however, I realised he wasn't wrong. My first experience working with him on the night shift I was aghast at how little interest he showed in police work.

As much as I used to enjoy the work on a night shift, I came to realise that they are not good for your health. Night shifts are in fact positively the worst thing you can do to your body, short of stabbing yourself in the neck with a fork. They can throw your system completely out of sync. Lack of a proper good nights sleep takes its toll. The older you get, the harder they become and the more damage they do to your body. I read somewhere that scientists had evidence proving that working throughout the night opposes our circadian rhythm and distresses us at a molecular level. At a biological molecular level, the interactions between DNA and our various cell systems is affected. The interruption to regular sleep can cause the body to badly dysfunction. When I worked the night shift, my molecules all gathered together and hung around in a dark mood in the pouches below my eyes.

Despite that, I actually liked working on a night shift. The early part of the evening can be busy but the second half quietens down, and you have time to get your paperwork done. That's if you can keep your eyes open.

At my new station, the sergeants did not work any later than 10 p.m. and thus on night shifts we got left to our own devices. PC Goodwillie was to be in my charge. Despite being out of his probation, my Sergeant tasked me to keep an eye on him, watch his every step and ensure there were no embarrassing incidents. Well warned.

PC Goodwillie, it turned out, was a nice guy. He had just one fault - he had no interest in doing anything even resembling work, not even if it relieved the boredom. The first night I worked with him he arrived in at work half an hour late. He apologised before stating, "I'll go and put the kettle on." And off he went to the canteen.

After a while, I went up to see if he was ready to go out on patrol. Nope! He had settled himself into a chair and fallen asleep in front of the telly. He hadn't even put his boots on, far less make a cuppa.

I switched the telly and lights off and left him to sleep - how kind of me. Then off I went out on patrol. I reckoned that he must be exhausted and a little empathy wouldn't go amiss. If I let him sleep, it might help us bond and we could work well together as a team.

I toured round my beat on my own, attended a few minor calls and visited our regular problem areas before returning to the office for my break around 3 a.m. PC Goodwillie was still sound asleep in his chair. I had a cuppa, a sandwich and watched some dull programme on the telly without him stirring once.

I went back out on patrol for the second half of my shift and didn't return until 6 a.m. My entrance was enough to rouse my sleepy colleague. PC Goodwillie sat up, stretched and yawned in a prolonged and exaggerated fashion. He rubbed his eyes before focusing them on me at which point he stated, "I'm absolutely shattered. You don't mind if I go home early do you?" and, without even waiting for a reply, off he went.

The next night I moved one of the comfy chairs from the canteen to another office before he arrived at work. PC Goodwillie was too lazy to move it back, so he came out on patrol with me, only to fall asleep in the passenger seat.

Mischief making entered my head.

After driving around for about an hour, I went out to a deserted industrial estate. On entering the industrial estate, I built up a little speed before switching on the blue lights and siren. I then slammed on the anchors and came to a dead stop. As quickly as I could, I got out of the car shouting, "Quick follow me!" I then ran off round the back of a large building, the storage depot for a large local glaziers business. There I sat waiting for him, ready to pounce the second he rounded the building. I waited in anticipation of giving him the fright of his life.

After a minute the sirens in the car ceased wailing. He had switched them off. I thought, 'he will follow me shortly.'

I waited.

I waited so long I thought something was wrong, my imagination ran riot. Had PC Goodwillie fallen and hurt himself? Had he had a heart attack?. I made my way back to the car to check on his welfare. Nope!

There he was still sitting in the passenger seat, still looking sleepy and disinterested. He had roused himself enough to switch the sirens off and no more.

"What happened?" he asked showing little genuine curiosity.

My 'keeping an eye' on PC Goodwillie became an easy task. I just needed to remember where I had left him and wake him up at the end of the shift. To be fair, I probably became a little complacent. I lapsed into a false sense of security, his lack of interest in doing anything related to police work lulled me into thinking it would last. I, therefore, eased my foot off the accelerator.

A few weeks later we ended up dealing with a group of marauding youths in a park. There were hundreds of them. Aged between ten and sixteen all gathered to have nonsense, and by their sheer numbers, they upset the locals, triggering numerous complaints.

There were kids from all walks of life. Good kids, not so good kids and some toerags. But always I remembered they were just kids. Yes, they could be loud, particularly in such a large group, but they were just kids. All we needed to do was show some patience, split them up, take a few names and threaten to make their parents aware. In the end, they would disperse, no harm done, and no more complaints. So I did.

I patiently split them up, talked calmly but firmly with them. Took some names and threatened to call their parents, cajoled and coaxed them into quietening down and dispersing.

It was with some consternation then when I turned around to find PC Goodwillie had had a run-in with an angry young teenager. The lad was about fifteen years old, drunk and being verbally abusive to PC Goodwillie. Despite warning him to move on several times the youth ignored this and squared up to PC Goodwillie challenging him to fight. PC Goodwillie snapped. His indifference to the world of policing was such that he didn't care most of the time. However, the youth had pushed him too far. PC Goodwillie's temper frayed, (probably because of actually having to do some work) so he grabbed the youth and wrestled him to the ground.

I turned and took in the scene. PC Goodwillie had the youth pinned to the grass with his left hand. With his right hand, he had reached around and grabbed his side handled baton and raised it above his head. The youth struggled all the more, but I had visions of the baton being used in earnest on the youth's head. The hundreds of youths milling around the park quietened at the sight of one of their friends getting manhandled to the ground. A hypnotic scene before them. With the noise abated the throng of youths became absorbed by the gruesome possibility that one of their numbers would imminently receive a baton strike to his head.

The baton reached higher above PC Goodwillie and just before it came crashing down on the prone teenager I grabbed the end of the baton. I held on to it for dear life. It took a moment for PC Goodwillie to extricate himself from his fog of anger and realise that there would have been hundreds of witnesses to him hitting this youth. He released his grip on the baton. The youth underneath him sobered at the thought of being batoned and stopped struggling.

Crisis and possible charges against PC Goodwillie averted we continued to disperse the youths until order restored.

Fortunately for the public, PC Goodwillie resigned from the job a few months later.

Without PC Goodwillie I didn't notice much of a difference. For a while, I paired up with whoever was available. I liked to work with different people, there were some good characters among them.

There were some people I worked with that didn't need looking after - but, for a different reason, I still had to watch them. PC Sylvester McDougan (Uncle Sylvester) was the one person I had to watch the most.

It all started one hot summer's day when I was sitting, thinking my own thoughts, in the front passenger seat of the marked police car. My colleague, Uncle Sylvester, was driving.

Uncle Sylvester is one of the easiest people with whom to get along. Nothing fazes him, well other than standing up in front of a class full of kids to give a talk (his knees would buckle at the thought). However, you stick him into a pub full of fighting drunks and he would be in his comfort zone. He is one of those rare officers who just got on with the job. He had no thoughts for promotion, no ego that required massaging. He wanted to come in and do his work, have fun doing it then go home and drink beer. I think we had similar outlooks on life, the universe, and everything.

As part of our 'having fun while doing the job', he would try to wind me up, and I would try to wind him up. There was a bit of rivalry as well. We always tried to beat each other in the number of cases we reported. No matter how hard he worked he never quite achieved the same caseload as me. I always ended up with more cases than him. I simply worked smarter. (*I put that in just to wind him up*).

So there I was sitting in the front passenger seat of the car quietly minding my business. Uncle Sylvester driving along a perfectly normal road in a perfectly normal town. We passed by people walking their dogs, men running into the bookies to get their bets on in time, and young mothers pushing prams with one hand and holding the older sibling with the other. It was an ordinary day or an ordinary week, nothing unusual to see. Uncle Sylvester turned and asked if I could roll down my window.

Now, I can sometimes be daft, but I am not stupid. The old 'roll your window down trick' was a favourite of mine. If you see a great big puddle up ahead and ask your passenger to roll down their window. If you time it right, just as the window gets rolled to the bottom, you drive through the puddle. The resultant spray splashes past the open window soaking your passenger. It is even funnier if they realise at the last second and don't have time to get the window back up. It's all about timing.

My eyes narrowed with suspicion the second Uncle Sylvester asked me to roll my window down. I looked ahead, but the road was clear of puddles, in fact, it was a beautiful hot and parched summer's day. There was not a puddle in sight. I looked at him and without questioning why I rolled my window fully down and sat back and relaxed back into my daydreaming.

TWOOOOMPHHH!!!

There was me quietly minding my own business with my window rolled down when Uncle Sylvester turned his head and spat his chewing gum - Twoooomphhh!!! - right past my nose and out my window. And that was how it started.

The sticky, saliva covered gum couldn't have passed any more than two inches from my nose. Jesus! I turned to him and looked. Uncle Sylvester just smiled. I thought to myself 'seems a shame to waste such an opportunity.' So, calmly, I picked up Uncle Sylvester's side handled baton and threw it out the window. We were driving through a residential street but there was no-one around that I could see. The baton struck the ground. Side-handled batons are made from a hard plastic composite, so I didn't think the ground would do it any damage. We only travelled about 30 mph. However, the baton landed with the side handle hitting the road first causing it to kick the baton back into the middle of the road. It spun back behind our car. The lorry following us drove right over it.

The driver of the lorry remained oblivious to having driven over the baton. It would have caused only a ripple up in his cab.

Uncle Sylvester slowed down and turned the car at the first opportunity. He returned to the scene and retrieved his baton. Remarkably he seemed unperturbed. The baton ended up slightly bent with minor cuts and abrasions. In due course, he had to submit memo detailing how 'the accidental' damage had occurred before he could get the baton replaced.

So that was how I got my revenge. Tit for tat. Matter closed. No need for further reprisals. At least, that is what I presumed.

Occasionally I cycled to work. A journey of eight miles, but I worked up a sweat so I would arrive at work, sit at a computer and brief myself before going for a shower, this gave me a chance to stop sweating before donning my uniform.

One day, not long after the baton incident, I was sitting in my cycling gear, at my computer reading the briefing logs when Uncle Sylvester offered to make a cup of tea.

"That would be nice," I told him and shortly after, he appeared with steaming hot tea. Alas, he had chosen not to use a cup or a mug but presented this steaming hot tea in one of my work boots. I've tasted better tea.

I let it go for a while. My lack of retaliation gave Uncle Sylvester a false sense of security and after a week or two he thought I had forgotten about it. That, I learned, is when you hit back. It is always better when it is least suspected.

My current partner and I detected a Theft by House-breaking.

Theft by Housebreaking is the Scottish legal term for un-lawful entry to a building. In England, they call it 'burg-lary,' Australians call it 'home invasions,' Americans call it 'breaking and entering,' and I think there are some places in the world it has the graphic title of 'violation of property,' which is quite inspired. Almost everyone everywhere, how-ever, who finds that someone has broken into their home, will call the police and say 'I've been robbed.' A robbery is defined as stealing property from a person using violence or threats of violence. It has nothing to do with breaking into a building, but people all over the world still call in and say 'I've been robbed' to describe the fact that they had their house entered illegally and their property stolen.

We recovered a load of stolen property in the process

of arresting our housebreaker. Included in the seized property was a battery powered handheld cordless screwdriver.

The cordless screwdriver was a novelty in those days; they were new to the market. We found a box of two-inch screws and secured things to walls and doors. I recall being impressed with the efficiency of the machine. I can tell you that an 'emergency procedures' poster, for example, can be screwed to a notice board by four two inch screws in just under twelve seconds, although it took a little practice setting that record.

It struck me that this tool would be handy in getting my own back on Uncle Sylvester for serving me tea in my police boot. Uncle Sylvester's drawers were the middle set of a large wooden old style bench. I tried the cordless screwdriver on the handle and removed the two screws supporting in two seconds flat. I placed the handle upside down and reinserted the screws. Now, the drawer looked as if it was upside down.

What if I turned the drawer upside down?

So I duly turned the drawer upside down stuffing its contents in as I closed it up. Now, Uncle Sylvester had a drawer that looked as if it was the right way up but on opening it, he would spill all the contents on the floor. I might have stopped there, but I was in the mood for stupidity.

I removed the drawers either side of Uncle Sylvester's drawer and inserted a screw either side, attaching the frame of the desk to the wooden drawer. I was delighted to find that his drawer remained resolutely closed. Secured in place by hidden screws. Quite a giggle.

Uncle Sylvester, on the other hand, didn't have

quite the same opinion of the prank. I later heard he pulled the handle so hard it broke. With no leverage to open the drawer, he spent ages trying to get it open. Eventually he figured it out, removed the drawers on either side and found the screws. He had to use an ordinary screwdriver to remove the screws and construct a makeshift handle on to the front of the drawer. When he managed to pull open the drawer, its contents tipped all over the floor.

It was a practical joke that kept me giggling for some time. As the days passed, all I needed to do was to think of it, and a smile would come to my face. As time went on, my smile gave way to a little niggle in the pit of my stomach. What was Uncle Sylvester going to do to me next? He would seek to mete out revenge. Tit for tat. I didn't have to wait long to the tit-for-tat shenanigans to continue.

When I started out as a cop, I bought a small A5 lined book and used this to record every case I ever did. I used just a few lines for each case and detailed the crime number, the accused and the charge. I had a column for remarks in which I would note anything interesting.

After twelve years in the job, my A5 lined book was half full and was a great record of my career. I could see at a glance how many cases I did every year. I always did more than Uncle Sylvester, despite his tendency to deal with easy matters and my tendency to take on the more involved cases. (*That should rankle with him too*).

It was a nice record to have kept. I could have used it to help me recall all my stories, and, it was something I might have cherished in my dotage. I use the past tense because my little lined A5 book is no more.

I came into the office one day, opened my tray to find my little lined A5 book sitting staring out at me in a sorry state. Uncle Sylvester had opened the cover then inserted all the pages into the office shredder. Each page shredded right down to the spine. He then reversed the shredder and closed over the covers of the book before replacing it in my drawer. When I opened it up, I saw hundreds of thin shreds of book flapping about all over the place; my little A5 lined book was utterly beyond repair.

Revenge for my shredded A5 lined book was weeks in the planning. A prank carefully executed and somewhat spectacular in the outcome.

I had got a firework, not a huge one but big enough. I extended the fuse on it by bastardising other fireworks. With a bit of testing on the timing, I ended up with a plan of action. So one day, early in the evening, I lay in wait for Uncle Sylvester in excited anticipation of my explosive prank.

Uncle Sylvester was due into the office for a 6 p.m. start. He wasn't prone to starting much earlier than five minutes to the hour, so I didn't look out the canteen window for him until about 5.50 p.m. Sure enough, a couple of minutes later he arrived in his car, parked up and headed into the office. The changing rooms are opposite the entry door, and he made his way straight in to get ready for work. He didn't see me spying on him from the canteen. I checked the time on my watch.

I had timed Uncle Sylvester the previous nights and discovered that he took an average of four minutes and twenty-five seconds to emerge from the changing rooms before making his way to the report room. His timing didn't vary by more than ten or fifteen seconds.

After three minutes and twenty-five seconds, I lit the fuse on the firework, popped it into Uncle Sylvester's drawer and left. I tiptoed out of the report room and made my way out of the office. Once outside I ran around to the report room window where I had set up a chair to stand on. I peeked into the office and watched.

Uncle Sylvester entered the room. He made his way across to his drawer, oblivious to me watching from outside. Just as he put his hand down to open his drawer, the firework inside exploded. A puff of smoke exited from the gaps in the drawer and clouded around Uncle Sylvester as he stood frozen to the spot. I couldn't have timed it any better. NB. Please don't try this at home.

Work was busy, but we had fun. I was being paid to enjoy myself. Almost everyone at the station got on well with everyone else. I say 'almost everyone' because we had a brief spell where PC Dingleberry also worked with us. At work PC Dingleberry was miserable and crabbit. Away from work he was the opposite - crabbit and miserable. Some people have an almost vampire-like ability to suck the joy out of any situation. Dingleberry was the embodiment of such a person. His grumpiness made everyone grouchy. Like a dark cloud filling the sky he blackened the mood.

Dingleberry's reputation preceded him. His father had been a rather crabby senior officer in the job, but Dingleberry hadn't made it past a cop, despite his protestations that he deserved an instant promotion. He was full of himself. An incessant moaner who showed little interest in doing anything other than self-aggrandising to get himself sergeant stripes. He had little interest in others and few redeeming features.

I worked with Dingleberry only once, during a major enquiry. Dingleberry and I were just two of many cops seconded to assist in the operation. I found his attitude to be appalling. The major operation involved a lot of officers being called out at short notice for locus protection. There were several houses requiring twenty-four-hour police presence. On the second day (having spent the first day standing in the pouring rain for fourteen hours with another colleague without a break) I got the job of organising relief breaks for the officers on the locus protection. It meant travelling around the houses picking them up and dropping off at the office where they received a brown bag containing a sandwich, crisps, juice, and a chocolate bar. To ensure that everyone was refreshed and afforded toilet facilities, I limited the breaks to thirty minutes. It meant everyone could enjoy two breaks. Any longer and some officers would not receive their second break.

On the third day, I was driving the first load of officers back for their break; Dingleberry was one of them. He could do nothing but moan about the standard of food the force provided. When I returned to the office to pick them up and take them back to their points, Dingleberry was missing. One of the others told me he had left the office, grumbling about the canteen food and said he was going to the fish and chip shop. Eventually returned to the office but refused to get on the bus until he had eaten his fish supper. That delayed the breaks and kept seven others waiting on a bus and eight others waiting at their various points in the rain - inconsiderate of him. When he returned, he continued to whine and nit-pick at everything and everybody. That was my first experience of him.

When Dingleberry entered the mini-bus, I gave him a big hearty smile. He took this as a cue to moan some more. He moaned about the job, the food, the senior officers, his colleagues and even the state of the mini-bus. I offered him all the sympathy I could; nodding in the right places, I agreed with his complaints and empathised at his outrage. I then dropped him off at the furthest point away from the office and forgot to pick him up for the rest of the week.

I was disappointed then to learn that he was coming to work at our station as a tutor. He had pestered the bosses to distraction to get himself promoted. So much so they moved him out of the way, all the way to our station. They did it under the guise that they were giving him responsibility in the form of a probationer to see how he coped. I think they knew, full well, that it was fated to be a disaster. PC Quentin Thorpe, a probationer straight from the Scottish Police College, started at our station at the same time. Dingleberry's future promotion prospects would depend on how well he could tutor Quentin.

Quentin was the complete opposite of Dingleberry. He was a people person. He was bright and enthusiastic and the type of person who would do well in almost any occupation. However, there was a lot riding on Dingleberry making sure Quentin completed his probation. Dingleberry didn't leave him alone for a second; he made his life a misery. Working with Dingleberry was a constant struggle. Quentin had to deal with Dingleberry's constant moans, his lack of humour and his ill-manners. Quentin would arrive back at the office, after working with Dingleberry all day, and we could all see his spirit drained. His natural exuberance knocked for six. He might perk up after a cup of tea and chat with others in the office, but we all feared that if he was to work with Dingleberry for any length of time, he might not have the desire to carry on. Dingleberry-caused him so much angst that Quentin was almost ready to quit.

Then one day Quentin came back into the office with a great big beaming smile on his face. His delight was plain to see; enthusiasm radiated from him again.

"What are you grinning at?" I enquired.

It turned our Dingleberry had been showing Quentin how to deal with a sudden death. Not the kind of thing that we looked forward to so I was surprised and keen to hear more. This particular sudden death was straightforward in that the elderly male had died in his sleep and there were no suspicious circumstances. Procedures still required Dingleberry and Quentin to call an undertaker and remove the body to the mortuary. Once at the mortuary, they had to strip the poor deceased man in readiness for a post-mortem examination. Not a pleasant task, but someone has to do it.

It was evident, from the stink, that before expelling his last breath this cadaver had also expelled his bowels.

Dingleberry and Quentin managed to get the body stripped right down to his underpants. Dingleberry then stood at arm's length and pulled the deceased's pants down from the front. The pants eased their way down the cadaver's body, and Dingleberry continued to pull with his outstretched arm, remaining as far away from the offending soiled pants as he could.

It was a plan that worked well until the underwear reached the heels of the deceased. The extra weight of the feet caused the pants to get caught, and the elastic stretched as Dingleberry continued to move away and pull on them. The pants remained stuck, so Dingleberry pulled harder until they gave way.

Then the inevitable happened. The elastic stretched as far as it would go and the pants came free of the heels of the body, slowly at first but just as soon as they reached the tipping point the pants shot out towards Dingleberry. The stored energy in the elastic caused the waistband to contract violently, returning it to its natural shape. Dingleberry's outstretched arm gripped tightly to the pants, he didn't want them landing on him. Unfortunately, the contents of the pants were no longer restricted and just like a catapult the pants came to a sudden stop, but the contents didn't. The contents propelled through the air and splattered over Dingleberry's immaculately-ironed white shirt.

Quentin dropped to the floor in delight. Holding his stomach, he took twenty minutes to stop laughing. When relating the story to us, we could see the joy on his face and hear the glee in his voice.

Shit happens (sometimes to the right people).

CHAPTER 27

IT WISNAE ME; IT WAS HIM

In the meantime, I had to watch out for Uncle Sylvester as his shenanigans continued. I expected a response to the 'firework blowing up in his drawer incident.' I was right to expect some form of retaliation, oddly it turned out to be a minor inconvenience, but it led to an idea that made me laugh so much I had sore sides for weeks. Even now I crease up when I think about it.

I started my night shift and came in to find my locker taped up. Now when I say taped up, I mean really taped up. There was no doubt in my mind who was responsible. Uncle Sylvester had excelled himself. The locker was taped round and round, up and down, side to side, over and over. I took an age, even with a sharp kitchen knife, to get the locker open and even longer to get it all off. A nuisance but funny, I thought to myself.

Uncle Sylvester was on early shift the next day, and I decided to get him back. Tit for tat.

In the middle of the night my colleague, Kevin, assisted me in removing Uncle Sylvester's locker from the locker room. The lockers came bolted in twos, so Gentleman George's locker also came with it. We took the lockers downstairs and outside. We then placed them in the back of the police van. The lockers were too tall to fit all the way in so Kevin had to sit in the back of the van holding it down as the end stuck out the back door. I then drove the van to Uncle Sylvester's house and parked just around the corner.

Kevin and I were in full uniform so God knows what anyone would have thought if they had seen us. We carried the lockers along the street, giggling all the way and placed them right outside Uncle Sylvester's front door. The first thing to meet Uncle Sylvester when he opened his front door in the morning would be his locker. 'How convenient for him,' I thought.

That was an excellent prank. It caused no real harm to anyone. It genuinely made me guffaw all night in anticipation of his reaction. It still makes me smile to this day.

About 6.45 a.m. the office phone rang - it was Uncle Sylvester. "Good morning," he said not giving away whether he had opened his front door and seen my present to him or not.

"Good morning," I replied.

"Any chance you could ask Mark to come and pick me up this morning," (Mark was his partner who was also due to start at 7 am).

"Yes no problem," I said, "I will ask him when he comes in."

"... and could you ask him to bring the big van with him," and at that point, I knew he had seen his locker on his doorstep and I burst out laughing, again.

When Mark came in, I asked him to pick up Uncle Sylvester, but I made a little omission as regards needing a big van. So Mark toddled off to pick up Uncle Sylvester in a car.

They had to carry the lockers back up the road in the van during the morning rush hour and had received a quizzical look from a boss who had driven behind them. Strangely, the boss never took the time to find out why his troops were moving lockers in a van with a cop sitting on them and the back door open.

That night Gentleman George was back shift and asked me if anyone had been in our lockers.

"No, why?" I asked him not letting on.

"Because someone has been in my locker and strewn everything all over the place. I wondered if the bosses had been in and had a rake around.

It was years after he retired before I told him what happened.

The shenanigans with Uncle Sylvester continued. Tit for tat. In between dealing with thefts, fires, neighbour disputes, and people causing a bloody nuisance of themselves, Uncle Sylvester and I amused ourselves with our pranks on each other. Before I tell you about the next prank, I need to tell you about my Dad.

My Dad used to say he was the worst singer in our Scotland. That was until he married my Mum (she had Van Gogh's ear for music) - then he became the second worst singer in Scotland. In the fullness of time my older brother came along, they nurtured him, and he grew from a tiny baby into a toddler, he learned to walk and then talk. The day came when he too tried to sing, and on that day my Dad realised he had become the third worst singer in Scotland. Regrettably, all four of his children (including myself), inherited his 'tone-deaf' gene. So with a wife and four children, my Dad confidently pronounced he is now only the sixth worst singer in Scotland.

I, in fact, come from a long line of musically inept and tone-deaf forefathers, but there is a reason for telling you this.

One Saturday night Uncle Sylvester and I received a call, Willie Gibbon had started his nonsense again. His neighbours phoned to complain about him shouting abuse at them. Willie Gibbon was a regular on our beat. He had an incorrigible appetite for rubbing people up the wrong way and, due to our numerous dealings with him, he had a chronic dislike for the police. We spent a full hour mediating between Willie and his neighbours. They were exasperated with him, and he showed nothing but contempt for them.

Willie Gibbon was the most intolerant of men and incapable of showing any form of empathy to anyone. We spoke to the neighbours, calmed them down and warned Willie that if we had to come back, he would end up spending a night in a cell.

Uncle Sylvester and I returned to the office. I sat down at my desk to get on with some report writing. Uncle Sylvester disappeared upstairs to make tea. Halfway through boiling the kettle, he phoned down from the kitchen to ask me what I took in my tea.

Now, this is where the problem arose. The phones in the office have two different rings. One ring to indicate an external call from a member of the public and another to identify an internal call from elsewhere within the office. My inborn genetic inability to differentiate between tones meant that both rings sounded the same.

All I heard was the phone ring, so I answered the phone in the appropriate way, expecting it to be a member of the public.

"Hello, this is the police office, PC McEwan speaking, how can I help you?"

Uncle Sylvester was quick to cotton on to the fact I had not realised it was an internal call. Without the slightest delay, he put on a drunken voice, not dissimilar to Willie Gibbon's drunken voice, and said, "Constable McEwan this is Willie Gibbon! You better get down here right fecking now, I want to make a complaint and don't bring that arsehole you were with earlier or I'll fecking kick him in the nuts."

I fell for it hook, line, and sinker. "What is it now Willie?" I asked, exasperated, "Who do you want to complain about?"

"Just get fecking down here, or I will complain about you too," and at that, he hung up.

I couldn't believe it. We had just left his house, and he wanted us back to make a complaint. Heavyhearted I made my way upstairs to give Uncle Sylvester the bad news, little knowing he could hardly contain himself.

"That was Willie Gibbon again; he wants to make a complaint."

"What about?" Uncle Sylvester asked innocently.

"He just said he wanted to make a complaint and hung up, but would complain about me if I don't go. I had better go."

"I'll come with you," Uncle Sylvester offered all angel-faced.

"No. No. Willie said he didn't want you there. I'll deal with it."

Uncle Sylvester must have been delighted with the way his ingenious impromptu prank had played out. He even jumped into the car and drove me round to Willie's house. He dropped me off outside and said he would nip to headquarters to get the mail while I dealt with Willie. I said I would walk back to the office, and off he drove.

Willie answered the door and gave me a quizzical look. "What the fuck do you want now?" was his opening gambit.

"You called me. What do you want to complain about?" I asked him.

Well from there it degenerated. One confusing conversation later, after a tongue-lashing from Willie, I left. I had to leave before I got even more infuriated with him.

I walked back to the office, mumbling away to myself about Willie Gibbon and cursing at him for once again wasting my time. As I approached the office, there was Uncle Sylvester standing at the top window looking down at me. He had a cup of hot steaming tea in his hand and a great big knowing smile on his face.

Following on from the Willie Gibbon incident, I decided it was time to step up with my revenge on Uncle Sylvester for his misdemeanours.

I was on night shift, and Uncle Sylvester was working from 6 p.m. to 2 a.m. He and his partner dealing with calls. I took the opportunity to have a rake in his drawer. There I found a key for his locker, so I had a wee trip to the locker room. I then had a shufti in his locker. There wasn't much of note other than his car keys, which gave me an idea.

Armed with his cars keys and a socket set. I went out to his car, a Renault Laguna, parked in the rear car park. The front seat of his Renault Laguna was bolted to the floor but proved no match for me and my socket set.

I removed the driver's seat in minutes. I locked his car up then hid the car seat in the attic space of the office.

Uncle Sylvester returned to the office about 1.30 a.m. along with his partner. They completed their required reports on the computer. At 2 a.m. I informed them I was going for my break and headed up to the canteen which overlooked the rear car park.

A few minutes later, as I peeked around the curtain, I saw Uncle Sylvester leave the office and head towards his car. He got to about two steps from the driver's door and then came to a sudden stop. Frozen like a statue, his car key in his hand stretched out towards the lock. He stood there and stared at his car in disbelief.

Eventually Uncle Sylvester composed himself and opened his car to confirm that what he saw was correct. His driver's seat was missing, gone, no longer an integral part of his car. He turned and looked up at the canteen window. The lights were out, and I remained behind the curtain peeking out. Uncle Sylvester could only have seen a shadow with its shoulders bobbing up and down (me trying to control my laughing).

Uncle Sylvester made his way back into the office and up to the canteen by which time I had moved from behind the curtain and sat eating a sandwich, drinking tea and watching TV, trying to look innocent.

"Right," he said, "where is it?"

"What?"

"My car seat."

"Dunno."

Give Uncle Sylvester his due; he didn't pester me any more than that. He did a systematic search of the office and found his car seat within ten minutes (search team trained). He then found tools and replaced his car seat to its rightful position.

Later he told me that one of the bolts wouldn't go on properly and he had to sell the car with a wonky seat. I did wonder what the hell he would come up with to top that.

Well, top it he did, with a wonderfully creative off the cuff prank of real cunning and inventiveness. A prank that had him rolling on the floor, tears in his eyes and grabbing his sides because his repeated guffaws made them sore. His ingenious wind-up caused me to swear at a superintendent which was one reason I ended up having to do two stints as a temporary sergeant before I got promoted.

But that is another story.

You can read all about it in *'The really STUPID thing about being a SERGEANT.'*

A WEE NOTE
FROM MALKY.

Oh good, you made it to the end. I hope you enjoyed it. Would you be so kind as to give it a rating on Amazon, please? One way to help establish this book's status as an entertaining source for others is to read your esteemed opinion and customer review of the book. (Click link)

Many thanks.

Malky

Malky McEwan writes to tickle, inspire, and make you think.

For police humour to tickle and delight:

THE REALLY STUPID THING ABOUT BEING A SERGEANT

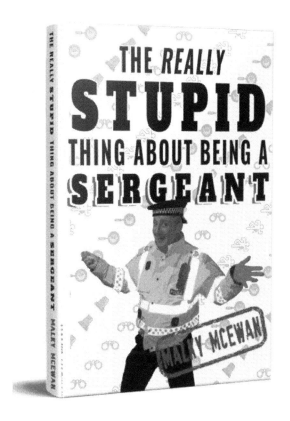

"A very enjoyable read this, many funny anecdotes but the best was the one about anger management, I was sniggering about that for the rest of the evening." - White Camel.

"I so enjoyed the first in this series I had to get the Sergeant sequel, and was not disappointed. Malky writes a really good yarn and helps me to start my day with a smile on my face. Another one please." - Carol

"He's done it again!! More stories of life on the beat, this time with some added responsibility as a Sergeant and some of the problems the cops create for you. A cracking read for the summer. Can't wait for the next one Malky!" - Kindle customer

"Great stories that had me laughing and showing my friends! Looking forward to the next one!" - Amazon customer

A LITTLE PREAMBLE

People sometimes ask me if I ever got flashed or propositioned to get themselves off with a ticket. An innocuous question with a salacious undertone. A desire to hear some spicy scandal?

I got an eyeful, once, when I went to deal with a noisy music complaint.

The normal procedure is to alert the householder to the complaint and request they turn the volume down. Should they refuse or ignore the warning we can charge them with a nuisance offence and take possession of their music playing equipment - problem solved.

On this occasion, a young lady answered the door, in the background I could hear the music blaring. It wasn't the first time I had been to her home; she had regular parties that kept her neighbours awake to all hours of the morning. When she came to the door, she opened it wide and stood facing my colleague and me. She was wearing a see-through negligee that didn't even reach below the waist. There were three steps up to her front door and because I was standing on the bottom step, my eye-line was level with her bushy pudenda. As magnificent as it was, I averted my gaze and looked her in the eye. I asked her to step back into her house, out of sight, and requested that she dress herself before we spoke to her. She went inside but refused to dress herself.

Instead, she took a seat in her lounge chair, unperturbed by her near nakedness. I turned her stereo off, gave her a warning and my colleague and I made a quick exit. We were very professional. I stopped outside to note the details in my notebook and the circumstances. Maybe she wasn't trying to proposition us, she didn't make a show of her body, she just seemed comfortable being naked. I didn't grant her any favours; she received a warning like any other person.

On another occasion, night shift, alone in my office. A woman came to the door dressed in a fur coat. I didn't know her, other than I had seen her around the small town where I worked.

It turned out she was looking for the services of a police officer that wasn't part of our duties; there was nothing under that fur coat (other than a garter belt and high heels). She was a good looking woman, and I was flattered - that was until she spoke.

"Is Constable Herman not on tonight," she said, wrapping her fur coat tightly around herself when she realised she had mixed up his shift pattern.

I went scarlet.

However, the most shocking proposition I received wasn't to get out of a ticket, it was to get out of a bollocking.

I was duty sergeant and had to have a closed door session with a female cop. She was an experienced officer and good at her job. Not only was she an asset, she had a sparkling personality and made the workplace a happier place.

I had to reprimand her for something - it must have been a minor matter because I can't recall what it was. I remember her attitude to it though. She laughed it off, fluttered her eyelashes and told me she fancied me. There I was trying to be serious and professional. She couldn't care about the reprimand. Instead she suggested that I come back to her flat when we finished work.

I was aghast. How could she be so dismissive of

my reprimand? What on earth possessed her to suggest such a thing to her sergeant? She must know I would not contemplate getting involved with a member of my team. That would have been totally unprofessional - a step into dangerous territory. It was a wholly improper suggestion. I need not tell you her proposal stunned me. I couldn't speak for a few seconds, appalled by her audacity.

She had a nice flat though!*

The *really* STUPID thing about being a SERGEANT is my second book detailing the funny incidents, the strange goings on, and the comic situations encountered during a thirty year and two-month career in the police. Guaranteed to make anyone with the slightest sense of humour laugh out loud. You can read these humorous accounts in any order. This book is worth reading for the one scene alone that had me, my custody assistant and every single prisoner in the custody suite laughing until our sides were sore; detailed in all its glory in the chapter entitled 'Hokey Cokey in the pokey'.

PC Penfold makes a return, but there are new characters too; Inspector Deadpan Dick who had me in stitches in a McDonald's drive-thru, Superintendent Amnesiac, and much more. There are even two bedroom scenes, the names have been changed, but my colleagues are utterly embarrassed when reminded of what went on.

*I couldn't resist this one liner - it is of course not true.**
** Her flat was actually a mess.

Click here to find out

HOW TO BE THE MOST OUTSTANDING COP IN THE WORLD - IN A SILLY WAY

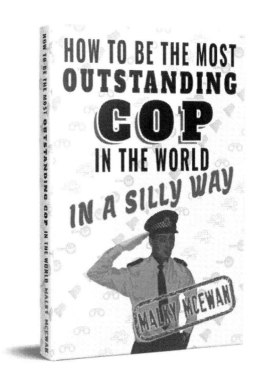

"This is the third in the trilogy and have to say, as an ex cop I enjoyed it thoroughly. It is entertaining, and shows the lighter side of what is an extremely serious profession (most of the time). Well worth the purchase if you fancy a light hearted read." - Kindle customer.

"I really hope that Malky tells lies and that this is NOT the final one. Another excellent series of tales and stories of his

Police 'career.' A cracking read!" - Adrian

"Another great read, read his previous books and it just gets better. This proves the statement 'the polis really are human after all'. Put a bit of sun in your life, buy the book!!" - GerryH

"Great stories. A feast of wisdom. La laughed my head off at the wind ups. Well written and almost made me want to join the police." - Kindle customer.

"I particularly enjoyed the "interview" running through it. It is very well written with a personal touch which made me feel part of the action." - Ineke.

A LITTLE PREAMBLE

I shouldn't be giving this one away because it is such a powerful technique - but nobody will read this, right?

If you ever get stopped while driving always tell the police officer, "I'm glad you stopped me because..."

That is a good start. It is non-confrontational. It will distract the officer from his original aim. Curious why you are glad he stopped you. That minor traffic offence you committed will go to the back of his mind.

The next part of the technique involves the 'why?'

Adapt the reason you give for being glad he stopped you to your situation. Your reason should fit in with what you are doing or where you are going. There should be no need to lie.

"I am looking for directions to..."
"Can you tell me where the nearest toilet/pharmacy/ petrol station is?"
"I'm lost."
"I'm not feeling well."
"My car has been playing up."

Police officers join the job to help people. Redirecting their attention from issuing a minor ticket to helping a member of the public is something they would prefer to be doing. It makes them feel good to help others. It works at a base psychological level. Thus, if you get it right, they forget their reason for stopping you and assist you with your problem. As an afterthought, they might say something like; *'Oh, by the way, get your taillight fixed,'* or *'keep your speed down,'* or *'remember to use your indicator.'*

It is a win/win situation. The officer will feel good for helping you, and you get away with a quiet word in your ear. The method does not work if you fall out of your vehicle drunk or have committed a hit and run or other serious offence.

STOP PRESS:

This technique also does not work if, like me, you get stopped by a police officer who has read this book,

therefore knows this modus operandi and doesn't believe you are bursting for the toilet (I wonder if I can sue
for a new pair of trousers?).

So without further ado, here is my final effort in the
trilogy of police memoirs documenting the amusing
circumstances, crazy scrapes, nonsense and shenanigans that went on. There is no central plot to follow.
You don't have to be a police officer to recognise the
characters - they appear in every walk of life. You don't
have to want to be an outstanding police officer either.
I wrote this book to record the comical cases and hilarious situations I experienced during my thirty-year
career in the police.

I changed the names to protect the guilty, embellished stories and took literary licence. Although,
the most ludicrous stories are probably true.

THE MICHAEL PARKINSON TELEVISION INTERVIEW

British broadcaster Michael Parkinson (best known for
his long-running talk show, *Parkinson*), said *'Muham-
mad Ali was the most extraordinary man I ever met'*. But
who was the second?

The following happened when Michael Parkinson came
out of retirement for one last chat show:-

Parky: I'd like to welcome to the studio tonight Malky

McEwan, best-selling and award-winning author of
How to be the most outstanding cop in the world.

APPLAUSE

Malky enters, embraces Parky and takes a seat.

Parky: Welcome, Malky. Can I call you Malky or should I
call you Inspector McEwan?

Malky: Malky is fine. I'm no longer an inspector.

Parky: Now, Malky you have written *'How to be the most
outstanding cop in the world'* do you think anyone can become an outstanding cop?

Malky: In a silly way, yes.

Parky: In a silly way?

Malky: Yes, in a silly way. That's the title of the book.
*'How to be the most outstanding cop in the world - in a silly
way!'*

Parky: I see. What I'm interested in sharing with the
audience is your experience with the not so outstanding cops you came across in your career.

Malky: That's not fair. They were all outstanding... in
their own way.

Parky: PC Penfold?

Malky: Er... um... Yes, PC Penfold, in his way was outstanding.

Parky: Not as a cop though.

Malky: Probably not.

Parky: In your previous books you have described cops who were a little inattentive. If there is a puddle on the road, they would step in it and get wet. There are others you described as unlucky; they see the puddle, sidestep to avoid it and still get soaked as a car drives through the puddle splashing them. You say PC Penfold was both inattentive and unlucky?

Malky: Yes. He would be the one that would jump the puddle to avoid getting wet, then land on a jobbie, slip and fall back into the puddle and then get splashed by the passing car.

Parky: Does he appear in this book?

Malky: He makes a brief appearance, yes. Like the time he they asked him to play in goal for the police football team.

Parky: What happened?

Malky: They were only ten minutes into the game and he had already let three goals passed him. He kicked the ball so far out of play it cleared the fence surrounding the ground. PC Penfold shouted, 'I'll get it,' chased after it, climbed the fence and didn't come back. Everyone thought he went to the pub. Nobody bothered because without him they only let in another two goals the whole game.

Parky: Oh that's funny?

Malky: That wasn't the funny part. The next week they were ten minutes into their next game when PC Penfold climbed back over the fence into the ground. He raised the ball above his head and shouted, 'Found it!'

Parky: So will the reader learn anything from him about being an outstanding cop?

Malky: Of course, learning from other people's mistakes is way better than learning from your own.

Parky: Is that how you learned to be an outstanding cop?

Malky: I don't profess to have been an outstanding cop. For me policing was like sex.

Parky: Like sex?

Malky: Yeah, I fumbled around for a bit, not really knowing what I was doing and I was never sure how long it would last - but, oh boy, it was fun!

Parky: Do you have any good advice for anyone who

wants to join the police?

Malky: I think the main thing is to have good posture.

Parky: Good posture will make you a good police officer?

Malky: Pretty much, the two words that help there are 'nipples leading'.

Parky: Look the part, project a good image, I get the idea. So this book is all about the funny incidents that you came across?

Malky: The silly incidents, the crazy characters and the stupid things that happened, yes. I think reading about what happens in the police and thinking about how you will deal with those situations will prepare you for what you may encounter.

Parky: It pays to be prepared?

Malky: Yes, but if not - at least you will get a laugh.

Parky: So Malky, what was it like when you first got promoted to Inspector?

Click here to find out

Keep your colleagues amused and never be bored at work again with the *Lateral Thinking Puzzle* books.

'Outstanding' Fiendish & Fun Lateral Thinking Puzzles

My favourite puzzle here is 'The milk container' which always gets the biggest 'AHA' moment.

Click link

'Even Better' Fiendish & Fun Lateral Thinking Puzzles

'My favourite puzzle here is 'Skiving' which was an absolutely, fit to burst, hilarious scenario that really did happen. It still makes me smile to this day.'

Click link

'The Ultimate' Fiendish & Fun Lateral Thinking Puzzles

My favourite puzzle here is 'How to deal with time wasters' which has such an elegant solution. I genuinely used at work to stop time wasters in their tracks. It never offended anyone and worked every time. There is a slight twist if you want to get to the right answer.

Click link

Royalties from these books are donated towards antibiotic research.

Why has there only been one new antibiotic developed in the last thirty years?

There has only been one new antibiotic developed in the last thirty years due to lack of money. It stems from many large pharmaceutical companies closing down antibiotic research programmes. It is not as profitable for them as drugs taken by patients for the rest of their lives. This is despite antibiotic resistance growing, already 700,000 people a year die from antibiotic resistant infections. It will get worse unless something is done. Someone you know could do something simple like cut their finger and die.

Made in the USA
San Bernardino, CA
19 January 2020